SOCIAL DEATH

NATION OF NEWCOMERS: IMMIGRANT
HISTORY AS AMERICAN HISTORY
General Editors: Matthew Jacobson and Werner Sollors

Social Death

Racialized Rightlessness and the
Criminalization of the Unprotected

Lisa Marie Cacho

NEW YORK UNIVERSITY PRESS
New York and London

NEW YORK UNIVERSITY PRESS
New York and London
www.nyupress.org

References to Internet websites (URLs) were accurate at the time of writing.
Neither the author nor New York University Press is responsible for URLs
that may have expired or changed since the manuscript was prepared.

LIBRARY OF CONGRESS CATALOGING-IN-PUBLICATION DATA
Cacho, Lisa Marie.
Social death : racialized rightlessness and the criminalization of the unprotected / Lisa Marie
Cacho.
p. cm. — (Nation of newcomers: immigrant history as American history)
Includes bibliographical references and index.
ISBN 978-0-8147-2375-3 (cl : alk. paper)
ISBN 978-0-8147-2376-0 (pb : alk. paper)
ISBN 978-0-8147-2377-7 (ebook)
ISBN 978-0-8147-2542-9 (ebook)
1. Immigrants—Civil rights—United States. 2. Minorities—Civil rights—United States.
3. Illegal aliens—United States. 4. Marginality, Social—United States. 5. Criminal liability—
United States. 6. Racism—United States. 7. Illegality—Social aspects—United States. I.
Title.
JV6456.C33 2012
323.173—dc23   2012024957

New York University Press books are printed on acid-free paper,
and their binding materials are chosen for strength and durability.
We strive to use environmentally responsible suppliers and materials
to the greatest extent possible in publishing our books.

Manufactured in the United States of America

c   10 9 8 7 6 5 4 3 2 1
p   10 9 8 7 6 5 4 3 2 1

To David Coyoca, for everything . . .

CONTENTS

ACKNOWLEDGMENTS

This has been a difficult book for me to write, and because it was, I had to rely on many people during all its stages. While I claim all its flaws and shortcomings, the people I acknowledge in these pages helped me conceptualize and clarify all its best and most interesting parts. First and foremost, I would like to acknowledge Liz Gonzalez, my first-rate research assistant; I would not have been able to come close to deadlines without her. I extend my appreciation to her with deep sincerity. Kevin Dolan's early edits provided me with expert help in clarifying my arguments and making the book clearer overall. His assistance, too, was invaluable.

Eric Zinner, the best editor ever, has been more than supportive of this project. I am so grateful for all his help, his patience, and his persistence. I also thank Eric for choosing my excellent reviewers. My anonymous reviewers and my non-anonymous reviewer, James Kyung-Jin Lee, pushed the book in important directions I didn't even know it could go. I believe it is a *much* better book because of their comments and critiques, recommendations and encouragement, and I really appreciate the care and attention that each person provided.

At the University of Illinois, I've been lucky to have support from the Center on Democracy in a Multiracial Society and from the Illinois Program for Research in the Humanities, where I completed my postdoctoral fellowship. I thank the university for granting me humanities release time, and I thank the Latina/Latino Studies department for awarding me much needed course release right before tenure. I've been fortunate and privileged to work with exceptional faculty on this campus. I would like to recognize my colleagues Ricky T. Rodríguez, Eileen Díaz McConnell, Mireya Loza, Jonathan Inda, Julie Dowling, Edna Viruell-Fuentes, Gilberto Rosa, Alejandro Lugo, Rolando Romero, Arlene Torres, William Berry, Yutian Wong, Junaid Rana, Moon-kie Jung, Susan Koshy, Yoon Pak, Nancy Abelman, Esther Lee, Caroline Yang, Augusto Espiritu, Lisa Nakamura, Kent Ono, Karen Flynn, Ruth Nicole Brown, David Roediger, Antonia Darder, Jose Capino, Adrian Burgos, Dara Goldman, Clarence Lang, Erik McDuffy, Mark Perry, C. L. Cole, and Sundiata Cha-Jua. I also thank Siobhan Somerville for making the campus such a productive space for intellectual engagement by bringing scholars to campus, and I thank her for reading pieces of my work and offering me very helpful comments.

To Martin Manalansan and Angharad Valdivia, I owe a special thanks as my senior faculty mentors in Asian American Studies and Latina/Latino Studies. As they learned, I am not an easy person to mentor. I am grateful for their invaluable insights about my research, teaching, and professionalization. I also thank Martin and Anghy for helping me to navigate the more difficult aspects of a joint appointment, for being advocates and strategists, and for having confidence in me when my own tended to waver.

This book itself would not have been possible to write without the mentorship of the brilliant scholars who taught me how to be thoughtful, careful, analytical, and responsible. George Lipsitz's support has been essential, and I am grateful that he has always been so giving. His remarkable ability to find hope anywhere in anything can make writing about the most depressing topics still rewarding. Yen Espiritu, Lisa Lowe, and Denise Ferreira da Silva have always pushed me intellectually as well as supported me professionally and personally. I thank Denise Ferreira da Silva for training me to be smart enough to read her book and teach it and for teaching me how to question what is easier to take for granted. I thank Lisa Lowe for teaching me to look for the politics of poetics, for making literature so important to life, and for helping me to articulate what I mean to say. I would not be where I am—in fact, I would not be who I am—had I not had the privilege of working with Yen Le Espiritu. Yen's undergraduate ethnic studies class gave my life a new story and a new direction. And in graduate school and afterward, I carried around her books as models for how to make and write smart arguments as clearly as possible. Whenever I have one of those teaching moments— when what I've been saying finally "clicks"—I believe I am channeling Yen Le Espiritu.

While my committee members trained me to be careful and socially accountable, the men and women with whom I spent most of my free time during graduate school taught me how to take risks, how to find my writing voice, and most importantly, how to ask questions that I was not yet smart enough to answer. (If only they could have given me the answers too . . .) After talking with the occupants of the Marlborough House and their many guests, I always left awed, inspired, and humbled—I am ever grateful to and still inspired by Albert Lowe, Barry Masuda, Boone Nguyen, and Randall Williams. I thank Randy also for reading parts of this manuscript and for always being so generous with his time and expertise. Ofelia Cuevas and Tony

Tiongson—I thank both for going through all the hard parts of graduate school with me and for making it worthwhile.

I also feel indebted to Grace Hong, Rod Ferguson, Chandan Reddy, Victor Bascara, Gregory Lobo, Dylan Rodríguez, Rachel Buff, Suzanne Oboler, Jane Rhodes, Jordana Rosenberg, and Mike Murashige for producing and supporting paradigm-shifting work that has been really important to my intellectual development as a scholar. I thank Jodi Melamed for exchanging her amazing work with me and providing me with thoughtful comments. I thank Helen Jun for being brilliant and giving, for making sure I don't take myself too seriously, and for always making it worth waiting for the next high tide. Ruby Tapia always gave me the help I never could ask for and that I didn't always know I needed. I thank Ruby for being a beautiful writer, profound scholar, and beloved friend, whom I can always count on to take my side.

When I first came to Urbana-Champaign, people told me it was like the Berkeley of the Midwest. That's not true at all, but because Urbana-Champaign lacks the wonderful distractions of urban spaces, I've made relationships here that nurture and sustain me. I thank Steve Hocker for intellectually engaging conversations and delicious desserts. I thank Ian Sprandel for feeding me, fixing my clothes, worrying about me, and for keeping me smart outside my areas of knowledge and always in the most entertaining way possible. I thank Luciano Molina-Sprandel for reminding us to let hope happen and for motivating us to look for everyday magic. I thank Soo Ah Kwon for her friendship, support, and remarkable ability to make sure we're all on task. I also thank Soo Ah, Dustin Allred, and Max for hosting gourmet dinners and spontaneous activities afterward to burn all the calories. I am thankful to Fiona Ngô for being a wonderful writing partner, careful reader, and easygoing deadline enforcer. I am grateful to her for being generous with her time, for keeping me on track, and for helping me let the work go. Fiona has read many parts of the manuscript at various stages, and for this I am deeply thankful. When I get lost in my own words, her genius always points me in the right direction. I thank Mimi Nguyen, who has read very difficult drafts of this book and yet somehow still understood it; I'm especially grateful that she helped me organize it and clarify it so that others could understand it too. I am very appreciative that Mimi has been so generous with her time and her expertise, so giving in all her friendships.

For Isabel Molina-Guzmán, my gratitude overwhelms me. From "check-ins" through tenure, from drafting to revising, Isabel has worked through this book with me on so many levels. I thank her for helping me to work through arguments, brainstorm examples, talk out contradictions, and find "what's another word for . . . ?" It has been my honor to work with her in the truest sense of the word. I thank Isabel for caring so much and for working so hard, for always being right and for putting herself wholeheartedly into everything she does. I profoundly appreciate that she uses her many powers for good—fierce and savvy, courageous and passionate, brilliant and incredibly stubborn. I thank her for ensuring that travelling with her is always an adventure and that everyday life in Champaign is amusing, exciting, rejuvenating, and precious. My life is better because of Isabel.

I thank my parents, Joy and Bob Cacho, for trying to explain to friends and family what ethnic studies is and then for being okay with not really being able to brag about it. I thank my brother Lyle Cacho for making sure I will never fully grow up and my sister Leilani Moore for teaching me that so much of life really is just a matter of perception. I thank my brother Joel Cacho for finding humor where awkwardness should be, and I thank my sister Ariana Cacho for her relentless, quiet support. Though she rarely says it aloud, I know she's always taking care of me and always standing up for me. I thank both Joel and Ariana for giving me every free moment of their time when I visit. My niece and nephew, Nicci and James, I thank for being cute and entertaining. And for always caring, I also thank my extended family, especially my aunts, Val Morrow and Christine Martinez, my uncle Jesse Martinez, and my cousin Trisha Martinez.

Lastly, I extend my deepest appreciation to David Coyoca. David read every draft of every chapter in every stage—and this has gone through many stages. He worked through this project with me intellectually, analytically, conceptually, emotionally, creatively, and painfully, and when he wasn't doing that, he did all the cooking and cleaning. I thank him for giving me the critiques I needed even though I rarely heard them graciously. I thank him for taking care of me when it was too hard, for being angry on my behalf when I was too tired, and for being happy for me when I was too cynical to notice when good things happened. I thank him for continuing to be so giving even at the moments when we both know all I can do is take and ask for more—I thank him for knowing all those moments were temporary and for pretending it didn't matter whether they were. I thank him for making all the nonwriting moments fun and meaningful, for being someone I love to be around all the time in any place, and for being an example that writing is a means for our survival as well as an outlet to detour all the crazy-making of everyday life. This book is dedicated to David because it would not exist without him.

Introduction

The Violence of Value

Hurricane Katrina decimated the poorest, the brownest, and the blackest neighborhoods along the Gulf Coast in Louisiana, Alabama, Florida, and Mississippi. By almost all accounts, the people most devastated and the places most damaged were disproportionately black and impoverished. And while not all coverage was without sympathy, some articles' portrayals of Katrina victims were disconcerting. News media and conservative weblogs stigmatized and criminalized poor African American victims of Hurricane Katrina, particularly the residents of New Orleans. Among the most publicized examples of these incriminating images were snapshots of black people allegedly "looting" abandoned grocery stores. Several bloggers juxtaposed two virtually identical photos on the internet with very different and very telling captions. One read, "A young man wades through chest deep flood water after looting a grocery store . . . ," while the other said, "Two residents wade through chest-deep water after finding bread and soda from a local grocery store . . ."[1] The pictures told us that African Americans "looted" while white people "found." It seemed that news media presumed white people's innocence and the black poor's guilt, but the example also elucidated much more than individual journalist's stereotypes.

The captions illustrated not only that young black males are persistently stereotyped as criminal; they also revealed that criminal activity was *unrecognizable* without a black body. Without a black body, the same action was interpreted as a (white) survival strategy. The difference between seeing a stereotype and recognizing criminality is not insignificant. A stereotype is about perception and deception. Its colloquial use often refers to a certain kind of intellectual laziness that prefers to interpret situations through ideological shortcuts, rather than searching seriously for what's "really true." But if the black body is *necessary* for an audience to *recognize* criminal activity, then the difference between "looting" and "finding" is not just a stereotype, not just proof of a distorted image that obfuscates "truth" and complexity. The example illustrates that race is much more than a fraudulent mask that we have been forced to wear that prevents other people from "truly seeing" who we "really" are.

The example also demonstrates that race, gender, and sexuality are ways of knowing that make sense of social reality in the United States. Two practically indistinguishable images could have been interpreted in multiple ways, but they were not, and they were not because social differences made sense of the scenes that were seen. They were not because a single black man and a white couple (heterosexual by all appearances) provided the context for abandoned grocery stores and floating loaves of bread. Black masculinity gave a different meaning to chest-deep waters and hurricane-wrecked lives than the meanings conveyed by white heteronormativity. As ways of knowing and methods of meaning-making, race, gender, and sexuality simultaneously erase and make sense of what should have been a contradiction by making racial contradictions commonsense. It should have been contradictory to interpret the same action as unlawful for one person but resourceful for two others, yet the contradiction was dismissed, explained away as merely the simple "truth" of photojournalists' observations.

The Associated Press (AP) essentially argued that the photographer saw a person who seemed to have engaged in the act of looting and that it was no one's fault that the looting body happened to be black: "AP's policy is that each photographer can describe only what he or she actually sees."[2] Both photographers described what they saw, but race was the way of knowing that made sense out of their observations. As the *New York Times* reported,

> Mr. Martin had seen the man in his photograph wade into a grocery store and come out with the sodas and bag, so by [the] A.P.'s definition, the man

had looted. . . . Mr. Graythen [photographer of the Agence France-Presse photo (AFP)] described seeing the couple near a corner store from an elevated expressway. The door to the shop was open, and things had floated out to the street. He was not able to talk to the couple, "so I had to draw my own conclusions," he said.[3]

The explanation for this racial contradiction was simple: Nothing needed to be explained because nothing was contradictory. To make these contradictions no longer contradictory, interpretations of the photographs had to bracket bodies of racial difference, refocusing the controversy by directing us to "see" the Katrina victims' conduct and contexts instead of their color.[4] After all the controversy and such blatant evidence, we are left only with a picture of black looting and a photo of white finding, each verified as and representative of the color-blind truth. What we were really seeing, we were told, was a photo of "looting" officially defined and a photo of "finding" credibly presupposed.

Racial stereotypes are not degrading because race is devalued. Stereotypes are degrading because they link race to other categories of devaluation, just as race is redeemed when linked to other properties of personhood universalized as socially valuable, such as heteronormativity or U.S. citizenship. In these examples, racial commonsense-making pivots on the concept of "looting." "Looting" links black racial difference to criminality. And although this is an association adamantly disavowed, the disavowal itself falls one step short. The looter, as a criminal figure, is also a signifier for a fiction, a fictional figure that people have made real and consequential. The looter is given a life of his own, affixed with an amoral nature and ascribed shameful meanings that justify why certain people need to be targets of state violence and abandonment. Disavowing criminality was possible in part because bloggers took the looter out of the photograph; the looter was erased and re-presented as a survivor who had been misrecognized as a criminal. His particular black body was delinked from criminality and given back personhood, but criminality was not delinked from black bodies in general. The criminal was and could be renounced only because the figure of the looter was no longer a part of *this* picture. The juxtaposition of black looting and white finding lends itself to outrage, disavowal, and repudiation, but none of these responses help us to reveal how Hurricane Katrina victims of color are transformed into criminals or how communities are criminal*ized*. One photographer saw a survival strategy, rather than a criminal activity. We reproach him because he saw a Hurricane Katrina survivor instead of a criminal figure, because he seemed selectively empathetic, because he had a definition of "looting" that some looters did not seem to fit.[5]

Social Death

Social Death: Racialized Rightlessness and the Criminalization of the Unprotected examines how human value is made intelligible through racialized, sexualized, spatialized, and state-sanctioned violences. Although we know that social value is assigned and denied on racial terms, less attention has been given to examining the ways in which social value is also contested and condoned through legally inflected notions of morality. Because the law is presumed to be both ethical and irreproachable, the act of law-breaking reflects poorly on a person's moral character. If following the law (legitimate or not) determines whether a person is moral or immoral, it is all but impossible for people assigned to certain status categories to represent themselves as moral and deserving.

In no small part, our analytical limitations can be traced to past solutions. Part of the difficulty is connected to our own victories: Today's "racial progress" is heavily indebted to the state and its legal apparatuses, and for some populations that is precisely the problem. For the poor of color, the stakes are always high. The poor of color are affected most often and most intensely when criminal and immigration laws are altered to be more efficient but less humane. This happens, in part, because the criminal, the illegal alien, and the terrorist suspect are treated as obvious, self-inflicted, and necessary outcomes of law-breaking rather than as *effects* of the law or as produced by the law. When law targets certain people for incarceration or deportation, it criminalizes those people of color who are always already most vulnerable and multiply marginalized.

The practices and processes of criminalization, however, are often concealed when we reject criminal stereotypes. The term "criminalization" has been used to refer to being stereotyped as a criminal as well as to being criminalized, but it's important to maintain a distinction between the two. Even though being stereotyped and being criminalized are not mutually exclusive and often overlap, these have different relationships to U.S. law. To be stereotyped as a criminal is to be misrecognized as someone who committed a crime, but to be criminalized is to be prevented from being law-abiding. To be stereotyped as a gang member means that someone, perhaps a law-abiding citizen, was misrecognized as a gang member because of his or her racial background. In contrast, gang members are criminalized because they have a different relationship to criminal law and the U.S. justice system, because they face regulations other people do not have to follow, such as gang injunctions, and because they deal with harsher and longer sentences because of gang enhancement charges. Racial profiling both stereotypes nongang members and criminalizes gang members. For the person who is racially profiled as well as misrecognized as a gang member, the injury is not just the act of racial profiling but also the act of misrecognition. Not only does criminalization preempt sympathy for and empathizing with gang members, it ensures outrage on behalf of those who are misrecognized and falsely accused of *being* (not behaving like) a gang member.

In this vein, people who occupy legally vulnerable and criminalized statuses are not just excluded from justice; criminalized populations and the places where they live *form the foundation* of the U.S. legal system, imagined to be the reason why a punitive (in)justice system exists. Although they are excluded from law's protection, they are not excluded from law's discipline, punishment, and regulation. Their position evidences what ethnic studies scholar Yen Le Espiritu terms "differential inclusion."[6] As Espiritu argues, marginalized groups are "deemed integral to the nation's economy, culture, identity, and power—but integral only or precisely because of their designated subordinate standing."[7] Certain vulnerable and impoverished populations and places of color have been "differentially included" within the U.S. legal system. As targets of regulation and containment, they are deemed deserving of discipline and punishment but not worthy of protection. They are not merely excluded from legal protection but criminalized as always already the object and target of law, never its authors or addressees.

As the foundation of law, certain racialized populations are excluded from its protections and its processes of legitimation, but they are not quite imagined as completely outside the law because to be outside the law suggests that eventual inclusion is possible. When immigration law excluded people of particular races and national origins from immigrating, it was not permanent. Because these laws explicitly criminalized identities, they could be changed or rescinded to incorporate previously excluded groups. They did not, however, fundamentally change the criminalized statuses such laws produced. For instance, Chinese Exclusion (1882) produced Chinese "illegal aliens."[8] Repealing Chinese Exclusion (1943) enabled more immigrants from China to enter the United States legally, but it did not change the vulnerable legal status of the "illegal alien." The "illegal" or unlawful alien is a status that forms the foundation of immigration law, and, therefore, the unlawful alien cannot be incorporated into immigration or naturalization law. Laws that have tried to address the problem of having an undocumented, rightless population have only been able to make exceptions. The Immigration Reform and Control Act of 1986, for example, provided a path toward legalization and citizenship for a specific contingent of undocumented immigrants, but it did not change or decriminalize the rightless status of the "illegal alien." All those who did not qualify (or could not prove that they qualified) under the exemption would still be criminalized, demonized, and rendered rightless. Recent proposals for a federal Development, Relief, and Education for Alien Minors Act (DREAM Act) also propose to create exceptions to current immigration law (i.e., by giving a path to legalization to undocumented college educated students and undocumented persons who serve the military). But the DREAM Act proposals do not address the fundamental problem of immigration law: that it creates a permanently rightless status.

To say that some groups form the foundation for law is to say that law is dependent upon the *permanence* of certain groups' criminalization. These permanently criminalized people are the groups to whom I refer as *ineligible for personhood*—as populations subjected to laws but refused the legal means to contest those laws as well as denied both the political legitimacy and moral credibility necessary to question them. These populations are excluded from the ostensibly democratic processes that legitimate U.S. law, yet they are expected to unambiguously accept and unequivocally uphold a legal and political system that depends on the unquestioned permanency of their rightlessness. As I will argue, targeted populations do not need to break laws to be criminalized. Their behaviors are criminalized even if their crimes are victimless (using street drugs), even if their actual activities are not illegal at all (using health care), and even if the evidence is not actually evidence ("looking like a terrorist"). Criminalization can operate through instituting laws that cannot be followed. People subjected to laws based on their (il)legal status—"illegal aliens," "gang members," "terrorist suspects"—are unable to comply with the "rule of law" because U.S. law targets their being and their bodies, not their behavior. They are denied not only the illusion of authorship but even the possibility of compliance.[9]

Certain populations' very humanity is represented as something that one becomes or achieves, that one must earn because it cannot just be.[10] These populations are denied what political philosopher Hannah Arendt calls "the right to have rights."[11] The bodies and localities of poor, criminalized people of color are signifiers for those who are ineligible for personhood, for those contemporary (il)legal statuses within U.S. law that are legally illegible. These statuses are legally illegible because they engender populations not just racialized but rightless, living nonbeings, or, in Judith Butler's words, as "something living that is other than life."[12] To be ineligible for personhood is a form of social death;[13] it not only defines who does not matter, it also makes mattering meaningful. For different reasons, undocumented immigrants, the racialized poor of the global South, and criminalized U.S. residents of color in both inner cities and rural areas are populations who "*never* achieve, in the eyes of others, the status of 'living.'"[14] In her study of death, race, sexuality, and subjectivity, Sharon Holland observes that in the space of social death, "there is no full embrace of the margin here, only the chance to struggle against both a killing abstraction and a life-in-death; neither choice is an appealing option."[15] The killing abstraction is not itself abstract. It references the ways in which racialized populations are made unduly vulnerable by global capitalism and neoliberal restructuring, and it refers to the way they are positioned absolutely and necessarily beyond legal recourse. Urban geographer Ruth Wilson Gilmore names these killing, abstracting practices and processes "racism":

> Racism is a practice of abstraction, a death-dealing displacement of difference into hierarchies that organize relations within and between the planet's sovereign political territories. . . . Indeed, the process of abstraction that signifies racism produces effects at the most intimately "sovereign" scale, insofar as particular kinds of bodies, one by one, are materially (if not always visibly) configured by racism into a hierarchy of human and inhuman persons that in sum form the category of "human being."[16]

Racism is a killing abstraction. It creates spaces of living death and populations "dead-to-others."[17] It ensures that certain people will live an "abstract existence" where "living [is] something to be *achieved* and not *experienced*."[18]

Engendered by corporate capital and the neoliberal state, ineligibility to personhood refers to the state of being legally recognized as rightless, located in the spaces of social death where demands for humanity are ultimately disempowering because they can be interpreted only as asking to be given something sacred in return for nothing at all.[19] By definition an inalienable right cannot be taken or given away, and, therefore, it cannot really be reconferred. Regardless of citizenship status, whether people of color deserve rights and resources is often questioned because those with social privilege often still interpret economic, social, political, and/or legal integration as a (conditional) "gift."[20] Ineligibility to personhood is the contemporary manifestation of what Orlando Patterson refers to as the "inalienability problem."[21] In his seminal work on slavery and social death, Patterson explains that the act of freeing slaves, specifically their transformation from possession to personhood, was legally, economically, and conceptually illegible. Because the master already owned anything a slave could give, freedom could only be conceived of as granted, never actually purchased, so "even though slaves paid dearly in one way or another for their freedom . . . freedom itself was still regarded as a gift from the master or mistress."[22] When slaves bought their freedom, the transaction did not give them what their master possessed by owning them, "for the master does not convey dominion or power to the slave; he merely releases him from his dominion."[23] Buying "freedom" did not transmit empowerment; it reconfigured the slave's relationship to the master's power.

Current examples of the "inalienability problem" can be found in popular arguments over extending welfare benefits to the unemployed of color because all sides of both debates accept the premise that working (or independently wealthy) U.S. citizens have something to lose and nothing to gain. This is why such debates—over welfare, deportation, detention, etc.—frequently revolve around questions of morality and ethicality—whether Americans should or shouldn't "freely give" rights and resources to the destitute and undeserving. To extend legal recognition to those already recognized as ineligible for such rights is also about the empowered population's "sacrifice," as if legal recognition was a contract between unequals that formalizes the dominant populations' willingness to share their power and privileges. Whether marginalized and aggrieved groups have access to legal recourse becomes a moral and ethical question for the privileged population. Hence, the transformation from nonbeing to legal personhood is always and already framed as someone else's "freely given decision" to relinquish power and privilege in exchange for nothing at all.[24]

To use the term "ineligibility" underscores that legal recognition is not and cannot be a viable solution for racialized exploitation, violence, and poverty. For all legally uncertain populations, the law punishes but does not protect, disciplines but does not defend. Because the state renders criminalized populations of color ineligible for personhood and, consequently, ineligible for the right to ask for rights, they cannot be incorporated in rights-based politics. Another way to think about populations "dead-to-others" is to think about those populations whom a politics of misrecognition needs to bracket, disavow, and/or repudiate because they are either self-evidently undeserving, politically illegible, or (and usually) both. As criminal by being, unlawful by presence, and illegal by status, *they do not have the option to be law abiding*, which is always the absolute prerequisite for political rights, legal recognition, and resource redistribution in the United States. When subjugation is engendered, justified, and maintained by the law, legal recognition cannot be a permanent or meaningful solution to subjugation. Criminalization justifies people's ineligibility to personhood because it takes away the right to have rights. Consequentially, criminalization makes sense of the contradictions that ensue when according unequal access to legal universality.

The Eyes of Others

To transparently recognize a black man or a black woman as a "looter" is not equivalent to misrecognizing a hurricane victim as a criminal. Seeing a looter rather than a recognizing a victim does not emerge from an inability to conceive of certain people as entitled to personhood. This way of seeing emerges from the *refusal* to see them as such. Cultural studies scholar Sara Ahmed's work on "stranger fetishism" helps to clarify why transparent recognition is not just seeing a stereotype, not merely an act of misrecognition. As she explains, the stranger is not just someone whom we don't know, but the one whom we *know* to be a stranger.[25] The stranger becomes a figure with a life of its own because its transparent recognition as the other we don't know "fleshes out" its given form. In other words, the act of transparent recognition places a looter into a body of color. The looting black body, as the stranger's given form, comes to contain all we think we know (and all we think we don't know) about the nature of strangers, who register as out of place when in our space. The figure of the stranger, Ahmed argues, "assumes a life of its own only insofar as it is cut off from its histories of its determination."[26] The figure of the stranger is, thus, *ontologized* "as a way of being in the world";[27] it is "assumed to have a nature" and turned into "something that simply *is*."[28]

Akin to "the stranger," so-called "unlawful" people (looters, gang members, illegal aliens, suspected terrorists) and so-imagined "lawless" places (totalitarian regimes, inner cities, barrios) are ontologized. These grossly overrepresented, all-too-recognizable figures with lives of their own—the looter, the gang member, the illegal alien, the suspected terrorist—have *real world referents*. We can transparently recognize criminals (with their disreputable traits and deceitful nature) *only* if we refuse to recognize the material histories, social relations, and structural conditions that criminalize populations of color and the impoverished places where they live. To transparently recognize a looter where a survivor should be depends on erasing the state's neglect of poor African American victims of Hurricane Katrina. When transparently recognized, such figures are abstracted from the social relationships that effect them, assumed to represent ways of being in the world, defined only by people's claims and conclusions about their nature. Acts of transparent recognition are integral to the processes that criminalize people of color in the first place.

One of the strategies for exposing moments of transparent recognition is to apply double-consciousness. W. E. B. Du Bois' concept of double-consciousness works well as an analytical lens for examining photos of black crime and white survival because the photos evidence and validate what we feel we know but rarely can prove. Du Bois defines double-consciousness as "this sense of always looking at one's self through the eyes of others, of measuring one's soul by the tape of a world that looks on in amused contempt and pity."[29] According to Du Bois, African Americans are keenly attuned to the ways in which other people "see" and perceive them. Double-consciousness explains how we might interpret reading stories and seeing photographs through how we imagine what other audiences see, read, and transparently recognize.

Explicit contrasts like the example of looting and finding, however, are not the most prevalent images of racialized criminality and criminalized rightlessness. In addition to coverage about Hurricane Katrina victims, the other topics explored in this book—hate crime, gang violence, undocumented immigration, the war on terror, and the immigrant rights movement—are rarely presented in ways that expose how news media participate in creating or fabricating criminals by providing us the tools that enable us to see and simultaneously deny what we are seeing. Like the AP's explanation of why looting was not finding, news media suggest that what we see (looting) is not dependent on what we see (a single black man). This becomes even more complicated when pictures do not accompany the text or when the narrative leads us to picture certain images but then takes no responsibility for doing so. While few would admit they imagine specific racialized bodies when reading words such as "crime," "terrorism," or "immigration," social differences such as race, gender, class, sexuality, and legality shape not just how we choose sides in political issues but also how we interpret social reality. This charges scholars of culture with the critical tasks of not only decoding familiar narratives that tell us what to see but also illuminating invisible pictures that most people will deny they see, let alone imagine. As Ruby Tapia writes, "Between images and in the interstices of how we have been taught to see, there are so many necessary and invisible forms. As fiercely as we struggle to say things that are pictures, we must work to picture things that are not, the things inside the gaps in images, the content of spaces between time(s), the dynamic imperatives of power taking shape."[30]

We need an analytic that enables us to analyze how criminality is recognized when the perspective of power and privilege is not represented but also not necessarily not there, such as when the American public "sees" through *another other's eyes*. In 2009, the *New York Times* reported on "an under-the-radar crime epidemic" in the Big Easy, which was attributed to corporate opportunism, law enforcement apathy, and a resentful residential displaced out-of-workforce. Characterizing New Orleans as "one of America's most crime-ridden cities," the article declared undocumented workers had become "the prey of choice."[31] In this news story, the local poor of color in New Orleans were criminalized through interviews with undocumented immigrants who reported being beaten and mugged by African American assailants. Geovanny Billado, an undocumented immigrant from Honduras, was one of many unauthorized workers who had been mugged. Billado interpreted the reason for the attacks as African Americans' anti-Latina/o racism: "The blacks are waiting for us. They'll beat you up. They'll take your money."[32]

The photos of looting and finding provided us the pictures and the captions to use our "double-consciousness" to illumine how black people were criminalized, but in the story about crime in New Orleans, undocumented Honduran immigrants represented "the eyes of others." Undocumented immigrants' eyes were used to facilitate the transparent recognition of black criminality, to enable U.S. Americans reading this story to simultaneously "see" and deny "seeing" black criminality. Like the Associated Press's and Agence France-Presse's contradictory captions of black looting and white finding, respectively, Billado's comments and the news story in general tell us how to recognize crime in relation to blackness.[33] He, too, sees crime when no crime is occurring as implied by his phrase "the blacks are waiting for us," as well as by his predictions "they'll beat you up" and "take your money." Yet his allegations are contextualized much differently than the Associated Press's official recognition and definition of "looting." Because Billado's assumptions are grounded in a past experience, his claims feel factual in a way that makes it more difficult to challenge than the pictures of anonymous looters and finders. Like the photographs betrayed by their captions, this news story, through informants such as Billado, teaches us how to see crime and criminality, how to interpret "waiting" as a crime-in-the-making. In fact, the story has much in common with the captions, which not only attached criminality to black bodies in the photos of looting but also made black bodies necessary to recognize crime. In the absence of black racial difference (the white couple), a photo of looting becomes evidence of finding. Stories such as Billado's do the same ideological work as the captions attached to the AP and the AFP pictures, yet unlike the juxtaposed pictures and their betraying captions, Billado's observations and the news story that cited him held none of the characteristics that make it easy to repudiate racialized criminality, that make it easy to reproach people who "see" looting where finding should be or who "recognize" a crime-in-the-making instead of waiting or wading.

To make matters more complicated, the article's ideological work functions to decriminalize undocumented immigrants. Drawing upon criminalizing stereotypes of African Americans works to represent undocumented

Latinas/os in New Orleans as hardworking, exploited laborers. When figures of criminality are displaced onto the African American community, journalists undercut the criminalization of "illegal" status. The *New York Times* article cites an official to speak for undocumented laborers, which redeems Latina/o "illegality" through connecting the men to families while naming their African American attackers as the comparatively unredeemable or the "true" criminals.

> "It's very sad that they're here helping us rebuild, yet you have an element that's targeting them," Officer Janssen Valencia said. "They work all week. Then comes the weekend, they get robbed."
>
> "What they really voice is: 'That money was for the family. We don't harm anybody. Why does anybody mess with us?'"[34]

The article on crime against undocumented immigrants allegedly by African Americans makes it appear as though both groups harbor racist sentiments toward each other. By citing undocumented workers' claims that African Americans are racist, journalists conveniently displace the American public's anti-Latina/o nativism onto the African American out-of-work poor. At the same time, citing such statements also accomplishes the converse because it represents undocumented immigrants as racist for interpreting the attacks as racially motivated. As the press reported, "The accusation of racism does not ring true to some city leaders . . . and in the eyes of some in New Orleans, they have mistaken simple opportunism for racism."[35] This is highlighted with a quotation from African American community leader Reverend John C. Raphael Jr. a minister who leads anticrime rallies: "'I think it's not directly racial,' Mr. Raphael said, but rather 'the fact that they were vulnerable, they were taken advantage of.'"[36] In this way, "respectable" African Americans are cited to undermine undocumented immigrants' interpretations of their experiences, but not to undermine the experiences themselves. Hence, representations of black criminality remain intact while undocumented immigrants are held responsible for originating and disseminating stereotypes about African Americans as criminal, displacing not only Americans' anti-black racism but also Americans' role in reproducing stereotypes about African Americans as criminals.

To analyze the voice of racism when it speaks through the voice of another debased and criminalized group, it's important to employ a comparative analytic that examines how human value and humans' values are assumed and assigned, justified and denied. How do we analyze racialized representations if undocumented Latinas/os are cited as both the voice of American anti-black racism and the victims of African American criminality? Is there a way to disavow the figure of black criminality without reifying the figure of Latina/o illegality when it's precisely the figure of Latina/o illegality that enables the recuperation of the African American citizen? To represent either aggrieved group as deserving of rights and sympathy, the criminalized figures that their bodies signify must be disavowed or vindicated. But the criminalized figure does not disappear; more often than not, the figure is displaced and mutates into other easily recognizable figures of criminality, such as the "illegal alien."

Unlike the juxtaposition of black criminality with white ingenuity, the criminal figure cannot be exposed through denial and disavowal in stories that quote Latinas/os, African Americans, Asians, and indigenous peoples to be both the voice and victim of racism. Particular bodies of color cannot be recuperated because no counter evidence or alternative framework reinterprets the figures of criminality, exposes how people of color are criminalized, or uncovers how whiteness is valued.

Because different racial groups are variously marked as criminal and unincorporable, conflict and competition between two marginalized groups are often represented as extraneous to white/nonwhite binaries, but these narratives actually reinforce racialized value hierarchies and binaries—criminal/not criminal, illegal/not illegal, terrorist/not terrorist. Represented as if in constant conflict, aggrieved groups are placed within different racialized binaries and value hierarchies that *overlap and intersect*—criminal/illegal, illegal/terrorist, terrorist/criminal—in a way that essentially hides, disguises, and displaces American racism, stabilizing rather than subverting practices and processes of criminalization. Our analytical frameworks for making sense of race and race relations in the United States are thus limited when applied to criminalized people of color. This book explores those limitations and, in doing so, elucidates why repudiating criminality and recuperating social value so often reproduce the problems we mean to resolve.

Value and Its Violences: Using a Comparative Analytic

Value is made intelligible relationally. According to literary critic Lindon Barrett, value *needs* negativity. As he theorizes, the "object" of value needs an "other" of value because "for value 'negativity is a *resource*,' an essential resource. The negative, the expended, the excessive invariably form the ground of possibilities for value."[37] Hurricane Katrina literally established the watery grounds that made the land and its resources extremely valuable to developers precisely because the land was now worthless to everyone except the poor of color whose lives were not deemed worthy of rebuilding. As wealthy New Orleans developer Joseph Canizaro said, "I think we have a clean sheet to start again. And with that clean sheet we have some very big opportunities."[38] His "big opportunities" required razing New Orleans. Rather than seeing the destroyed city as a national disgrace, he saw it as a "clean sheet," but this sheet can be clean only if poor, displaced African Americans are conceived of as a population easy to abandon. Value and violence, Barrett emphasized, are not simultaneously engendered, but rather "value introduces itself by way of a violent agency that it subsequently seeks to deny."[39] Hurricane Katrina was not the source of violence; it was the cover story that made it easier to deny the past and present violences of abuse and abandonment, of profit and privatization, which brutally paved the way for corporate elites to accumulate surplus value as they rebuilt a drowning city on newly devalued land. The more worthless the haunted grounds and the more forsaken its residents, the cleaner the sheet, and the cleaner the sheet, the more possibilities big businesses could seize for profit.[40]

But the relationship between human value and human disposability is a bit more complex, conflicted, and even confusing when we aren't talking about the ways in which Halliburton/KBR finds economic value in the violent devaluation and dehumanization of the poor of color. How might we revise our strategies for analyzing anti-black racism when it works through anti-Latina/o and anti-Asian nativism, when the coded comparison is meant to be the insult? For instance, when identified as "refugees," black Katrina victims were devalued on multiple levels. Both President George W. Bush and Reverend Jesse Jackson felt it was inappropriate, even offensive, to refer to American citizens displaced by Katrina as "refugees." As Bush emphasized, "The people we're talking about are not refugees. . . . They are Americans and they need the help and love and compassion of our fellow citizens."[41] Jackson maintained that referring to Katrina victims as refugees used "racist language" because it suggested that African Americans were not Americans.[42] His disapproval of "refugee" was grounded in indicting the federal government for its incompetence and indifference, foregrounding African Americans' unrecognized relationship of privilege to the state: "We are American citizens. We are not refugees. We are citizens who have not been well served by our government."[43] Both Bush's and Jackson's remarks illustrate refugees' presumed relationships to the federal government and the American public —as un-entitled to Americans' "love and compassion" and as even less entitled to government resources and services—a relationship that most journalists characterized as "second-class citizenship." However, to reclaim entitlement by adamantly denying resemblance to refugees also renders less worthy the many refugees who were also Hurricane Katrina victims, such as New Orleans' resident immigrant populations from Viet Nam and Honduras.

Like Bush and Jackson, those who rebuked the use of "refugee" were not disagreeing with the definitions of "refugee" provided by the Oxford English Dictionary or the United Nations. They repudiated the way in which "refugee" was used and how it could be interpreted metaphorically—in which case, all the characteristics of "refugee" would be transferred to the victims of Hurricane Katrina, including the meanings assigned to the racial groups currently associated with the category "refugee." When race works analogically, comparatively, and relationally to make sense of systemic and systematic racism, the state recruits people of color to demand their due recognition as deserving U.S. citizens or law-abiding immigrants, but the manner of their recruitment requires that they do so by disavowing another devalued racial other of U.S. citizenship and American empire. The source of one racial group's social value (African Americans' Americanness and citizenship) was contingent upon and made legible through the devaluation of an/other (refugees' un-Americanness and noncitizenship).

Calling African Americans "refugees" was not only criminalizing; it was alienating and distancing. Journalists used what they believed to be "true" of the Third World to apprehend what they were witnessing, to make sense of post-Katrina New Orleans for themselves and their audiences. "Refugee" evoked racialized regions of the Third World in order to explain a First World disaster. National Public Radio correspondent Mike Pesca's explanation for why "refugee" was an apt description reveals that some reporters did not identify with Katrina victims and needed to use "refugee" as a way to make sense of tragedies that happen to "other" people and places.

They're refugees because circumstance is turning them into refugees. . . . If you watched this situation on television, you might not realize how dirty and foul-smelling these people were. There was a reluctance on the part of the rescuers to touch the people. There was a total unwillingness to walk among them. The reaction was understandable. Many of the people they were trying to help had swum through sewage water to get here, and no one was showering anytime soon.

The dynamic I witnessed was clearly of the dirty masses on one side and the soldiers and police on the other. There was a justification for this separation because security was a concern in New Orleans and law enforcement was on edge. But if you looked at the armed men in fatigues on one side of metal barricades, and thousands of grieving people in tattered clothes on the other, you couldn't help but think of Haiti or Kosovo.

The people of New Orleans who finally made it out of town, and who are still being plucked from attics weren't people on their way out of town. The people who heeded warnings and had the wherewithal to leave town before Katrina hit were evacuees. These beleaguered people who had lost everything were something else.[44]

Essentially, Pesca could not reconcile how he imagined America with that part of America beyond his imagination, and so he "couldn't help but think of Haiti or Kosovo." Pesca differentiated between Katrina evacuees and Katrina refugees, in part, because he identified with the evacuees, with the people "who heeded warnings and had the wherewithal to leave town," whereas those "beleaguered people" left behind were "something else." Though perhaps unwittingly, "refugee" was deployed to foreclose empathy for the impoverished African American victims of Hurricane Katrina, and it did so through likening them to differently devalued people of color, whom the debate over the use of "refugee" erased as victims too.

The erasure of victim status also recruits people of color to demand due recognition, as if being represented (no matter how negatively and irregardless of purpose) is in and of itself a sign of social value. Writing for the higher education magazine *Diverse*, Lydia Lum took a different approach toward explaining why the Vietnamese victims of Hurricane Katrina were "swept into the background."[45] She began the article by calling attention to how

[t]he entire world saw the images of Black New Orleans residents left homeless, jobless, and helpless by the arrival and aftermath of Hurricane Katrina. The pictures and stories dominated mainstream news outlets for weeks. What hasn't been widely publicized, however, are the Katrina-related ordeals of Vietnamese Americans, another socio-economically disadvantaged population along the Gulf Coast.[46]

Lum illustrates the underrepresentation of the Vietnamese by situating them in relation to the global coverage of the black poor, challenging portrayals of impoverished African Americans as representative of Hurricane Katrina victims by posing equivalency ("another socio-economically disadvantaged population"). And although Lum and her interviewees make a concerted effort to describe Vietnamese and black relations in New Orleans as just ordinary (as neither wrought with tension nor as an untapped coalition), the article can't help implying that audiences care more about what happens to African Americans than to Asian Americans and immigrants.

Although she does not indict African Americans for their supposed overrepresentation, Lum does suggest that news coverage is a measure of social value in the United States. However, proposing that "visibility" is an unearned privilege that evidences racial inequality in media and popular culture evades questioning these institutions' roles in criminalizing the black poor; it also presupposes that criminalized representations are better than none at all—perhaps even suggesting that criminalized representations must be at least partially accurate. Engaging a politics of representation, the article communicates two messages: that poor blacks cannot stand in for America or for all people of color, and that the lives of impoverished blacks always seem to overshadow the lives of other U.S. minorities.

In these narratives about Katrina "refugees" of color, race is the methodology of social value; it's used to contest erasure, reveal neglect, call out contradictions, claim injustice, and make explicit hidden assumptions that justified and reproduced narratives about already not-valued lives of color. Journalists utilized comparative and relational methods to explain and narrate the initial denial of and consequent demand for the (re)conferral of social value. I call attention to these examples not to say that these groups are racist toward one another or that one group pulls another down in order to get ahead. To the contrary, I highlight these examples to demonstrate that *there is no way out of this dilemma* because recuperating social value *requires* rejecting the other Other. Ascribing readily recognizable social value always requires the devaluation of an/other, and that other is almost always poor, racialized, criminalized, segregated, legally vulnerable, and unprotected. These racial/ethnic groups are not actually selling each other out; they are simply reasserting the truth of their existence, which has been erased or distorted not only by likening them to already not-valued others but also by not representing them when writing about differently devalued others. Thus, the fact of their existence (I am a citizen, not a refugee or I am a Hurricane Katrina survivor of color, too) is already linked to the devaluation of an/other.

Because (re)valuing always implies devaluing a not-valued "other," it makes sense to employ a comparative analytic when we analyze the ways in which aggrieved groups are devalued and why aggrieved groups are aggrieved.[47] A comparative analytic centers relational, contingent, and conditional processes of devaluation, which makes it particularly useful for examining how interconnected processes of valorization, devaluation, and revaluation (i.e., race, gender, sexuality, class, nation, legality, etc.) work interdependently to reify value and relations of inequality as normative, natural, and obvious. Although it is informed by the differential devaluation of racialized groups, this approach does not necessarily entail an explicit comparison of two or more racial groups because relations of value are not always explicit. Processes of differential devaluation often work invisibly and implicitly, or they may be referenced abstractly as what we are *not* (i.e., we are not "refugees," "illegal aliens," "terrorists," or "criminals"). In a sense, a comparative analytic assumes that in the United States, human value is made legible in relation to the deviant, the non-American, the nonnormative, the pathologized, and the recalcitrant—the legally repudiated "others" of human value in the United States.

The production and ascription of human value are both violent and relational, both differential and contextual. Value is ascribed through explicitly or implicitly disavowing relationships to the already devalued and disciplined categories of deviance and nonnormativity. When we distinguish ourselves from unlawful and outlawed status categories, we implicitly insist that these socio-legal categories are not only necessary but should be reserved and preserved for the "genuinely" lazy (welfare recipients), "undoubtedly" immoral (marrying for citizenship), and "truly" dangerous (gang violence). When we reject these criminalized others of color, we leave less room for questioning why such status categories are automatically and categorically devalued. While these tactics may be politically strategic and even necessary at times, it is important to be cognizant of the fact that they work because a sympathetic public can register that some people are the wrong targets of legitimate laws. They work only if a sympathetic public already accepts that discrimination against not-valued others is legitimate and necessary.

Legal Discrimination

A comparative analytic that centers and denaturalizes the space and the state of social death can help us to reframe familiar narratives about race relations. In many black-Latina/o conflict narratives, for instance, there are unspoken juxtapositions that run the risk of reifying figures of criminality. When rejecting or recontextualizing criminal activity, the disavowal is displaced, directly or indirectly, onto the other. For example, the claim that "law-abiding" undocumented immigrants reside in the United States without authorization is implicitly juxtaposed against the claim that African American citizens engage in criminal activities only because "illegal aliens" steal American jobs. But if we suspend the impulse to recuperate either of these demonized groups, we might find that the debate itself is a lose-lose story—that the official narrative of black-Latina/o conflict and competition works to pathologize both groups, regardless of which side we take.

Both claims obscure the ways in which neoliberal ideologies and values ontologize figures of criminality by treating them as if they were real examples of poor people's (ir)rational choices for making a living. According to Lisa Duggan, neoliberalism scripts disempowered and unprotected people as primarily responsible for their vulnerabilities to state exclusion and capital exploitation: "Neoliberals have promoted 'private' *competition, self-esteem,* and *independence* as the roots of *personal responsibility,* and excoriated 'public' *entitlement, dependency,* and *irresponsibility* as the sources of social ills."[48] The values neoliberalism publicizes, naturalizes, and universalizes also make indigent groups of color unable to prove they experience discrimination.

Even when one possesses ample evidence of employer fraud and worker abuse, neoliberalism makes it difficult to substantiate such claims because in some ways neoliberalism renders capital exploitation conceptually impossible. Neoliberal values of private competition, self-esteem, and independence benefit corporations: If everyone is an "entrepreneur" of him or herself, then individuals cannot be exploited by capital. As "entrepreneurs" of themselves, individuals exploit *themselves* and should take "personal responsibility" for doing so.[49] Interpreted through a neoliberal value system, "illegal" status is a choice made by rational individuals who are ultimately resigned to being underpaid, cheated, and abused because after "calculating" the risks or "gambling" against the odds, each person presumably decided that undocumented status would still be "worth" it.

In the era of American neoliberalism, social value and moral behavior are interpreted through and evaluated on economic terms, and, as a result, capitalist logic and ethics prevail in the social sphere as well as the economic and political realms. As put simply by Michel Foucault, American neoliberalism demands an "economic analysis of the non-economic."[50] We can see how this logic permeates narratives of black-Latina/o competition. When allies of undocumented immigrants describe certain occupations as jobs that "no one wants," they are decriminalizing unauthorized workers by describing them as valuable laborers who help rather than harm U.S. citizens and legal residents. This appeal, however, constructs poorly paid jobs as a privilege and poor U.S. citizens as the "no-one-who-wants" unskilled labor-intensive jobs. This appeal also naturalizes the notion that arduous jobs should not only be underpaid and exploitable but also that the poorest people, regardless of citizenship or immigration status, should feel lucky to be exploited if they are paid at all. The human value of undocumented laborers is measured only in terms of their economic value for the American middle class, whereas the human value of unemployed citizens of color is negated altogether. In this attempt to revalue undocumented workers, the middle-class and socially privileged consumer assumes the position of America's valued population.

Furthermore, it is virtually impossible, especially for those without co-pious resources, to press charges against corporations for nonemployment practices that keep people not just unemployed but out of the workforce and excluded from the labor pool. It is all but legal to discriminate against unemployed citizens—most of whom are African American or Latina/o.[51] How can unemployed workers provide concrete evidence of racial bias in hiring practices when they aren't given the opportunity to apply?[52] Claiming racially discriminatory practices in unemployment cannot be addressed by current equal opportunity laws or proven to have "disparate impact" in part because the unemployed are not a protected class and thereby have no basis to sue employers for discriminatory recruitment and hiring practices.[53] Per-haps even more significantly, online job ads and recruitment agencies betray that businesses routinely discriminate against the unemployed. For instance, some job ads require that applicants be currently or recently employed. Re-quiring up-to-date security clearances or training in brand new technology are other examples of the methods companies use to eliminate people who have been out of work for longer than a year or who are entering the work-force for the first time.[54]

To make matters more complicated, law-evading employers' criminal ac-tivity is not transparently recognized as criminal or punishable. By hiring workers unauthorized to work in the United States, employers commit a se-ries of labor law violations often accompanied by violations of health and safety laws that may be recognized as against the law but not necessarily seen as "criminal" (unlike statuses of rightlessness, such as "illegal aliens" or "gang members," who appear always already criminal). As such, employers are held less accountable for white-collar law-breaking than their legally vulnerable employees, scripting corporate crime as a consequence of, rather than the cause of and catalyst for, undocumented immigration, deindustrialization, and depreciating wages. Because unlawful corporate behavior is not rec-ognizable as criminal, the victims of corporate violence are not recognized as victims.

In fact, neoliberal reasoning would praise and privilege the "rational" logic of unscrupulous, self-preserving, self-determining corporations over unemployed African American U.S. citizens' rights to living wages and health care. "Neoliberal rationality," as Wendy Brown elaborates, "involves extending and disseminating market values to all institutions and social action," essentially "prescrib[ing] citizen-subject conduct in a neo-liberal order."[55] Under neoliberalism, corporations are read as more moral than the poor of color in part because a person's economic standing reads as evidence of one's character, moral standards, and values. As chronically unemployed, poor African Americans are subjected often to the disparaging judgments of neoliberal disciplining.

Under Neoliberalism, impoverished African American citizens' consumption patterns are under constant scrutiny. Poor African Americans are not only represented as unentitled to "luxuries"; they are also denied the power to decide what constitutes a "luxury" and the power to define what they need and what they can live without. They are chastised for spending "taxpayer" money on items derided as "frivolities"—notwithstanding the fact that poor people of color also pay taxes. After Hurricane Katrina, online postings accused victims of improperly using relief money, implying that survivors' spending habits should be under stricter surveillance. In one posting, a Katrina volunteer provided the following first-hand observation of victims' budget mismanagement:

> Houses in crappy neighborhoods with blue tarps on the roof to keep out the rain and a new HumVee sitting in the drive way. . . .
>
> Women in high dollar shops buying Louis Vitton [sic] handbags with FEMA money. . . .
>
> It's not that these people were left out in any way. Instead, they spent the money on HumVees and new SUVs, big screen TVs, and the jewelry stores were booming. By the time I left there, I hated the damn state and everyone in it. . . .
>
> Anyone that doesn't have a job in Mississippi five years later, damn sure doesn't want one.[56]

The poster's impressions were also evaluations that judged the financial choices of people assumed to be Katrina victims as extravagant and indulgent because they purchased nonessential items allegedly with money from FEMA. Although many similar postings of self-reported first-hand accounts berate Katrina survivors' spending habits, there was no space to allow the victims themselves to define what they considered essential—i.e., for people who lost everything because they lacked transportation and could not evacuate, buying trustworthy cars might be more than essential. Because they were already framed and interpreted as wasteful and irresponsible, African American victims' financial decisions were difficult to recontextualize without sounding defensive because any engagement puts not only their purchases but also their values and their rationales up for debate, inviting more surveillance over their spending habits. They could only disavow or deny the claims of indulgent irresponsibility.

Because poor people of color are not entitled to define or to decide what they need and what they don't, it is easy to accuse them of "mismanaging" their lives because they are held up to standards that are not always in their best interest to observe. Impoverished African American U.S. citizens are stigmatized and disciplined for being structurally positioned in ways that make *adhering* to neoliberal principles a form of entrapment.[57] Working to become "ideal" neoliberal citizen-subjects requires that they undermine their own demands for living wages, fair employment practices, and rights as citizens so they can compete for jobs with undocumented immigrants. What many forget (or willfully neglect) is that even a willingness to be exploited does not provide employers enough incentive to hire poor U.S. citizens of color because, unlike undocumented immigrants, citizens are legally protected from retaliation if they contest unfair employment practices and abusive working conditions.

Although some state laws include protections for undocumented immigrants in the workplace, such as minimum wage, overtime pay, workers compensation, and disability insurance, undocumented workers are not entitled to legal recourse to recover back pay if they are fired because they are unauthorized to work. If undocumented workers exercise their few legal rights to report workplace and labor violations, they also put themselves at risk for incarceration and deportation.[58] Furthermore, employers use the threat of Immigration and Customs Enforcement (ICE) raids to scare and intimidate workers before paydays.[59] Undocumented labor enables corporations to bypass labor and antidiscrimination laws as well as health and safety regulations because undocumented workers are made too vulnerable by immigration law to be able to utilize their rights as workers under state labor laws.

Since U.S. laws cannot offer redress to socially "dead to other" populations, such as undocumented immigrants and chronically unemployed African American citizens, access to legal recourse becomes understood as something the population in power decides to give freely or deny absolutely. It is, therefore, understandable that appealing to dominant populations' sympathies and sense of morality is a popular political tactic. Because poor people of color are legally disempowered, they are positioned by law as having to rely on those whom the law empowers—those who, consequentially, take it upon themselves to evaluate whether marginalized groups deserve the rights, recognition, or resources their members are requesting. Both undocumented immigrants and unemployed, impoverished citizens are legally ineligible for personhood because they cannot invoke the laws that address unlivable wages or unfair hiring practices. Unemployment and illegal status leave people legally vulnerable *because of* U.S. law, rather than protected by it, because it is all but legal to discriminate against both groups. Hence, because permanently criminalized, rightless statuses are also always already racialized, law ensures that there will always be a population of color rendered permanently rightless in the United States.

Whiteness as (Private) Property

The reason why persons ineligible to personhood are always people of color —or the reason why rightless statuses are always racialized—is because whiteness has a legal history very different from racial difference. Because of its privileged legal history, whiteness benefits from its contemporary relationship to U.S. law. As I argue in chapter 1, this relationship protects white law-breakers from occupying criminalized statuses; white people who commit crimes are more likely to be judged individually, on the basis of their conduct and perceived degree of culpability. In contrast, impoverished people of color, who occupy rightless statuses—such as gang members or illegal aliens—are more likely to be categorically criminalized without regard to their actions or intentions. Put simply by legal scholar Cheryl Harris: "Whiteness has value, whiteness is valued, and whiteness is expected to be valued in law."[60] According to Harris, whiteness has functioned in law as a property interest deserving of protection.

> The set of assumptions, privileges, and benefits that accompany the status of being white have become a valuable asset. . . . Whites have come to expect and rely on these benefits, and over time these expectations have been affirmed, legitimated, and protected by the law. Even though the law is neither uniform nor explicit in all instances, in protecting settled expectations based on white privilege, American law has recognized a property interest in whiteness that, although unacknowledged, now forms the background against which legal disputes are framed, argued, and adjudicated.[61]

The state produces both eligibility and ineligibility to personhood by formalizing or legally recognizing "inalienable rights" as "natural" properties inherent to personhood. As Grace Kyungwon Hong explains, "property is better understood as describing a set of *social relations*. . . . Ownership describes not only the relationship between oneself and the thing one owns, but a system in which the state protects one's right to own something by ensuring no else does."[62] Explicating John Locke's well-known proclamation that "every man has *property* in his own *person*," Hong argues that Locke was not only defining "property" but also defining *personhood*. As she argues,

"The subject is defined by his ability to own . . . the first and foremost thing he owns is himself."[63] Thus, when Lisa Lowe succinctly argues that "the most powerful contradiction of liberal democracy arises from the condition that each individual man's right to property violates the rights of others," we might see this contradiction not only in relation to property traditionally defined but also as it relates to property in one's person.[64] The institutionalization of white privilege institutes "inalienable rights" as a property of whiteness and personhood.

In the United States, rights, freedom, and property are intertwined, and this interconnection determines one's eligibility for personhood. Historically, race and property interacted in ways that not only established whiteness as property but also defined property ownership in racial terms and made property ownership contingent on racial status. Only white people could define property ownership, which meant denying that Native Americans' land was also Native Americans' property, and only white people could define other people as property, which included enslaving black people as white people's personal property.[65] As Harris articulates:

> According whiteness actual legal status converted an aspect of identity into an external object of property, moving whiteness from privileged identity to a vested interest. The law's construction of whiteness defined and affirmed critical aspects of identity (who is white); of privilege (what benefits accrue to that status); and, of property (what *legal* entitlements arise from that status).[66]

When the state divests targeted populations of their civil and human rights —through criminal law, immigration legislation, the institution of U.S. citizenship, etc.—the very personhood of unprotected residents in this nation is formalized in law as irrelevant.

Because whiteness was/is a property in law, whiteness itself was historically fraught with tensions and contradictions. Although Mexicans were legally defined as white by the Treaty of Guadeloupe-Hidalgo (1848–49) and the much later court case *In re Rodríguez* (1897), Mexicans' citizenship rights were continually subverted both by and outside law.[67] As ineligible to citizenship, Asian immigrants' struggles for political enfranchisement were about challenging the definition of whiteness. In 1922 and 1923, in two different cases, Asian immigrants Takao Ozawa and Bhagat Singh Thind were denied naturalized citizenship because the court rejected their claims to whiteness on the basis of skin color and Caucasian ancestry, respectively.[68] Ozawa's claim to whiteness based on his literal skin color was denied because

Japanese were not members of the Caucasian race; however, Thind's claim to whiteness premised on his Caucasian ancestry was denied because he did not look phenotypically white and would not be considered white according to the "understanding of the common man."[69] Although these cases contradicted each other and were decided only months apart, together they helped to define whiteness and reinforce how it was protected by law as a property interest that required protection from those who would taint or threaten it. As legal scholar Ian Haney López reminds us, black immigrants were also eligible for naturalized citizenship, but there was only one reported case (*In re Cruz*, 1938) in which the petitioner sought U.S. citizenship on the basis of being African, which was also unsuccessful.[70] Even though some nonwhites were eligible to become citizens in status either by law or birth, whiteness determined whether citizens had access to the rights, privileges, and immunities of U.S. citizenship.

Ultimately, whiteness defined itself through what it was not, and this definition was protected vehemently even when it worked against white people's interests.[71] In *Black Reconstruction*, for instance, W. E. B. Du Bois elucidated how working-class whites' investments in racial superiority affected them detrimentally by preventing them from forming class alliances with African Americans.[72] David Roediger has argued that the white working class actively used the perception that people of color were innately inferior to bolster support for the white working man's political and economic demands. Roediger posits that blacks were considered "anticitizens" because it was believed that enfranchised African Americans would be easily manipulated by the rich and powerful.[73] Thus, it was not a coincidence that extending the vote to more white men in the 1800s by taking away property requirements corresponded with the increasing disenfranchisement of African Americans.[74] As Harris argues, opening up political rights to unpropertied white men during the time that African Americans were being actively disenfranchised reveals how law changed the "property requirements" for voting—from land ownership to whiteness.[75]

The legal protection of whiteness as a property interest worked to undermine hard-won civil rights. For instance, *Brown v. Board* (1954) defined racial integration as the only solution to racial inequality. Even though the court outlawed legal segregation, it also refused to recognize African Americans' right to equal resources, accepting racial inequality "as a neutral base line."[76] Anti–affirmative action cases, Harris explains, "speak the formal language of equality, but subordinate equality" by protecting white expectations that "what is unequal in fact will be regarded as equal in law."[77] In other words, white people expect to be overrepresented on a neutral playing field. If inequality is taken to be the "neutral base line," all practices and policies that seek to redress racial discrimination will (if remotely successful) alter the base line from unequal to less unequal. George Lipsitz terms this expectation of white entitlement a "possessive investment in whiteness." As he explains, because whiteness is a social identity with a cash value and legal benefits, people invest in whiteness as an investment property, or a means to accumulate assets and advantages.[78]

As Harris, Lipsitz, Roediger, and López argue, the institutionalization of white privilege has normalized and protected white expectations of entitlement and empowerment. Hence, whiteness as property figures prominently in contemporary political debates. For example, whiteness has a vested property interest in maintaining the exploitation of undocumented immigrants. The everyday conduct of "illegal" but law-abiding immigrants is often made intelligible as "criminal" by likening immigrants' actions to "property crimes," which are characterized as the theft, fraudulent use, and/or depreciation of someone else's entitlements. When immigration opponents appeal to concerns over resources by portraying immigration as an infringement on rightful ownership (e.g., immigrants take jobs that belong to American citizens), they are appealing to the expectation of white entitlement. This expected entitlement has a history in anti–affirmative action cases. Several anti–affirmative action cases validated the expectation that white Americans should always be able to compete for 100 percent of all jobs (as well as 100 percent of college admission slots and business contracts).[79] Hence, even if poor African Americans are named the mostly likely beneficiaries of anti-immigrant legislation, the argument is grounded in a legal history that has negated black people's rights to higher education, job opportunities, and socioeconomic mobility. In fact, even immigrant rights activists appeal to white Americans' expectation of entitlement when countering the argument that undocumented immigrants "steal" resources, such as the expectation of unfettered access to the goods and services undocumented labor keeps affordable. In other words, the conflicting property interests of whiteness underlie immigration debates.

The Objects, Methods, and Narrative Arc of Social Death

Rather than trying to rationalize criminal or illicit behavior, this book seeks to denaturalize crime, criminality, and criminal conduct by taking what we know about criminalized statuses and making this knowledge unfamiliar. Making narratives unfamiliar means asking different questions of evidence and situating that evidence within different contexts. I do this through reading texts symptomatically and diagnostically for what they can tell us about the criminalization of the disempowered, about the production of vulnerabilities, and about the foreclosure of empathy for the unprotected.

My archive is eclectic and unruly. I rely heavily on news media because of its public accessibility, but I also examine a range of other texts such as congressional reports, police bulletins, court cases, legal transcripts, and books by self-proclaimed gang experts—texts that produce official narratives and texts that are likely to be in conversation with one another, directly or indirectly. I follow the texts that either help to produce the categories and narratives about criminalized populations of color or participate in the discourses that shape each chapter's case study. What the narratives illustrate is that the debates themselves, precisely because they ascribe value and deservingness, depend on and therefore support the permanent criminalization of unsympathetic racialized statuses. These statuses are made unsympathetic in part because the texts engage in what Isabel Molina calls "symbolic colonization." Molina defines "symbolic colonization" as "the story-telling mechanism through which ethnic and racial differences are hegemonically tamed through the media."[80] News media colonize images and narratives of criminalized populations and places through information-gathering practices that not only produce one-dimensional portrayals but also reproduce the official stories that work to justify policing practices, deportation policies, and increased incarceration. These narratives "tame" racial differences by reducing them to criminal natures, by making them all too easy to recognize, to "know" as unknowable and irrational, thereby foreclosing identification and empathy. There are alternate and oppositional texts that give a more complex story than the one I present in this book, but my focus on official narratives is intentional. I am not arguing that poor people of color devalue each other. Rather, I argue that the most vulnerable populations in the United States are often represented as if they are the primary sources of the other's social denigration. And because they are represented in this way, they are recruited to participate in their own and others' devaluation.

In the conclusion, I demonstrate how we are all recruited often unwittingly and/or unwillingly to devalue lives, life choices, and lifestyles because valuing them would destabilize our own precarious claims to and uneasy desire for social value. By narrating the ways in which the texts and narratives analyzed in this chapter unsettled me, I provide both an explanation and a demonstration of my analytical approach to the eclectic texts of my unruly archive. Alongside my analysis, I point out the moments when my evidence or analysis reaches a dead-end, compels me to follow a detour, and/or demands that I ask a different question altogether. In that final chapter,

I examine the official narrative about the death of my cousin alongside the narratives my family and I produced about him. This is a story of my many failures to ascribe him social value on terms that felt true to him and his memory. Employing a politics of misrecognition could not ascribe social value to him. A politics of misrecognition is a politics that relies on tactical arguments that construct only some members of a group targeted for state violence as having been falsely and unfairly misrecognized by U.S. law. My cousin was a Mexican American male, and he was often racially profiled, but pointing out the devalued categories of which he was not a part was not enough to ascribe social value to him. It was not enough to say that "he was not a gang member" because he did not leave us with something to say next. Part of the power in denying stereotypes comes from the "truths" we offer in their place. But my cousin was not a straight-A college student who was misrecognized as a gang member or an undocumented immigrant. He was not a family man, leaving behind a wife and children. Neither was he a doctor, a teacher, or an activist. He was a high school dropout who was often unemployed and lived with his parents. He had habits and hobbies considered self-destructive, dangerous, and socially deviant. Although he was not ineligible to personhood, like gang members or undocumented immigrants, his personhood was nonetheless illegible because he did not fit socially valuable categories either. A politics of misrecognition could not ascribe value to him because it relies on criteria that he did not meet.

My other chapters examine how the criminalization of impoverished communities of color informs, naturalizes, and reinforces the racialized criteria for social (de)valuation. To delve deeper into how and why such criminalizing processes are so tenaciously attached to bodies of color, chapter 1 examines how whiteness is decriminalized and how processes of decriminalization are also relational. The refusal to recognize young white males as criminal relies upon recognizing the figure of the criminal as not only always already racialized but also as one whose conduct and character must be imagined as proportionately more depraved than that of a white person who commits comparable crimes. The chapter's case study is set in San Diego, California. In 2000, seven white youth and their half-Cuban-, half-white-identified friend violently attacked five Mexican migrant workers without provocation. Changes to the California penal code earlier that year mandated that the teenagers be tried as adults. In mainstream media accounts, the young men's guilt was never questioned nor was the "wrongness" of their actions disputed. What was left up for debate was whether or not they should be punished according to the new laws, which many thought affected only gang members and other/ed unredeemable youth. In other words, the primary question regarding the assailants' case was whether their irrefutable guilt tainted their innate innocence. I argue that the case was thought about in this way because criminality is racialized and spatialized and because their violent vigilantism was aligned with state-sanctioned violences against Mexican immigrants in general and undocumented immigrants in particular.

While the first chapter examines how criminality is recognized through scrutinizing the ways in which whiteness is decriminalized, chapter 2 analyzes how criminality is produced. Unlike stereotyping, which refers to the multiple ways law-abiding people of color are misrecognized as criminal and treated by others as such, criminalization refers to the various ideological and material processes that turn some people into criminals by making it all but impossible for them to be law-abiding. In this chapter, I examine the criminalized figures of the gang member and criminal alien as simultaneously embodied by a Cambodian refugee. Kim Ho Ma was detained indefinitely for his participation in a gang-related murder. Ma's overlapping (il)legal statuses —noncitizen, criminal alien, refugee, and gang member—worked to convey and deny sympathy by deploying race relationally to make his value legible. Official narratives used "cultural difference" to normalize violence within refugee communities, as if violence directed against Southeast Asian immigrants can be traced to either cultural difference, as violence imported from over there, or to inner-city irrationality, as space-specific American violence, expected and inescapable but not excused. The notion that violence only happens elsewhere, I argue, justified the ways in which immigration legislation was revised to function like criminal law, instituting punishment. These various representations of Southeast Asian violence help us see how legislation such as the Antiterrorism and Effective Death Penalty Act (AEDPA) and the Illegal Immigration Reform and Immigrant Responsibility Act (IIRIRA) could be narrated as preemptive even though many of their harshest penalties were retroactive.

While chapter 2 analyzes the ways in which common criminalizing narratives about African Americans were deployed to contextualize and minimize Southeast Asian social deviance, chapter 3 examines how new racialized and sexualized threats can unsettle seemingly stable narratives of commonly criminalized figures. In this chapter, I trace how the production of the racialized status category of "suspected of terrorism" both upset and reinforced the racial and gendered signifiers of the "illegal alien." During the war on terror, "suspected terrorists" were racially profiled and legally produced through the same laws (such as the AEDPA and the IIRIRA) that had already rendered criminal aliens and undocumented immigrants ineligible to personhood. As the signifier for legitimate discrimination through legal racial profiling, "illegality" marks certain people as not just outside law but also subject to lawlessness and unregulated state violence. Because Middle Eastern immigration was rendered "suspect" and "fraudulent" through immigration law and represented as "illegal" in mainstream news media following 9/11, Latina/o racial difference was temporarily destabilized as the contemporary signifier for unlawful immigration. The war on terror also created opportunities for the racialized un-incorporable to be socially and legally integrated through military service, expedited naturalization, or posthumous citizenship. Arab/Muslim racial and religious difference was deployed by media to manage the contradictions that emerged when Latinas/os were portrayed as both the face of illegal immigration and the face of the multicultural military, as both the threat to and the protector of the American way of life. Although this limited Latina/o incorporation provided powerful political tactics for undocumented activists and their allies, these other, distinct, and disparate racialized "threats" were quickly reconsolidated under U.S. immigration law, grafting terrorism onto "illegality."

Because the "terrorist" was at times represented as an "illegal alien," antiterrorist discourses impacted undocumented Latinas/os in various ways —from proposals for harsher immigration laws to the political strategies that protested those laws. Chapter 4 examines how those political strategies were represented in news coverage of the 2006 immigrant rights marches. Explicitly positioning hard-working, family-oriented undocumented immigrants against incorrigible "criminals" and "terrorists," movement activists and sympathetic reporters highlighted immigrants' claims to respectability. Unlike the anti-Latina/o family campaigns of the 1990s (touched upon in chapter 1),[81] the 2006 demonstrations for undocumented immigrant rights framed "family rights" as "civil rights" and also narrated the immigrant rights movement itself as the next chapter of U.S. civil rights history. Movement leaders' invocation of the U.S. legacy of civil rights, however, was represented in news media as controversial, as if the comparison devalued rather than honored the African American civil rights leaders of the 1950s–1970s. In chapter 4, I analyze how the black-Latina/o conflict and competition narrative was used as a means to undermine both Latina/o immigrants' and African American citizens' claims to rights. In particular, I argue that the focus on civil rights frames African Americans' entitlements to citizenship as "earned" (achievable) rather than inherent (universally inherited). The debate sets terms, which demand African Americans to demonstrate time and again their "deservingness" for rights. (This was a demand never made of the eight young assailants in San Diego analyzed in chapter 1.)

Toward Unthinkable Politics

This book is not a critique of activists and academics who ascribe social value to devalued people and places but rather an analysis of our limits and an examination of the reasons why other options are less accessible, less influential, and, perhaps more often than we think, less intelligible. Contemporary progressive politics must rely not only on what dominant groups find palatable (i.e., the family, legality) but also on the "value practices" that will make social statuses recognizable as valuable to (and often for) the very privileged of U.S. society. Because "value is fundamentally relational despite all appearances to the contrary,"[82] to ascribe (legible) value to devalued populations, we have to evaluate them in relation to differently devalued groups and according to normative criteria. Indeed, as an explicitly comparative race project, my analyses cannot escape these contradictions; nor can they offer a politics that finds a way out of the violence of value. Because we cannot escape the devaluation in revaluation, I instead take up Barrett's challenge: "to re-member the Other by dismembering value."[83] For me, this means suspending the impulse to reject criminalizing stereotypes precisely because the mere chance to recuperate social value is contingent on that rejection. As Hong reminds us, a politics that rejects social value is inconceivable.

> When the alternative to social value is social death, and social death means brutally exacerbated conditions of racialized violence, incarceration, and coercion, the allure of legibility is undeniably difficult to resist. Indeed, imagining a politics based on the refusal of social value is an impossible, unthinkable option, one, in truth, outside of any available notion of the political.[84]

Dismembering social value by refusing "the lure of legibility" re-members the other because it gives us the space to be more critical of the automatic, understandable impulse to deny and be offended by criminalizing stereotypes. In this space, the space of social death, we can re-member the other by asking ourselves: Whom does this rejection really benefit and whom does it hurt? This project is not concerned with whether something is politically practical or logistically possible because these approaches need to assume that legal apparatuses are legitimate and fixable. If we suspend the need to be practical, we might be able see what is possible differently. A focus on social death enables us to start at the places we dare not go because it enables us to privilege the populations who are most frequently and most easily disavowed, those who are regularly regarded with contempt, those whose interests are bracketed at best because to address their needs in meaningful ways requires taking a step beyond what is palatable, practical, and possible. Like Barrett, Hong, and Holland, I find "empowering oppositional narratives" in the devastating spaces of social death and their populations' abstract existences, but empowering narratives do not necessarily give us happy endings. Nor do they always leave us inspired.[85] In the spaces of social death, empowerment is not contingent on taking power or securing small victories. Empowerment comes from deciding that the outcome of struggle doesn't matter as much as the decision to struggle. Deciding to struggle against all odds armed only with fingers crossed on both hands is both an unusual political strategy and a well-informed worldview. It is a choice premised upon what Derrick Bell calls "racial realism."

Racial realism is a form of unthinkable politics because it proposes that we begin battles we've already lost, that we acknowledge and accept that everything we do may not ever result in social change.

> When implementing Racial Realism we must simultaneously acknowledge that our actions are not likely to lead to transcendent change and, despite our best efforts, may be of more help to the system we despise than to the victims of that system we are trying to help. Nevertheless, our realization, and the dedication based on that realization, can lead to policy positions and campaigns that are less likely to worsen conditions for those we are trying to help and more likely to remind those in power that there are imaginative, unabashed risk-takers who refuse to be trammeled upon. Yet confrontation with our oppressors is not our sole reason for Racial Realism. Continued struggle can bring about unexpected benefits and gains that in themselves justify continued endeavor. The fight itself has meaning and should give us hope for the future.[86]

Although racial realism takes failure for granted, it does not equate failure with defeat. Accepting hopelessness is not necessarily equivalent to abandoning hope. As Sara Ahmed writes in her critique of happiness, "To kill joy . . . is to open a life, to make room for life, to make room for possibility, for chance."[87]

To take unthinkable politics seriously, we need to entertain counterintuitive thoughts and practice imagining otherwise. "To imagine otherwise," Fiona Ngô argues, "failure need not be overcome, rehabilitation need not be desired, subjectivity need not be recovered." Instead, she insists, "we must conceive of an ethical stance that refuses to cover over the violence that brought us to the present."[88] If the critical task is *not* to resolve the contradictions of reintegrating the socially dead into a capitalist society that sees most of humanity as a necessary but negative resource, then it makes sense to mobilize *against* preserving this way of life or the ways of knowing that this life preserves. Rather than "breathe life" into the spaces of social death (gentrification, privatization, and democratization), we might conscientiously work against the logic of survivability,[89] which in the United States sees the preservation of U.S. capital as central and indispensable to the "American way of life." In neoliberal ways of knowing, the *value of life* is subjected to an economic analysis and assessed accordingly: How has this person contributed to society? What will he or she accomplish in the future? Is it worthwhile to invest in this neighborhood and its residents or will such an investment be only a waste of resources?

Lives are legibly valuable when they are assessed comparatively and relationally within economic, legal, and political contexts and discourses, framed by a culture of punishment according to the market logic of supply and demand. This means that, for the most part, value is not ascribed to living life in meaningful ways, and it also means that those who are socially devalued do not get to decide what makes a life meaningful or the terms by which their lives are evaluated as meaningful or meaningless, as valuable or valueless. By figuring out new contexts and ways of framing "why life is valuable," we might figure out how to talk about social problems in ways that do not require us to appeal to market values or to redirect juridical and social repudiation toward other populations that constitute the "negative resource" to American value. Of course, we cannot discount that fighting for basic survival needs in immediate, practical, and strategic ways is urgent, important work, but at the same time, a meaningful life is not a luxury but rather the purpose of the struggle itself, the difference between surviving and living.

1

White Entitlement and Other People's Crimes

High school teenagers Morgan Manduley, Bradley Davidofsky, Adam Kets-dever, Nicholas Fileccia, Steven DeBoer, and Kevin Williams (ages 15–17) set out to "hunt" undocumented Mexican migrant workers on July 5, 2000. They cased an area near their homes in Rancho Peñasquitos, an affluent suburb of San Diego, California. They found Andres Roman Díaz (age 64) walking back from work, carrying groceries and drinking water. They shot him with BB guns from their Subaru station wagon, then got out of the car to chase him on foot. Roman ran back to the nursery where he worked, and the young men got back in the car to pick up their friends Michael Rose and Jason Beever (ages 15 and 14), as well as more weapons and more ammunition.[1] This time they went to the encampment where Roman lived. According to some accounts, they concocted an elaborate plan to pretend to be Immigration and Naturalization Service (INS) agents. They demanded money and documents from migrant workers, and then robbed and beat those who didn't understand them.[2]

At the encampment, nursery workers Anastacio Irigoyen Najera, Alfredo Ayala Sanchez, Atanacio Fierros Juarez, and Juan Miguel Ramos (ages

64–69) were assaulted with whatever blunt or sharp objects their assailants could find at hand, which included a pitchfork, rocks, and pipes. The men were shot with pellet guns at point-blank range and robbed—all while listening to their attackers shout racist epithets. The teenagers tormented the workers for three hours. They riddled Ayala's face and body with BBs and tried to set his home on fire. When 69-year-old Irigoyen tried to help Ayala, the assailants beat him unconscious—and so badly that on the way home to their comfortable suburban lives, the assailants worried that they might have killed him. Their worries did not lead to calling an ambulance because they were not concerned for Irigoyen; they were concerned that they might be caught. They returned to the encampment to drag his body behind the bushes, leaving him for dead. A few of the teenaged assailants later confessed that they had assumed their victims were undocumented and would be too afraid to report them. All five workers, however, were living and working in the country legally.[3]

The adolescent attackers might have believed they would not be punished for their actions because the encampment where the elderly Mexican workers set up their temporary homes did not discriminate by legal status. Perhaps because mostly Mexican men lived in the camp where little English was spoken, the space seemed to be an "illegal," un-American place. And for the teenagers, perhaps race and language were more than enough signs of illegality and nonpersonhood to justify their malevolent and sadistic behavior. There even appears to have been a sense of righteousness motivating their violence: By pretending to be immigration officers, these teenagers aligned themselves with the state, planning to act how they imagined INS agents would act (or could act) toward undocumented Latina/o migrant workers.

Although the teenagers' deplorable exploits might be characterized as senseless, they were not random. The high school students targeted a group they believed to be too vulnerable to fight back physically or legally; they targeted a category of persons who they imagined did not carry enough social and human value to compel others to fight on their behalf. The teenaged assailants grew up in a place and a political climate audaciously and openly hostile to undocumented immigration and the Latina/o populations that signified it (irrespective of their actual legal statuses). Only six years earlier, in 1994, the California populace passed Proposition 187, which tried to deny necessary services and resources, such as education and health care, to undocumented immigrants. Perhaps the adolescents assumed their violence would be more than tacitly condoned because it was directed toward Latina/o workers assumed to be not just vulnerable as "illegal" but deserving punishment as criminal.

Ironically (and yet fittingly), the same racist anxieties and nativist animosities that motivated the San Diego adolescents' violence also motivated California voters to pass Proposition 21 in March 2000,[4] just a few months before the teens' arrest. Proposition 21's newly implemented amendments to adult and juvenile criminal law were both extensive and arbitrary. Referred to as California's "Juvenile Crime and Gang Violence Initiative," Proposition 21 not only instituted harsher penalties for crimes considered "gang-related," it also required that more juveniles be tried as adults and increased the penalties for various violent or serious offenses.[5] Under these draconian provisions, the suburban adolescents could be tried as adults, and each could have received an adult prison sentence of twelve to fifteen years. In fact, because the crimes were so openly racist, nativist, and violent, they were charged with committing a hate crime, which could have added an additional four years to their sentences. The adolescents' families led legal challenges against the proposition's constitutionality. Even though they were not able to overturn Proposition 21 in court, not one of the young men's "adult" sentences seemed to reflect this legal loss. No one was sent to state prison; two were sent to a county jail; and five were sent to a California Youth Authority facility. (Four of the five were sentenced for terms of less than one year.)

In this chapter, I urge us to think about why certain crimes and criminals cannot be recognized as such. Why are some acts of violence and the people who commit them interpreted as less criminal than others? What makes it difficult for the criminal justice system to recognize young white men as criminals and, for that matter, to recognize racially motivated anti-immigrant violence as a crime deserving of criminal punishment? It is telling that the young assailants impersonated INS agents. They aligned themselves with the state as they attacked the elderly Mexican workers. Their vigilante exploits were essentially illegal demonstrations of state-sanctioned violence. As imitations of violence deemed necessary and legitimate by the state, their actions had the potential to be interpreted as unfortunate and inappropriate—not justifiable but understandable. Thus, this particular case exposes how certain bodies and behaviors are made transparently criminal while privileged bodies and their brutal crimes are rendered unrecognizable as criminal or even as violent. Processes of criminalization regulate and regularize targeted populations, not only disciplining and dehumanizing those ineligible for personhood, but also presenting them as ineligible for sympathy and compassion.

Although race might appear to be the determining factor in the lenient judgments against the youths, it also seems too simple to assert that their whiteness and their victims' nonwhiteness are evidence enough to make this argument, especially because the brutal attacks could not be condoned or even rationalized. Because these suburban teenagers broke laws intended to criminalize others, their lawbreaking was unintelligible (even to themselves). Along these lines, we see that processes of *de*-criminalization are just as dependent upon the same racial and spatial norms that render criminality and personhood recognizable on some bodies but irreconcilable with others. In effect, race is not so much a code for criminality (although stereotypes do function in this way); rather, race and racialized spaces are the signifiers that make an unsanctioned action legible as illicit and recognizable as a crime. This means that the interpretation and application of criminal law is never race-neutral, no matter how race-erased individual laws appear to be. Recognizable as rights-bearing subjects and able to access pervasive discourses of white innocence, injury, and entitlement, the eight affluent teenagers were read and represented as explicitly not criminal and even unable to become criminal in a way that effectively rendered their intent and their culpability irrelevant. They would be rendered innocent even if guilty.[6]

Illegal by Presence

Only six years earlier, in passing Proposition 187, California voters had tried to formally deny undocumented immigrants not only life-bettering resources but also life-sustaining services.[7] In California, the ballot initiative process allows citizens to change laws directly by majority vote without going through legislative representatives. Touted as "direct democracy," California ballot campaigns require large amounts of funding as well as legal counsel. Most propositions on the ballots are drafted primarily by wealthy citizens and politicians, and many are aimed either at expanding state powers in order to police marginalized populations or at decreasing state resources that help these same aggrieved groups. This is a central contradiction of neoliberalism. As social services and health care are cut, more of people's incomes have to cover the costs of an always-shrinking social safety net, even as hourly wages and employee benefits remain stagnant at best. For impoverished and legally vulnerable populations, these conditions essentially make welfare necessary, but those who need it are denigrated as eschewing their "personal responsibility" to care for themselves and their families.[8] The middle and wealthy classes, who can afford to absorb the costs of privatizing public services and resources (a process that promises to make services more "efficient" and of higher "quality"), find themselves with less discretionary income. However, they blame this decrease on people presumed "irresponsible"—welfare recipients, noncitizens, people without health insurance, children of the undocumented—who either don't make enough money to cover costs or don't "deserve" to use public services. Easily ratified by the voters but overturned by the courts, Proposition 187 would have instituted and exacerbated these contradictions. Among its provisions, Proposition 187 would have denied undocumented mothers prenatal care; it also would have required doctors and teachers to report undocumented children to the INS for receiving a polio shot or attending fifth grade. Criminalizing not just the act of receiving assistance but also giving it, Proposition 187 would have charged state workers in the health, welfare, and education professions with the policing functions of the state. These professionals would have been required to report their clients' and students' immigration status to the INS if they "reasonably suspected" any one of them was not authorized to reside in the United States.

Proposition 187 was promoted as a way to deter immigration, but in actuality, the ballot measure pursued *punishment* rather than prevention. The institutionalized neglect that the initiative proposed was totalizing, and sadly, the measure was not an anomaly, but a foreshadowing. In subsequent years, California voters proposed, passed, and implemented a series of initiatives that also targeted vulnerable groups either by making it easier to incarcerate people or by eliminating much-needed policies and programs. In 1994, Proposition 184, the "three-strikes-and-you're-out" initiative, mandated a life sentence upon conviction of a third felony. (Consequently, most of the youth convicted after the passage of Proposition 21 found themselves with felony strikes before they became adults.) In 1996, voters took away affirmative action by passing Proposition 209, ironically titled "The California Civil Rights Initiative." Proposition 227 eradicated bilingual education in 1998. Two years later, and the same year that Proposition 21 was passed, Proposition 22 denied gays and lesbians the right of state-recognized marriage.

The Rancho Peñasquitos attackers targeted the same population that supporters of Proposition 187 had targeted—those most vulnerable within an already vulnerable community, including not just the elderly but also children, mothers, and those with disabilities, illnesses, and/or chronic conditions requiring medical care. Mistaken for and marked as "illegal," the teenagers' Mexican victims occupied a de facto "illegal" status that positioned them outside law, empathy, ethical obligation, legal protection, and justice. If the victims aren't recognized as deserving of justice, how can the teenagers be seen as deserving of punishment?

(Con)fusing Status and Crime

The young men of Rancho Peñasquitos thought they might not be arrested because they believed their victims were "illegal." On some level, it seems the teenagers were under the assumption that legal vulnerability excludes migrants completely from legal protection, all but inviting vigilante violence against Latina/o immigrants. And yet the attacks were also much more than opportunistic. They were also hateful, as if the assailants had learned that violence against some people was not just overlooked but legitimate, as if personhood did not actually apply to all people. The boys targeted men they believed were not only vulnerable to ridicule and robbery, but also vulnerable to being intimidated, beaten, dragged behind bushes, and left for dead.

To explain how certain bodies are marked as disposable and violable, as legitimate targets of state and vigilante violence, it is necessary to examine the ways in which law works to affix assumptions about behavior onto bodies. Historically, law has criminalized the recreational activities, survival economies, and intimate relationships of people of color so the status of "being of color" was inseparable from conduct assumed to be "criminal." Before anti-racist legislation was implemented following the civil rights movement, law criminalized and reified marginalized identities as statuses. Being "colored" was a status that formed the basis for exclusionary, discriminatory, and regulatory laws, such as Jim Crow. What we call "identity categories" in the contemporary era functioned historically as excludable or includable statuses in segregation, naturalization, and immigration law. Today's laws that criminalize conduct contingent on status have inherited this history.

In immigration and naturalization law, this history was one of restriction and privilege, and it was this history that shaped the political landscape of California in ways that made being an undocumented Mexican immigrant a de facto status crime, not just vulnerable to violence but designated both criminal and disposable. As legal scholar Leti Volpp argues, status has been historically fused to conduct in citizenship and immigration law, in spite of seeming to be distinct.

> We conventionally separate identity into realms of status and conduct, and have presumed that status (for example, one's race) as opposed to conduct (in the form of how one behaves) has constituted the primary barrier to citizenship. But what we remember as status-based exclusions in fact were premised on assumptions about appropriate conduct. Thus, history shows the impossibility of separating the realm of status from that of conduct.[9]

Volpp argues that ineligibility to citizenship was both premised upon status and justified by (presumptions about) conduct. As she explains, the Page Law excluded Asian women from immigrating to the United States on the basis of both status (Asian, women, unmarried) and conduct (sex, work). Like the Page Law, Volpp reminds us, the 1882 Chinese Exclusion Act was also premised on status and conduct because not all Chinese were barred from immigrating to the United States. Chinese laborers were excluded, but Chinese merchants and diplomats were exempt from these immigration restrictions. The Chinese Exclusion Act was premised on both status (Chinese) and conduct (laborer). The exceptions to the exclusion act were also premised on fusing status (upper class) and conduct (merchant, diplomat).[10] Eligibility for U.S. citizenship was also restricted on the basis of status and conduct. Naturalized citizenship was restricted to people of a certain status thought capable of self-governance (conduct). The 1790 Naturalization Law conferred naturalized citizenship on the basis of race, gender, and class status: Only white men who owned property could become naturalized citizens.

Lifting race-based status restrictions in immigration and naturalization law did not remedy status-based discrimination. Thus, although together, the 1952 McCarran-Walter Act and the 1965 Immigration and Nationality Act removed the final overt vestiges of status-based exclusions premised on race and national origin in immigration and naturalization legislation, at the same time they implemented "race-neutral" or "color-blind" preferences that privileged heteronormativity and discriminated against homosexuality.[11] As Siobhan Somerville has argued, normalizing race in law often works through universalizing heterosexuality and further demonizing and/or abnormalizing gender nonconformity and sexual "deviance."[12] Asians had been excluded and/or severely restricted from immigrating and naturalizing since the late 1800s, and those few in the United States were mostly male, which contributed to marking Asian relationships and residences as nonnormative.[13] Along with the War Brides Act, which allowed Asian American servicemen to bring wives from Asia, the 1952 and 1965 immigration acts recuperated and repositioned Asian Americans in the national imaginary because they enabled more Asian professionals and families to settle in the United States. The Immigration and Nationality Act of 1965 also gave all nations in the Eastern Hemisphere, including countries in Asia, the same annual quota of 20,000. Under the new family preferences, 80 percent of the Eastern Hemisphere's yearly quota of 170,000 went to family members of U.S. citizens and permanent residents.[14]

These color-blind policies, however, did not have race-neutral intentions or results. Due to decades of exclusion, the Asian population in the United States in the mid-1960s was not only paltry but also mostly male and therefore unable to utilize the new law's family preferences. Rather than greatly restricting Asian immigration, as legal historian Mae Ngai contends, the act restricted only Asians of certain class and occupational statuses.[15] Asians immigrated through the "preference" for scientists and educated professionals as well as through the preference created to alleviate alleged labor shortages in certain industries, such as health care. According to Ngai, by 1972, well over 80 percent of the scientists, engineers, physicians, and surgeons immigrating to the United States emigrated from various Asian nations.[16]

While the professional preference seemed to be color-blind, it had status-based results because it worked to create new race and class statuses. Removing the racial and national origin restrictions did not make all countries equal before immigration law because the new "race-neutral" preference system did not attempt to address already existing racial and ethnic inequalities. The "color-blind" regulations and quotas affected sending nations and impacted U.S. populations unequally and unevenly. Because the preferences were largely family-based, they were directly premised on the ways in which different U.S. racial and ethnic populations were historically shaped by the status-based determinations of race, gender, and national origin in previous immigration and naturalization law. Hence, not only did the race- and nationality-neutral restrictions still have status-based consequences, but the new preferences also functioned to fuse new assumptions of conduct to racial identities—transforming the Asian "illegal alien" in the era of Asian exclusion to the family-oriented and highly educated Asian model minority in the era of family and professional preference.

For the Western Hemisphere, removing immigration restrictions also had drastic ramifications. Although the act increased the annual immigration quota from 150,000 to 290,000, it actually greatly *decreased* the total number of legal immigrants admitted each year because it was the first time a numerical restriction was placed on countries in the Western Hemisphere —countries that included Mexico, Canada, Latin America, and the Caribbean.[17] Prior to 1965, immigrants from the Western Hemisphere were non-quota immigrants under the United States' "good neighbor" policy. When the 1965 Immigration and Nationality Act imposed a 120,000 quota on the Western Hemisphere, it caused a 40 percent reduction in immigration from the Western Hemisphere in general as well as a 40 percent increase in the number of Mexicans who were deported.[18] In 1976, the act was amended to establish the 20,000 per country quota for the Western Hemisphere, which further restricted legal immigration from Mexico, but not the demand for Mexican immigrant labor in the United States.[19] As Ngai argues, "The imposition of a 20,000 annual quota on Mexico recast Mexican immigration as 'illegal.' When one considers that in the early 1960s, annual 'legal' Mexican migration comprised some 200,000 braceros and 35,000 regular admissions for permanent residency, the transfer of migration to 'illegal' form should have surprised no one."[20] The "color-blind" quota imposed on countries in the Western Hemisphere had status-based results. It dramatically changed the long-standing pattern of legal immigration and commuter migration from Mexico, reinforcing the assumptions of Mexican illegality that had already began circulating during the Bracero Program.[21] Ideas about "illegal" conduct, such as criminality, were also fused to the racialized status of the "illegal alien" and to the Mexican body as its signifier. Although identity-based status restrictions, such as race, were removed from immigration and naturalization law, numerical restrictions criminalized migration patterns that had developed under the "good neighbor" policy, transforming Mexican migrants from "good neighbors" to "illegal aliens."

To be an "illegal alien" is an example of what I'm referring to as a *de facto status crime*. A person does not need to *do* anything to commit a status crime because the person's status is the offense in and of itself. In the United States, criminal laws that make status in and of itself a crime have been ruled unconstitutional, yet both criminal law and immigration legislation inherit broader meanings and tangled histories of status and conduct that have made it difficult (if not impossible) to regulate and reprimand conduct without status-based consequences.[22] The term *de facto status crime* also captures the ways in which criminalized conduct has been intimately linked to the use of "status" to refer to identity categories, such as race, gender, sexuality, and class.[23] To clarify, I have retooled the term *status crime* to refer to what I see as its contemporary incarnation. That is, a *de facto status crime* does not refer to illegal activity; rather it refers to others' perception that a person of a certain status is certain to commit future crimes and may well have already committed crimes unwitnessed. A de facto status crime is not contingent on criminal conduct; it is premised upon bodies perceived to be criminal. When conduct is only criminalized and penalized when committed by a person who occupies a legally vulnerable racialized status, it is essentially a de facto status crime.

De facto status crimes can be defined as specific activities that are only transparently recognized as "criminal" when they are attached to statuses that invoke race (gang member), ethnicity ("illegal alien"), and/or national origin (suspected terrorist). Hence, to be an "illegal alien" would not be technically or legally considered a status crime, but because undocumented immigrants are treated as if they are always already criminal, illegal, and fraudulent, "being" an "illegal alien" is essentially a de facto status crime. Some criminal activities cannot be committed by just anyone because they are identified according to status: Only gang members can commit gang-related crime, and only gang-related crime is subject to gang enhancement sentencing, which allows judges to add extra years to perpetrators' sentences. Because "status" assumes embodiment and fixity, *de facto status crime* captures the many ways in which people and places of color have become necessary signifiers to recognize illegality or criminality, thus marking certain behaviors as not only illegal but also innate, inherent, and inherited.

Therefore, even though "illegal alien" is not a legal term and to be undocumented is not crime, to be an "illegal alien" is to embody a criminalized status. The act of crossing the border without authorization is unlawful, and the act of overstaying one's visa is a civil (not criminal) violation of immigration law, but the passive act of *being* an unauthorized immigrant is not a crime. Undocumented/unauthorized immigrants are not eligible for most life-bettering resources and services, but being ineligible for them is not in and of itself an illegal activity. The term "illegal alien" facilitates the transparent recognition of racialized illegality and ineligibility to personhood; the words themselves convey a status of rightlessness justified by un-American origins and presumed criminal culpability.

When simply "being" is criminalized, there is little to no room for discussion of a person's reasons, motivation, or premeditated intent—all these details are assumed always already known, universal, and unchanging. The courts provide people accused of committing a crime the chance to defend themselves and confront their accuser, but a person accused of "being" an "illegal alien" is not given these same opportunities to explain his or her actions, state of mind, intentions, motivations, or degrees of culpability. As debates over Proposition 21 demonstrate, criminal law does not hold children as responsible as adults for most violent crimes because it's believed that children cannot comprehend the consequences of their actions. But a child who crossed the border before he or she learned to walk is still held responsible for "being" an "illegal alien" even though the crime committed—crossing the border unlawfully—was not committed consciously. Criminal law also does not hold parents responsible for their children's actions. None of the Rancho Peñasquitos attackers' parents were prosecuted for their sons' crimes. But in cases regarding the deportation of undocumented youth, parents are often blamed, and both parents and children are penalized for unlawful entrance. When people treat being an "illegal alien" as a status crime, they criminalize undocumented immigrants without having to engage the kind of arguments provided to judges and juries when adjudicating a criminal case.

The Not-A-Gang Defense

The perception that Proposition 21 targeted status rather than conduct was implicit in the teenagers' collective challenge to the initiative's constitutionality. They challenged Proposition 21's legitimacy on the grounds that youth gangs and gang sentencing enhancements should not be included with laws that impact adults and violent youth who are not in gangs. According to the amicus curiae brief submitted by the California Attorneys for Criminal Justice (CACJ) on behalf of Michael Rose and Morgan Manduley, one of the reasons Proposition 21 should have been overturned was because "the non-juvenile and non-gang-related portions of Proposition 21 violate[d] the single subject rule."[24] Under the single subject rule, an initiative can propose multiple laws and multiple amendments to current laws (such as Proposition 21) only if the issues are relevant to one another and/or if the provisions will further the initiative's goals. The single subject rule exists so that voters will not be asked to cast all-or-nothing votes on several unrelated issues.[25] CACJ pointed out that Proposition 21 dealt with "specific classes of minors and street gang members."[26] Although the assailants and their supporters did not argue explicitly that Proposition 21 was meant to target youth other than themselves, the insistence that the initiative misled voters suggested that criminal laws addressing gang violence were so disconnected from criminal laws for everyone else that when voters imagined one category of crime (gang crime), other categories of crime (hate crime, suburban juvenile violence, or adult crime) would never come to mind.[27]

Although gang membership is not an actual status crime, gang enhancement sentencing treats gang membership as a *de facto status crime*. The young men's actions could easily be recounted in terms similar to descriptions of gang violence—that is, as senseless, unprovoked violence directed against innocent victims over territory. But even though Proposition 21 expanded the definition of "gang-affiliated," being tried as a gang was never a concern for the teenagers or their lawyers because gang violence is not defined through a group's actions or conduct but by a group's status or identity.

Proposition 21 changed the definition of gang-affiliation from "active participation" in a gang to anyone who "benefits from" the actions of a gang.[28] The new meanings of "gang-affiliated" were more likely to affect gang members' family, friends, and neighbors than white suburban youth who act in ganglike ways. Prior to Proposition 21, a prosecutor needed to prove that the offender was a gang member. After the proposition passed, offenders no longer needed to be members of a gang to be charged as active gang members.

In fact, offenders do not have to participate directly in the crime at all; gang members can be charged as co-conspirators if a member of their gang commits a crime, and nongang members, such as family and friends, could be charged under gang conspiracy law if they "benefit from" gang crime.[29] Professor of law Harry Mitchell Caldwell and reference librarian Daryl Fisher-Ogden explain that there is no agreed upon definition of a "gang," and that one of the problems of keeping records on gang-related crime is that even within the same jurisdiction, different law enforcement agencies define "gang" and "gang-related" differently. The vague definitions that are used for gangs could "include any conspiracy as well as outlaw motorcycle gangs, the traditional American hate groups such as the Ku Klux Klan and the Neo-Nazis, and an assortment of militia groups"; even fraternities and sororities that "engage in certain 'college pranks'" could be defined as a gang.[30] As Caldwell and Fisher-Ogden clarify, although gangs could be defined as "conspirators and members of hate groups," law enforcement does not define these groups as gangs. Rather, individual state efforts (such as Proposition 21) "have been directed at 'street gangs' such as the Bloods, the Crips, the Mexican Mafia and so on."[31] Although the various legal definitions of a "gang" can be thought to encompass any number of groups and unlawful activities, only people of color are imagined with and criminalized by the term "gang." Racial masculinities of impoverished inner cities serve as the only signifiers for criminal street gangs.

Even when a white gang fits the legal definition of a "gang," it would not necessarily be recognized as a "criminal street gang." This is important because only criminal street gangs are subject to gang enhancement sentencing. In the book *Gangs in Schools*, written for high school administrators, psychologists and school counselors Arnold P. Goldstein and Donald Kodluboy argue that white gangs form for different reasons and commit different crimes than gangs of color. These differences, they assert, demonstrate that white gangs in schools should not be classified as "street gangs." As they write, "ideological, or single-issue, white gangs are not street gangs in that they generally do not engage in 'cafeteria-style' crimes (i.e., a range of diverse crimes, including property crimes, drug crimes, and crimes against persons)."[32] Although the San Diego youths' violence could be characterized as ganglike, it could also be read as a vigilante expression of state-sanctioned violence. Criminal street gangs, on the other hand, are engaged in the kinds of "illegitimate" activity that the state promises to punish, such as property crimes (vandalism, turf wars) and illegal economies (drugs, prostitution, stolen and pirated goods). White gangs are thought to form for "ideological" reasons or as a "business venture"; its members are characterized as purposeful and calculated, even political, but not as ganglike.[33] On the other hand, Goldstein and Kodluboy characterize black, Latina/o, Asian, and American Indian gang formation as more instinctual than deliberate, as an understandable (though not a rational or forgivable) reaction to poverty and racism. For youth of color, gang membership is described as an involuntary or impulsive response to their lack of power, property, and personhood, whereas the "nonstreet" gangs of socially privileged white youth are represented as a means to augment members' (entitlement to) power and property in misguided but not irrational ways. Subtle but immensely meaningful, this distinction reveals that disempowerment and disenfranchisement are central to the commonsense understanding of "criminal street gang."

In one of the more critical news articles about the attacks, journalist Thomas Larson referred to the adolescents as a gang in order to make their criminal intent and the seriousness of their violent crimes *recognizable*: "But it is clear from court documents that they attacked the Mexican men with gang-like terror—in the orderly nature of their plan and in the ravenous swarm of their rampage."[34] Usually, the term "gang" was avoided altogether. Even the prosecution did not describe the eight adolescents with terminology that would suggest they had acted like a gang; prosecutors referred to them as a "wolf pack" instead.[35] Whether these young adults are described and defined as a gang or a wolf pack, their crimes are not readily recognizable as crimes until they are represented in relation to the criminalized figure of the gang member, Proposition 21's explicit target. In effect, whiteness cannot signify de jure or de facto status-based crimes.

Because criminal street gang membership is recognized only by invoking disempowered racial masculinities of impoverished areas, the adolescents and their family members did not seem to realize they were subject to Proposition 21. Policy analyst Deborah Vargas stated that most voters did not believe Proposition 21 pertained to them: "We tried to warn voters that this was going to cast a wide net. . . . We said it was not going to be just gang members from L.A. who do drive-by shootings, but that this will be your grandchildren, your kids, your nieces and nephews. It will bring in stellar kids with no past records."[36] Indeed, the initiative defined "gangs" as persons who do not belong to a community (at least not to voters' communities) but who are threats to others' communities: "Criminal street gangs and gang-related violence pose a significant threat to public safety and the health of many of our communities."[37] Framed in this way as "our communities" and "your grandchildren" versus "gang members from Los Angeles" or "us" versus "them," Proposition 21 distinguished the subjects of law as different from those who were subjected to it. The assailants' parents and others who supported their legal challenges more than likely identified with the initiative's addressees, the threatened members of "our communities." They most likely imagined their children as potential victims of gang-related crime—not as the leaders of ganglike violences.

For a law to be read as legitimate, it is essential that people feel addressed by the law, that they are included as members of its protected constituency (whose "public safety and health" is a primary concern). Jürgen Habermas explains that in modern societies, laws acquire legitimacy through democratic discourse or political participation. In order to secure public endorsement of any given law as rational, self-legislated, and socially integrative,[38] members of a lawful community need to be able to imagine that they would have authored the laws that address and/or affect them.[39] This was at the heart of the combined Manduley and Rose challenges. The attackers' parents could imagine themselves as the initiative's authors and addressees only if their families were not actually subject to its consequences. Had they realized their own children would be subjected to the punishments that seemed fair and appropriate only when referencing others' crimes, it is more than likely that not one of them would have supported Proposition 21. Voters are supposed to identify with legislators seeking to protect the public, not with criminals from which the public needs to be protected. Proposing, passing, and implementing de jure and de facto status-based laws (such as Propositions 187 and 21) create a socially empowered and politically entitled population, who see passing laws they imagine pertain to others as a civic responsibility, a duty they owe to the state that purports to protect them.

The youth targeted by Proposition 21 could not vote. They could be legally charged as adults, but they could not politically participate as adults. These youth had no say over whether or not the law should be enforced, and they were not asked if the laws they were expected to follow seemed legitimate. Their legal disempowerment is not just due to age. Status-based criminal (and criminalizing) laws are assumed to be a priori legitimate; thus, acquiring legitimacy does not require the targeted, disempowered population's consent.[40]

Deserving Redemption and Respect

In San Diego County, 66 percent of voters supported Proposition 21, which was higher than the state's average. The Rancho Peñasquitos area was reported to be even higher, voting 70 percent in favor.[41] In 2000, the suburb of Rancho Peñasquitos was predominantly white, but not overwhelmingly so. Whites were just under 63 percent of the population; Asians approximately 26 percent; Latinas/os just more than 8 percent; and blacks and Native Americans together accounted for only 3 percent. Rancho Peñasquitos is not a low-income suburb. On the contrary, the median household income in 2000 was almost $78,000, considerably higher than the national median household income of just under $42,000.[42] Rancho Peñasquitos residents were more likely to hire undocumented immigrants (as landscape workers and caretakers) than compete with them for jobs or over poorly funded state services. The suburban neighborhood where the migrant beatings took place was both affluent and relatively diverse, which suggests that neither economic competition over resources nor ignorance from racial isolation can readily explain why the adolescents attacked the migrant workers.

Mainstream media characterizations of the young assailants revealed different degrees of racialized senselessness and sense-making at work. Descriptions of their backgrounds highlighted their higher income levels, educational advantages, and extracurricular activities, and these descriptions assumed the perpetrators' entitlement to an audience's sympathies: "The boys have been described as above-average students. Only one has had a prior brush with the law, and several are athletes at Mount Carmel High School, a public school that serves upscale neighborhoods."[43] Although it seems as if their economic backgrounds and neighborhood demographics cannot help but emphasize the "irrationality" of their brutality, their social circumstances and privileged positions are more often used as evidence for their hidden humanity.

Of course, not all representations of the adolescent attackers problematically correlated wealth with innocence.[44] For example, in an opinion piece, freelance writer Jacquelyn Giles challenged the coupling of money with morality (or poverty with immorality) by interrogating how the meanings of "good" are made.

> If what is being reported is true, where did these suspects, these seven boys from "a good neighborhood" get the idea that Mexicans, or any other minority were fair prey for their prejudice? What do we mean by the term, "good," as applied to a neighborhood and its residents, or a school and its students?
>
> When we say, "good," do we really mean, "affluent"? Do people think that their families' prosperity confers on them a humanity superior to migrant workers who toil with their hands and cannot afford to live in "good" neighborhoods?[45]

Giles does not, however, see criminal punishment for racist violence as an effective deterrence, asserting that prison would be more likely to "perpetuate unreasoning hatred."[46] She worries that incarceration would only turn young men into hateful citizens who "would go through life spewing hatred for a system that punished them and blaming Mexicans as being 'responsible' for ruining their chances for a college education and the bright future their privileged youth seemed to promise."[47] For Giles, the appropriate penalty should lead the perpetrators to repent, to feel remorse and regret, yet her alternative situates the victims as primarily responsible for the attackers' future feelings. In her ideal scenario, the victims would facilitate the adolescents' rehabilitation and reintegration.

> If the victims are willing, those convicted of these crimes and their parents could learn much from the life histories of the migrants. At what age did they first go to work? Did they have a chance to attend school? Did their homes have indoor plumbing or running water? Did they have dreams and hopes as teen-agers?
>
> The perpetrators and their parents should be required to learn Spanish, study Mexican history and culture and perform enough hard, manual labor to bring them to understand that the men whom they held in contempt and brutalized are real people deserving of respect.[48]

Not only does her idealized alternative presume that racist violence is easily redeemable with more education, but it also constructs learning from and about Mexicans as an appropriate punishment for violent hate crime. Giles is attempting to make less strange what Sara Ahmed refers to as "the stranger encounter." By welcoming the other, Giles assumes, the young adults would assimilate and master racial difference.[49] Learning from migrant workers in order to learn about them implies that knowing is humanizing, but in actuality, it is objectifying.[50] Giles' questions betray that she already knows what the teenagers would learn; indeed, the questions make and assume claims about migrant workers' "being," which "transform[s] the 'being' of strangers into knowledge."[51] As Ahmed argues, "the stranger is some-body [not *any-body*] we know as not knowing, rather than some-body we simply do not know. The stranger is produced as a category within knowledge, rather than coming into being in an absence of knowledge."[52]

If we follow Giles' logic, the next encounter the rehabilitated teenagers would have with migrant workers would no longer inspire the fear, anxiety, rage, or resentment that led them to commit the hate crime. After learning how to "be" the other by learning Spanish and performing arduous manual labor, the eight teenagers would become better people, people who speak for and on behalf of all oppressed groups. As Giles writes, "Imagine what good can result if young people not bigoted beyond reclamation can be led to learn empathy for others, 'unlearn' their prejudices and become messengers of peace and tolerance, rather than racist felons whose next hate crime could be murder."[53]

The two options she presents—learning to be the other in order to unlearn prejudice or perpetuating "unreasoning hatred" through imprisonment—both invoke an/other figure, different than the migrant worker. For Giles, prison holds and teaches people to be "violent bigots [who] blame their victims simply for existing," and the boys need not be destined for this fate.[54] Racist violence, however, was not something they were in danger of learning but an accurate description of acts they had already committed. Although Giles interrogates the problematic ways in which "good" is often linked to affluence, she cannot construct both Mexican migrant workers and the white criminals who violently assaulted them as "good," unless she affixes the meanings of "bad" to criminalized populations of color. She reads people of color already convicted and incarcerated as irredeemably immoral and permanently violent. In her narrative, prisoners are the only people who cannot be imagined as "good," who do not receive sympathy or empathy, who remain not "real people deserving of respect."

Becoming White through Anti-Mexican Violence

Most of the assailants' parents refused to talk with the media. Morgan Manduley's family was an exception. Morgan's mother, Debra Manduley, voted for the proposition that could have sent her son to prison for more than a decade. After his arrest, she claimed that she had been misled to miss "the fine print" that would have enabled her to recognize the penal code was being amended in ways that would affect nongang youth. She told reporters that she thought Proposition 21 "was directed at 'incorrigible' young criminals involved in 'serious sex offenses and murder.'"[55] "Instead," San Diego Union-Tribune reporter Alex Roth wrote, "the new law is being used against her son, whom she describes as a 'terrific kid who has been no trouble at all to raise.'"[56] These rhetorical moves avoid juxtaposing "serious" crimes such as "sex offenses and murder" with Manduley's equally serious hate crimes that encompass racially motivated robbery, torture, assault, and elder abuse. Rather, "sex offenses and murder" are contrasted with Manduley's status. His unambiguous portrayal as a "terrific kid" and an "obedient little boy" shifts the focus from his conduct (committing hate crimes) to his status (as a privileged suburban teenager).[57] His innocent, youthful, suburban body is juxtaposed against not just other bodies but also other people's crimes, against bodies belonging to "incorrigible young criminals" and crimes he did not commit. The nonparallel image underscores Manduley's bodily difference while subtly sidestepping his comparably criminal behavior.

Journalists elicited sympathy for Manduley and empathy for his family by representing him as an unintended casualty of Proposition 21, misrecognized by criminal law as a criminal.[58] Because journalists presume that "the audience must identify with the players in the narrative,"[59] they often write in ways that both assume and manufacture an audience thought to share "universal" values, morals, and ethics. In this way, newspaper articles about Manduley sought to elicit sympathy irrespective of the teenager's guilt or innocence. His guilt was irrelevant for his parents and relatives, who were more concerned with how much the penalties for his actions would affect the future he was entitled to enjoy: "No one that young and with so much promise should be condemned."[60] Manduley's criminal activity was narrated as a one-and-only time offense, an aberrant moment for an otherwise "normal" (i.e., white, middle-class, and suburban) teenaged boy: "His mother, Debra, said outside of court that the incident was out of character for an otherwise 'super child.'"[61] In this manner, Manduley and his family were portrayed as victims of a law that was not supposed to affect them.

Manduley's story, which on some level stands in for the other seven adolescents, reflects what communications scholar Carrie A. Rentschler describes as "victim-oriented journalistic practice."[62] Examining the media strategies and journalism training that was developed in response to the victims' rights movement, Rentschler argues that the family members of crime victims are constructed as a "class of citizens without rights."[63] The victims' perspective in media focuses the story on the individual victim without regard to structural and historical explanations, "defining the criminal event itself as oppression, where the individual 'right-bearing' criminal and the institutions of criminal justice become victims' oppressors."[64] But these tactics were not deployed on behalf of the migrant workers; they were deployed on behalf of their attackers. By writing the offenders' crime stories as if the assailants were the victims, journalists refocused the news story on frightened families fighting an unfair law, evading the young men's unforgivable acts of unprovoked violence.

Ironically, it was easier for the Manduleys to claim injury and innocence because Morgan Manduley's father was Cuban. Morgan's racial identity, as part Latino, complicated the hate crime charges because the victims were also Latinos. Cubans who immigrated before 1980 have often (but also inconsistently and unreliably) been conceived of as elite, as the "model minority" of Latina/o ethnic groups.[65] Their precarious privileged status was a result of immigration restrictions and U.S. refugee policies during the Cold War that created ethnic hierarchies within Latina/o communities and engendered discourses of Cuban exceptionalism. Referred to as the "golden exiles" in the 1960s, (anticommunist) Cuban refugees of this era were disproportionately from upper-class and privileged backgrounds, and their resettlement in the United States was aided by U.S. government grants.[66] Unlike many undocumented Mexican immigrants and the vast majority of undocumented Central American immigrants (many of whom sought to escape vicious regimes allied with the United States), Cubans arriving without authorization during this era were not imagined as "illegal" because upon arriving unlawfully, they could immediately adjust their status from "illegal" to "legal" by petitioning for asylum via the 1966 Cuban Adjustment Act.[67]

Manduley's Cuban-American father, Commander Octavio Manduley, felt constitutional protection was due to him and his son, protection against the legitimate accusations of illegitimate victims. In news reports, he emphasized his patriotism, his Americanness by reminding reporters that he was a career U.S. Navy officer: "I've spent 17 years of my life defending the Constitution of the United States. . . . I've put my life on the line. And now when I expect to get some protection under the Constitution, I and my family have none."[68] Octavio Manduley reminds us that "rights" and "protections" for U.S. citizens of color are always unstable because they are framed as earned through assimilation, obedience, loyalty, and compliance rather than simply self-possessed. But at the same time, his military background (like the teens' impersonation of INS agents) is also representative of state-sanctioned violence. Deployed strategically and purposefully, Manduley's Latina/o heritage obscured the emphatic racial hatred motivating the ruthless assaults by casting doubt as to whether the attacks could actually be categorized as racially motivated at all: "If the seven White kids hate Latinos, why were they hanging out with Manduley?"[69]

Their family's social value and class privilege were most legible when framed through and emphasized against the criminalized other's racial difference and/or unlawful status. When juxtaposed against criminalized youth of color, Morgan Manduley was able to access injury and innocence, legal universality, and even white entitlement. As one of Manduley's Juvenile Hall inmates reportedly told him "I'm going to kill you white boy."[70] Manduley was represented not only as white but also as an outsider to and out of place within the criminalized cultures of Juvenile Hall. His seven peers also dismissed Manduley's racial and ethnic difference in relation to the elderly

—and mistakenly undocumented—Mexican workers. When he purportedly told his peers that he was Cuban, one of the boys responded by emphasizing that his other half was white: "Oh well, you're only half-Hispanic."[71] Morgan Manduley was able to access white injury but could do so only in relation to others' real or perceived illegality and criminality, thereby reducing his Cuban heritage to mere "irony."[72]

Boys Will Be Boys

As one of the youngest attackers, Manduley was also portrayed as inherently innocent on account of his age. His violent conduct was often rescripted as merely a regrettable consequence of his callow, but not criminal, youth. In an opinion piece, Laurence Steinberg, the director of the John D. and Catherine T. MacArthur Foundation Research Network on Adolescent Development and Juvenile Justice, wrote on Manduley's behalf that "His crime was being insufficiently mature to extricate himself from a bad situation. When the 17-year-old leaders of the group ordered Morgan to get them BBs for their guns, he reluctantly did."[73] As in the earlier examples, Manduley's crime is never named or described for what it was: participating in the racially motivated, abusive hate crime against Mexican workers. His criminal conduct is portrayed as merely and only a consequence of his youth. He is characterized as not yet man enough to protect himself against his peers' disapproval, as reluctantly compelled to participate in the brutal assaults.

According to sports studies scholar Kyle Kusz, the youthification of the white male as victim trope encourages reading "the dominating and prohibitive behaviors that boys/men often enact on others" as "further proof of their own vulnerability, suffering, and need for compassion from our culture."[74] In other words, even unsympathetic or neutral portrayals can be interpreted as more evidence of white male youths' innocence. For instance, by age 15, Michael Rose, the only teenager charged as a juvenile, already had a juvenile record prior to committing the attacks.[75] Rose's record was read not as evidence that he might commit another crime but as evidence of an unspoken cry for help. The judge who sentenced him said that Rose should have "the benefit of substance-abuse programs and other services" that the California Youth Authority offers and prison does not. Judge James R. Milliken believed that "With treatment, Rose will be less likely to commit another crime when he is released," whereas in state prison, "he's just going to get a Ph.D. in criminal behavior."[76]

The issue of juvenile crime versus adult crime prompted one of the other perpetrator's fathers to speak to the media. Eric Davidofsky, Bradley

Davidofsky's father, apologized for his son's behavior: "All I would like to say is every parent I've talked to is sick and sorrowful about what happened to the victims and we wish them a full recovery."[77] And he stressed, "We would hope everyone would remember that the defendants are children and not adults."[78] Upon learning that all the adolescents would be tried as adults, Eric Davidofsky told reporters the ruling was "a little perplexing" but not surprising, insisting again that "I know my son, and I know my son is not an adult. . . . I guess there's a legal definition with regard to this case, but I know my son is not an adult."[79]

Whether an accused teenager is described as mature or immature is not legally insignificant. The legal system distinguishes youth who can be rehabilitated from youth who cannot by estimating the crime's "degree of criminal sophistication" or whether the crime committed seemed to be more adultlike (such as gang violence) than childlike (such as, apparently, hate crimes).[80] Attorney Nicholas Espíritu argues that even before Proposition 21 was drafted, judges determined juvenile "fitness" for rehabilitation through racialized criteria, such as whether youth were affiliated with a gang or whether youth had "strong school attachments" and "good families."[81] As Espíritu argues, "By 'sophisticating' or placing the full moral culpability that is reserved for adults onto youth, they [the courts] are creating different categories of youth."[82] Criminal "sophistication," Espíritu contends, is a racialized concept of crime, functioning to differentiate youth of color who are "unfit" from those who deserve second chances. It is not surprising that taking away judges' discretionary power to decide each individual's potential for reform and redemption was the primary concern for both Rose's and Manduley's legal challenges. As the CACJ's amicus curiae brief concluded,

> Petitioners have argued that by creating a distinct group of juveniles who by the definition of their crimes will no longer be dealt with according to the calculus used by a juvenile court, Proposition 21 offends a tradition and public policy at the core of modern criminal justice—namely the use of judicial review of the circumstances of a young person's life as a basis for potential salvation.[83]

The eight Rancho Peñasquitos young men would have benefited from judicial review because their parents' background and school involvement would have been considered favorably, but juvenile review rarely benefited youth of color. Before Proposition 21 passed, youth of color were already overrepresented in transfers to adult court. In 1996, 95 percent of the juvenile cases transferred to adult court in Los Angeles involved youth of color.[84]

When compared with white youth in Los Angeles, youth of color were 2.8 times more likely to be arrested for a violent crime, 6.2 times more likely to be transferred to adult court, and 7 times more likely to be imprisoned.[85] In 2002, three out of four youth admitted to the nation's adult state prisons were youth of color.[86]

Proposition 21 targeted those youth whose future actions were already evaluated as "undeserving" of second chances. As Barbara Herrnstein Smith reminds us, who and what we encounter are at least partly "pre-interpreted and pre-classified for us by our particular cultures and languages" as well as "pre-evaluated" because they exhibit "the marks and signs of their prior valuings and evaluations."[87] Prior valuings (and devaluings) of certain statuses and bodies work to assign, allocate, and legitimate social entitlements. Even though the teenagers' actions were found to warrant punishment, their social status—as white, heterosexual, male, suburban citizens—entitled them to second chances.

Of the teenaged assailants, one pleaded guilty and seven pleaded no contest to hate crime charges of elder abuse, robbery, and assault with a deadly weapon. Three—Adam Ketsdever, Bradley Davidofsky, and Michael Rose —also pleaded no contest to an additional charge that their actions caused great bodily injury.[88] Ketsdever, Davidofsky, and Manduley were also charged with assaulting another victim.[89] Even though Rose was described by Deputy District Attorney Hector Jimenez as "the biggest thug out there," Rose was the only one tried as a juvenile. He was sentenced to the California Youth Authority for a term of five to seven years.[90] Judge Milliken sentenced Ketsdever and Davidofsky to two years in the San Diego County jail, and Steven DeBoer to one year.[91] The rest were sentenced to spend less than one year at a California Youth Authority facility even though they were charged as adults. Nicholas Fileccia was sentenced to eight months; Jason Beever[92] and Kevin Williams each received six months.[93] Morgan Manduley received the lightest sentence with four months.[94] They each received five years probation and 200 hours of community service, including racial and cultural sensitivity training, programs, or counseling, consistent with California hate crime charge enhancements, though these are not the only options for enhanced sentencing. (They could have had four years added to a prison sentence.)[95]

Although their crimes were recognized and tried as adult crimes, the young men's sentences suggested that these adult crimes were not attached to the actual perpetrators. On some level, it appeared that the adult charges were about setting a precedent for future perpetrators, rather than punishing the current ones. The behaviors, but not the boys, were condemned. Judge

Milliken sentenced seven of the young men as adults because he believed that "the fact that this behavior is possible is a sad commentary on the community." He said trying the young men as adults would "tell the community that we are not going to put up with it."[96] While Milliken and the community were not going to put up with such heinous behavior, they were more than willing to put up with the boys responsible for it. Milliken was clearly convinced that each one of the teenagers deserved a second chance because not one of their adult sentences included serving time in state prison. As Greg Moran of the *San Diego Union-Tribune* reported: "[Milliken] was reluctant to send them to state prison, where rehabilitation programs are few and where they would be housed with adult criminals."[97] For those sentenced to jail time, Milliken had this message: "This is a chance for you to prove you won't spend the rest of your life in prison, and that you can become a good citizen."[98] The chance to become a good citizen was never offered to their noncitizen victims.

When we read representations of this case, we learn that lives are differentially valued. We learn that it is difficult for many to imagine that young white men from "good" families and suburban neighborhoods deserve to be imprisoned, even if such adolescents were intentionally and callously violent, and even if they willfully directed that violence toward people they believed would not be able to defend themselves physically or legally. We also learn that Latina/o agricultural workers can be simultaneously victims of violence yet not represented as victims of violent crimes if that violence was committed by young assailants believed deserving of second chances. The Rancho Peñasquitos perpetrators could have received twelve to fifteen years in state prison, but not one of them received a state prison sentence. Most were sent to California Youth Authority facilities, four of them for less than one year. Their sentences included attending classes to better learn the inappropriateness of brutally beating and leaving for dead people whom they see as unlike themselves.

The verdict might have been different if the attackers and/or victims were different ages, races, ethnicities, genders, or legal statuses. Manduley received four months in a California Youth Authority facility. Had he and the other young men been considered gang members, not only would it have been more likely that they each would have received twelve to fifteen years imprisonment (the maximum sentences), but they would also have been subject to gang enhancement charges, which could have added up to ten more years to their sentences.[99] The suburban adolescents' crimes were not less vicious nor more rational than gang-associated crimes, but the potential sentencing disparities are so glaring that it almost seems as if these youth were tried under different laws altogether, as if they were not really subject to Proposition 21 after all.

Value's Traps and Untold Stories

While Morgan Manduley and Michael Rose were the lead plaintiffs for the case against Proposition 21 that made it all the way to the U.S. Supreme Court, many youth had already been tried under the initiative. Of these, 17-year-old Manuel Ortega was the first tried after the initiative was passed. Ortega and two other youth were fighting on a well-travelled sidewalk in Riverside. Ortega was charged for beating the man who attempted to stop their fight.[100] Although he was the first adolescent tried as an adult after Proposition 21 was passed, he received very little media attention.[101] His story did not trigger outrage and empathy, nor did his experiences with the law provoke democratic discussions and public debate regarding the fairness and constitutionality of Proposition 21. In fact, even his defense attorney agreed that Ortega would have been tried as an adult whether the proposition had passed or not.[102]

Ortega's act of violence was not planned; nor was it a hate crime. Unlike the eight San Diegan adolescents, Ortega did not stalk, rob, or torture his victim for three hours. His actions were indeed violent, but they were not comparable to the actions of the eight attackers of Rancho Peñasquitos, who acted collectively and aggressively. While those suburban teenagers dragged an elderly man whom they had tortured for three hours behind bushes to die, they were given a second chance because they said they were sorry. Both the mainstream media as well as the judge who sentenced the attackers believed that the young men were sincere in their apologies and that they had suffered enough. Ortega pleaded guilty to assault and was sentenced to three years in custody.[103] Even though the ten-year maximum sentence Ortega could have faced was less than the twelve- to fifteen-year sentence faced by the Rancho Peñasquitos adolescents, Ortega's sentence was longer than the sentences of each of the other teenagers who had been charged as adults. Like Rose, who was charged as a juvenile, Ortega did have a record, but unlike Rose's record, Ortega's was used as evidence of his inability to be rehabilitated rather than a cry for help. Unlike all eight of the adolescents, Ortega was not represented as a "good kid," "obedient little boy," or even as a youth-not-adult who deserved another chance to be a "good" citizen. Ortega was convicted by the news media before he was tried, represented as a criminal before proven to be a criminal. In fact, prosecutor Creg Datig, who helped to draft Proposition 21, said Ortega's case was "exactly the kind of case we had in mind."[104]

Although Datig had cases like Ortega's in mind, most of the proposition's supporters had gang members in mind. California news media report often on the arrests of gang members, particularly for "sex offenses and murders," but less is published on whether accused gang members are convicted.[105] The vast majority of cases are not followed up with articles on suspects' pleas, trials, and sentencing. Journalists rarely represent gang members and drive-by shooters as complex people, let alone as victims of law or as teenagers and young adults who make mistakes. Communications scholar Kevin Dolan argues that the failure of journalists to delve deeper into complicated and multisided events originates from the pressure to represent stories "objectively." "To avoid accusations that they are making and not reporting the news," Dolan explains, journalists rarely write stories on their own, "often waiting for an official, a major player or someone else (rather than the columnists)" to provide them "unbiased" perspectives on a story.[106] Coupled with easily recognizable and popular news narratives about gang violence, these kinds of practices lead journalists to gravitate toward the most outspoken actors.[107] In stories about gang activity, those who are most outspoken and most official are often the police and the prosecutor, who are both invested in representing arrested gang members in ways that cast the arrests and the charges as legitimate. The defense attorney is often the sole spokesperson (if one is sought) for the "other side" of a gang member's story. Generally, journalists do not interview gang members themselves, nor do they seek statements from gang members' families, friends, and teachers.

Although the young attackers' case was often represented in binarisms, such as white versus Mexican or citizen versus immigrant, the case itself was not nearly this simple because the lines demarcating interests and allegiances were neither neat nor stable. The victims were not exactly the targets of the attackers, and the attackers were not quite the targets of Proposition 21. Manduley, half-Latino, was accused of participating in an anti-Latina/o hate crime. The adolescents attacked legal immigrants, but they believed they were assaulting "illegal aliens." Because youth of color were targeted by the proposition, they had the most to lose if the proposition was not overturned, and yet youth of color such as Ortega were not involved in the legal challenges at all. The assailants' minimal sentences and failed legal challenge assigned valueless-ness not only to their Mexican victims but also to undocumented immigrants and criminalized youth of color. The suburban youth aligned themselves with the state, which tells us that their attacks were not disconnected from but rather reflective of the state's sanctioned violence against undocumented Latina/o immigrants. The court's decision that Proposition 21 was legitimate ultimately evidences the valueless-ness of criminalized youth of color, while the young San Diego assailants' lenient sentences remind us that societal value is unequivocally accorded to white suburban boys.

As I write about this particular case's injustices, I struggle with the contradiction that U.S. law not only defines injustice but also institutes multiple punishments for those passively not committing de facto status crimes. When we insist that law recognize the value of victims' lives, we are essentially demanding that lawbreakers receive harsher prison sentences, which validates and substantiates the power of the criminal justice system to determine whose lives are socially valuable and whose are less so. As Rentschler writes, because "victims function as the corporeal texts of trauma and victimization," their suffering "proves the significance of punishing crime and its offenders."[108] The criminal justice system affirms and even partly determines a social group's human value. If the victims are socially valued, it seems more likely that their assailants will receive longer sentences, whereas if the offenders are assumed to be socially valuable, they are likely to be given more lenient sentences. In the latter case, the experience of being the target of a racially motivated and unduly violent hate crime is liable to be trivialized. Furthermore, because the "value of life" is measured by and made intelligible through the criminal justice system, the lives of the attackers and their victims are assigned value and valueless-ness not only in relation to one another, but also in relation to already not-valued others. Hence, the cost of securing value for elderly migrant workers Irigoyen, Ayala, Roman, Juarez, and Ramos is steep and paid by someone else—by youth and young adults of color whose bodies happen to be the real world referent for that always already criminal figure targeted by Proposition 21 and its draconian measures.

2

Beyond Ethical Obligation

> What makes a human monster a monster is not only that it is an
> exception to the form of the species but also that it introduces dis-
> order into the legal system.
> —Michel Foucault, *Abnormal*

Oun Roo Chhay was ambushed by members of a gang that called itself the
Local Asian Boyz (LAB) in the parking lot of his apartment building in
the Rainer Valley neighborhood of Seattle, Washington. He was 20 years
old when he was murdered. Four young adults were arrested for his murder; three were convicted. Kim Ho Ma, only a high school sophomore, was
among those convicted. Ma was tried as an adult because Washington state
law mandates that 16 and 17 year olds be tried as adults for first-degree man-
slaughter. He was convicted and sentenced to thirty-eight months in prison.
In 1997, he was released for good behavior after serving twenty-six.[1]

But because Ma was not just a gang member in the tenth grade but also
a Cambodian refugee,[2] when he was released for good behavior, he was

"released" into INS custody. Because he was a noncitizen and his sentence was for more than one year, his crime was defined as an "aggravated felony." This mandated his deportation under the newly implemented Antiterrorism and Effective Death Penalty Act (AEDPA) and the Illegal Immigration Reform and Immigrant Responsibility Act (IIRIRA) of 1996.[3] However, Cambodia did not have a repatriation agreement with the United States when Ma was convicted.[4] Once in INS custody, Ma had no release date to look forward to or to dread. He could have been held indefinitely along with a few thousand other immigrants who were given orders of removal but who could not be removed.[5] Referred to as "lifers" or "unremovables," these INS prisoners were either "stateless" or nationals of countries that did not accept criminal deportees, such as Cambodia, Cuba, Laos, Iraq, Libya, Vietnam, the former Soviet Union, and Iran. Some were like the Mariel Cubans, not criminal aliens but expected to become so if given the opportunity, and categorized by immigration law as simultaneously "inadmissible" and "unremovable."[6] Criminal, noncitizen, and essentially stateless, Ma and other lifers had no future and no rights.

Technically, the INS could not hold all immigrants indefinitely; it could detain people ordered deported for only 90 days, but "criminal aliens" were an exception. For "criminal aliens" who could not be deported, the rules were less clear, and the INS was less inclined to comply with them. The agency had leeway with "unremovables," which the government took to mean lifetime detention if necessary. During his detainment, Ma fought the INS for years, attempting to procure his freedom, and in 2001, he succeeded. In the consolidated cases of *Zadvydas v. Davis et al.* and *Ashcroft v. Ma* heard by the U.S. Supreme Court, the justices ruled that the INS could not hold "unremovables" for longer than six months if deportation was not likely within the foreseeable future. This victory did not pertain to the Mariel Cubans and other "inadmissible" nondeportable lifers.[7] For Cambodian detainees such as Ma, the victory was short and sardonic; the unforeseeable future became the sudden and unexpected present less than a year later. In March 2002, Cambodia signed a repatriation agreement with the United States, and the 23-year-old Ma was among the first deported in October of the same year.

Criminal aliens are difficult to defend because they occupy so many unsympathetic statuses. As both a U.S. gang member and a Cambodian refugee, Ma embodied the stereotype of the "criminal alien" that is so often deployed to bolster support for punitive immigration laws and policies such as the AEDPA, the IIRIRA, and California's Proposition 187.[8] Activists seeking public sympathy must repudiate gang members as people who matter because unlike undocumented workers and mixed-status families, gang members, whether immigrants or U.S. citizens, cannot be recuperated into U.S. norms or according to "American" values. They do not appear to make rational or normative choices. In fact, their choices do not make sense to most law-abiding U.S. citizens and residents because gang crime has already been interpreted as senseless and unprovoked. Gang members are too unsympathetic, too irredeemable, and too unreadable. They are rendered illegible as victims and irrational as victimizers. Ma's case would not be compelling at all if he could not be represented as rehabilitated, if gang membership was his present and not his past, if he had entered illegally rather than lawfully, or if his family had not fled Cambodia under Pol Pot's regime.[9]

Clearly, gang violence is nothing to celebrate or excuse, but being a member of a gang should not be a self-evident explanation for why contemporary gang members—inner-city gang members of color[10]—are depicted and dealt with so differently from other perpetrators who commit equally violent crimes. Gang-related crime is even classified as belonging to a different class and caliber of violence than the very same crimes committed by nongang members. This matters because, for all intents and purposes, gang members and those mistaken for gang members are almost exclusively conceived of as young men from impoverished neighborhoods of color. As a result, both how we make sense of gang membership and how we make gang violence make sense have consequences that extend far beyond actual gang members and their territories. How racial masculinity is constructed through the figuration of the "gang" impacts how surveillance and sentencing will be conducted. How race and space are imagined governs how neighborhoods of color and their residents will be managed.

Ineligible for personhood and beyond ethical obligation, gang members are, in Lindon Barrett's words, the "dismembered others" of so much that Americans value. As Barrett explains, "value remembers itself by dismembering the Other."[11] Literally and symbolically, criminalized people of color must be maimed or murdered, detained and disregarded in the name of "protecting" all that Americans are taught to value, such as family, private property, and U.S. citizenship. This is why gang members are so central to immigration debates and discourses of U.S. citizenship. Criminalizing gang members always simultaneously valorizes middle-class America and also validates the historical and present-day practices that work to isolate, segregate, and alienate criminalized neighborhoods of color. Suspending the demand and the impulse to disavow gang members and exclude them from our claims for justice enables us to consider how gang membership might be more than an identity and an affiliation. How can we read gang membership as a form of noncitizenship, and, along these lines, to what extent does the gang member as a social and cultural construct influence immigration legislation? How might we explicate the legal and political investments that discursively and juridically connect inner-city gang members to noncitizens of color? And how do these same investments recruit people of all colors from all legal statuses to repudiate young men of color like Ma so absolutely? The criminal justice system and immigration law depend on understanding crime, criminality, and criminals as evidence for and as emblematic of populations and places ineligible for personhood—legal universality's necessary fiction that violently yet surreptitiously divests communities of color of "inalienable" rights. Analyzing the justice system this way reveals the way in which criminalized people of color cannot access legal protection. They cannot access legal protection because they are the people against whom the law must discriminate in order to protect everyone else against discrimination. In other words, legal equality is possible for everyone else because criminalized populations of color are ineligible for rights and personhood. Hence, when we point toward representations of contemporary gang members as evidence for the ways in which entire communities of color are criminalized and stereotyped, we may miss how the gang member, like the "illegal alien," is both an effect and an object of criminalization, not the "truth" behind moments of misrecognition. To analyze otherwise, to scrutinize criminalization as a process of devaluation and state regulation, it is necessary to examine how gang members are (mass) manufactured as incorrigible criminals who are beyond even unsympathetically begrudged ethical obligations. This chapter offers a reading of criminality as a signifier for populations and places rendered ineligible for self-determination and sovereignty by examining how race, criminality, and irrationality are produced and naturalized as co-constitutive. Analyzing the logic, laws, and storylines that fuse gang membership to racial masculinity and impoverished spaces helps us to explicate why criminalization as both a disciplinary and regularizing process of devaluation does not just exclude some people from legal "universality" but makes their inclusion a necessary impossibility.

Criminal in Body and Being

In 1983, President Ronald Reagan established the President's Commission on Organized Crime.[12] In 1984, the commission held a hearing regarding Chinese, Japanese, and Vietnamese gangs, believed to be "emerging" organized crime groups.[13] According to the commission and its expert witnesses, Asian gangs did not act like U.S. black and Mexican American gangs because Asian gangs were not concerned with territory, which, in turn, made them difficult to locate and infiltrate. Although Southeast Asian gangs were not considered organized crime groups like their Chinese and Japanese counterparts, they were often included in the congressional hearings on organized crime because they were imagined to be more vicious and more villainous than other racial and/or ethnic gangs. For instance in 1991, Sergeant Douglas Zwemke of the San Jose, California, Police Department emphasized in his testimony that "in the nearly 16 years since the fall of Saigon, those Vietnamese predisposed toward crime have been involved in almost every type of crime, leaving virtually no illegal stone unturned."[14] At the same Senate hearing, FBI Director William S. Sessions insisted that "after the Vietnam War, the United States experienced a significant influx of Vietnamese gang refugees. The criminal element among these refugees rapidly formed street gangs, which now engage primarily in theft, home invasions, drug dealing, kidnapping and extortion."[15] Vietnamese criminal street gangs were also considered "extremely mobile" and "very difficult to identify," seemingly unconnected to a particular place and even disloyal to their own: "Gang members are frequently changing allegiances, if you call it that, from one group to another and moving on to a new jurisdiction quite rapidly."[16]

At a separate Senate hearing in 1986, national anxieties over Asian gangs prompted Congress to begin thinking about how to use immigration law as a way to complement criminal law, fearing that it had become too easy for "undesirables" to become U.S. citizens: "Chinese and Vietnamese crime members are often naturalized U.S. citizens, and we may need to look at the immigration laws to determine if we need to bolster them in order to deport those few among them engaged in violent crime."[17] Southeast Asian gangs were uniquely unnerving for law enforcement and legislators from the mid-1980s to the early 1990s because, unlike other gangs, Southeast Asian gang members could not be deported and were difficult to contain; they were simultaneously mobile and "unremovable."

The juridical recognition of personhood for legal immigrants and U.S. citizens does not protect gang members' inalienable rights because gang membership is a de facto status crime. De facto status crimes empower the criminal justice system in concert with other disciplinary apparatuses to revoke not only gang members' rights but their right to have rights. Although the "rule of law" is supposed to render all people in the United States formally equivalent,[18] it does not really apply to gang members because gang members are multiply constructed as criminal in "being." To examine how and why gang membership is criminalized in ways that can divest legal residents and U.S. citizens of color of their inalienable rights, it is crucial that we suspend the impulse to analyze the gang member as a racial stereotype or as a

race-neutral code word for race. Contemporary narratives of gang membership are key to understanding how racial difference works to signify ineligibility to personhood and how criminality works to reify that signification.

What differentiates the murder of Oun Roo Chhay from murders committed by nongang members is that Kim Ho Ma was criminalized before the
crime; he was guilty of being a member of the Local Asian Boyz and for as-
sociating with other members of the LAB. Ma did not need to be the person
who pulled the trigger to be guilty of Chhay's murder. The jury found him
culpable for the victim's death.[19] No one knew if he was one of the two shooters, but no one needed to know. The seriousness of the crime was not the
crime itself—the murder of another not-valued gang member.[20] The seriousness of Ma's crime was being part of a group of young men who identified
themselves as gang members.

For a gang member, to be criminalized is not contingent upon committing
a violent crime; the gang member is criminalized because he or she might
commit crimes in the future. Gang members are imagined as criminal in
being, as predisposed to criminality and as unreformable. This belief is con-
cretized in gang enhancement sentencing, and for Ma, it was also reaffirmed
by the Board of Immigration Appeals. Ma arrived in the United States with
his family in 1985 as a state-sponsored refugee when he was 7 years old.[21]
Until he became an adult at age 18, he could not protect himself against deportation because noncitizen minors cannot apply for naturalized citizenship on their own. They can acquire only derivative citizenship when their
parents are naturalized.[22] Ma would not have been charged with committing
an aggravated felony had he been tried as a juvenile, but under Washington
state's criminal law, he could be tried and convicted as an adult at age 17. In
other words, Ma was an adult in criminal law, but a minor according to the
Immigration and Nationality Act. He could be deported, but he could not
apply for naturalized citizenship to protect himself against deportation.[23] Ma
never had access to a second chance.

Although Ma's refugee status complicated and exacerbated his situation,
he was not unique. On the contrary, he was part of a population targeted for
early and repeat incarceration. For gang members, it is not just illegal to wear
specialized colors and clothing or to make a living through the underground
economy, it is also criminal for gangsters to associate with other people presumed to be gang members or to stand on street corners. Anti-gang legislation criminalizes gang members' relationships to public space, community
networks, and social institutions—even gang members' aesthetic choices are
demonized, disciplined, and regulated.[24] If everything and anything these
youth do and do not do is already a crime, what law-abiding options do gang

members have? How should we untangle the ontological processes that render them always already criminal in body and being?

Psychiatric Residues

the details don't matter

Because he was a gang member, Ma's motives could never have mitigating factors, and his actions would always receive harsher punishments, which is why the details of Chhay's murder were so much less important than the fact of his death. Ma participated in killing Chhay, but no one wanted to know why. The people making decisions about Ma's future already knew all they needed to know. Before he challenged the constitutionality of indefinite detention, Ma tried to apply for asylum and withholding of deportation. He was denied both, as well as bail.[25] As the immigration judge Anna Ho maintained, "no amount of bail would be able to guarantee the community's safety."[26] Part of Judge Ho's decision to deny Ma bond was premised upon psychologist Carla van Dam's report, which concluded that Ma was dangerous. Ho summarized the report by highlighting all the moments when Ma's responses did not correlate with the reality they already knew—all the moments when it seemed he lied. They believed he was in a gang. Ma said he was not, but then later admitted that he was. Ma denied drug and alcohol abuse, but the report stated he was drunk and high when he was arrested.[27] He was convicted of a crime that he believed he did not commit: "According to this information, respondent [Ma] did not admit that he had anything to do with the crime of which he was convicted. According to this [psychological] report, respondent states, 'There's nothing to talk about. I was charged with it [manslaughter]. I was there. I didn't know what was happening. I didn't have a gun. I didn't have nothing. I didn't know. I didn't say nothing in my trial.'"[28] Because Ma refused to recognize, and thus failed to recite, that the officially documented details of his case were representing a reality he had actually experienced, Ho could find no evidence of his regret: "Obviously, respondent feels absolutely no remorse for what he has done."[29] Ho's responsibility was to decide whether Ma was sorry for the crime he was not convinced he had committed. She believed his lack of regret was transparent ("obvious") because Ma did not accept (or respect) the premise of his conviction. Ho and Van Dam's imposed interpretation of Ma's actions directly opposed his performative answers as a suspect who pleaded not guilty. Ma was subjected more than once to the kind of power-knowledge that enabled psychologists, immigration judges, and INS agents to "know" all about him yet simultaneously render anything he said, perceived, or felt irrelevant.[30]

not following the script

This kind of power-knowledge emerged through psychiatry, which possesses what Michel Foucault calls a "Psy-function" (referring to "the psychiatric, psychopathological, psycho-sociological, psycho-criminological, and psychoanalytic function").[31] This, he argues, "became both the discipline and the control of all the disciplinary systems" by the beginning of the twentieth century,[32] as well as the discursive regime that "performed the role of discipline for all those who could not be disciplined."[33] Ma could not be rehabilitated if he could not accept that his experience was the same as Van Dam and Ho's interpretation of his actions. However, if he were to acknowledge and agree with their interpretation, he would be validating both the knowledge that had the power to convict him in the criminal justice system and the premise for his indefinite detention by the INS. He neither confirms nor denies, but his commitment to illegibility does not convey the complexity of his situation nor of his personhood. He reads simply as merely someone who lies.

His illegibility is a by-product of disciplinary power. According to Foucault, because disciplinary systems "tend toward isotopy" (in that different disciplinary apparatuses connect and converge with one another but not completely), disciplinary power will always produce "something like a residue. . . . There is always something like 'the unclassifiable.'"[34] An INS prisoner who has been ordered deported but who cannot be repatriated, who has already served his criminal sentence yet remains incarcerated as a civilian, is such an unclassifiable, "unremovable" residue. The "Psy-function" structures Ma's legal conundrum because his rehabilitation requires his confession (as a convicted criminal), but an admission of guilt only justifies his detention (as a noncitizen). He attempts to evade the charges altogether by refusing to acknowledge or affirm others' interpretations that the events leading to his conviction were ones he had actually experienced, admitting only that "I was there." The power-knowledge produced through the "Psy-function" also transforms the suspect who refuses to admit guilt into a pathological liar by transforming the suspect's not-guilty performance into a sign that he or she is a danger to society, into a symptom of the modern-day madness of monstrosity, a sociopathology.

The Sociopathic Condition of Irrationality

Sociopathology is the antisocial personality disorder often ascribed to gang members, and the absence of guilt is one of its primary symptoms. Lewis Yablonsky, criminologist and social psychologist, writes, "Guilt is an unknown experience for the sociopath who has no controlling superego. The sociopath has no automatic self-punishment that goes along with the commission of immoral and unethical acts. They behave irresponsibly, untruthfully, insincerely, and antisocially without a shred of shame, remorse, or guilt. . . . Their regret is not sincerely felt."[35] Yablonsky is a consultant and expert witness for more than 300 gang-related court cases; his opinions matter for many youth who face extended prison terms because they have been accused of gang activity. In most of his testimonies, Yablonsky is called upon to determine whether or not the accused is a gang member, which works against the common perception that gangsters are easily discernible from the rest of the population. Having spent fifty years studying the behaviors and personalities of gang members prior to and after becoming an expert witness, he believes that "many, if not most, gangsters are sociopaths."[36] He has deduced that a gang member "*does not have the ability to identify or empathize with any others*. He [the gang member] is thus capable of committing spontaneous acts of 'senseless' violence without feeling concern or guilt."[37] Interpreted in this way, "senseless" is not a conscious act of random violence that might be used to intimidate nongang members and neighborhood residents. For Yablonsky, "senseless" is much more literal: It is evidence of a "disabled" conscience, a conscience that lacks both sense and sentiment. As he asserts, "sociopathic youth" are "socially disabled" and have been "characterized by what has varyingly been called a 'moral imbecility' or a 'character disorder.'"[38] Yablonsky ascribes disability and illness to sociopathology in order to characterize gang members as persons inherently and permanently unequal in capacity and ability, not unwilling but unable to be compassionate and empathetic.

Disease and disability figure centrally whenever there is the need to represent state-sanctioned violence as necessary for national survival. Disability is the language of devaluation, contagion, and control. Metaphors of disease and infection are scattered throughout the 1997 Senate Hearing on Interstate Street Gangs, constructing gang members as physical threats to the health and well-being of the national body. Gang activity was represented as a "social disease of crime,"[39] young people could become "infected with gang violence,"[40] and the federal government needed to get "this epidemic under control."[41] Gang membership registered as dangerously viral, remaking victims of poverty into pathogens targeted for eradication.

Because they were evolutionary markers of disability or incapacity, race, culture, and world region were central to the scientific production of bodily difference as a signifier for *legitimate discrimination*.[42] For instance, in 1866, babies with Down syndrome, which was then called "Mongolism," were thought to be anomalies of the Caucasian race that evidenced a biological regression from the modern Caucasian to a primitive Mongol.[43] As disability studies historian Douglas Baynton writes, it was common for nonwhite races to be "routinely connected to people with disabilities" in the mid-nineteenth century because both "were depicted as evolutionary laggards or throw-backs."[44] As signifiers for various disabilities and evolutionary regression, race, nationality, and ethnicity justified social and material inequalities and were used to defend slavery and restrict immigration.[45] Women's bodily difference was assumed to evidence mental inferiority and was used to argue against women's rights and suffrage.[46] A woman's physical and mental fragility would ensure her disablement, anti-suffragists posited, if women were given the right to vote. Some even believed that a woman's reproductive organs would be debilitated if she used too much brain power by acquiring an education.[47] More recently, homosexuality was considered a mental illness and was used to exclude lesbian, gay, bisexual, transgender, and transsexual (LGBT) people from immigrating; people diagnosed with HIV or AIDS were also inadmissible until 2010.[48] Medical insurance requires that transgender persons seeking sex reassignment pathologize themselves and perform disability, mental illness, and/or psychological trauma.[49] Historically, social differences worked as signifiers for undeveloped minds and defective bodies. Race, gender, nationality, culture, and sexuality were variously deployed as markers for moral deficiencies, intellectual incompetence, compromised immune systems, and less-than-fit bodies.[50] As Baynton contends, "the *concept* of disability has been used to justify discrimination against other groups by attributing disability to them."[51] Because disability has figured so prominently in establishing the historical meanings of equality and in naturalizing the justifications for inequality, inscribing disability and disease onto criminalized bodies of color, whether as diagnosis or as metaphor, appears seamless.

Discrediting eugenic and related theories eventually rendered biological or physiological racial difference an unreliable signifier for various disabilities and susceptibilities. This enabled able-minded and able-bodied people of color to insist that people "equal in capacity" should be treated equally.[52] But normalizing racial difference as immaterial to "universality," "normality," and "rationality" stabilized and naturalized hierarchies of human ability and capacity, universalizing certain norms and ideals of bodies and minds as defining and definitively universal human properties. In other words, redefining who could be human also reified the criteria for who could not. Those perceived to have disordered minds and disabled bodies were the residue of these reconfigured disciplinary apparatuses, still leftover as "the proper subject for discrimination."[53]

Although sociopathology is defined as a personality disorder and described as a mental illness or as a social disability, it reads and functions as the manifestation of a "condition." According to Foucault, "The condition is a sort of *permanent causal background* on the basis of which illness may develop in a number of processes and episodes. In other words, the condition is the abnormal basis upon which illnesses become possible."[54] The concept of the condition emerged in the late nineteenth century,[55] when childhood became the focus of psychiatry and "the instrument of its universalization."[56] The instability of childhood as a fragile and unbalanced but not necessarily pathological state becomes the object of psychiatry's knowledge and the source of its power.[57] Generalizing psychiatric power depended upon the depathologization of its objects of knowledge and targets of discipline, which Foucault argues, gave rise to the condition[58] as "a privileged psychiatric object" precisely because it is "not exactly an illness."[59] The use of "condition" can avoid invoking discredited eugenic discourses while still labeling individuals and/or their behavior as fundamentally, inherently, and unpredictably "abnormal." As Foucault explains:

> A condition can produce absolutely anything at any time, and in any order. Both physical illness and psychological illness can be linked with a condition. . . . It allows any physical element or deviant behavior whatever, however disparate and distant they may be, to be connected with a sort of unified background that accounts for it—a background that differs from the state of health but nevertheless is not an illness. . . . It refers to nonhealth, but it can also bring into its field any conduct whatsoever as soon as it is physiologically, psychologically, sociologically, morally, and even legally deviant.[60]

ableism

Because it is unpredictable, abnormal, and illegible, sociopathic behavior is the manifestation of a condition, an incurable foundation for incorrigible conduct of all kinds, manifesting as both a moral deficiency and a social disability, as more than predisposed to violence and vice, degeneracy and deviance. In fact, because "abnormality" is the sociopath's afflicted core, even (what is presumed to be) socially acceptable behavior is transformed into a symptom of sociopathology. As Yablonsky emphasizes, "sociopaths, most of the time, appear to speak and behave in ways that are socially acceptable . . . a sociopath, to the untrained eye, can appear intelligent, charming and considerate. . . . The sociopaths' overt appearance belies their underlying amoral character disorder."[61] Even though how they act "most of the time" is "intelligent, charming, and considerate," it does not matter because such "socially acceptable" conduct is "abnormal" behavior for a social deviant and only provides further evidence of his or her sociopathology. If acting "normal" is symptomatic of sociopathology as a "condition," how would one ever demonstrate reform or rehabilitation?

↳ automatically assumed to be crazy

Spatial Disablement

iological

The fictive underlying "condition" that sometimes manifests as the sociopathic behavior of gang members has been imagined and managed as if it were inherited genetically and/or transmitted spatially. The emergence of the "condition" was accompanied by "the need to discover the background-body . . . that by its own causality confirms and explains the appearance of an individual who is the victim, subject, and bearer of this dysfunctional state."[62] According to Foucault, the "body behind the abnormal body" was traced to "the parents' body, the ancestors' body, the body of the family, the body of heredity."[63] Contemporary gang membership, however, has been inextricably linked not only to the body of the family and its ancestors but also to the segregated spaces where impoverished people of color live. In this logic, those who may or may not choose gang membership live in spaces that render them *already disposed to crime* "less capable" of resisting their latent but easily activated "sociopathic tendencies" and make them more susceptible to gang recruitment—a perspective behavioral geneticist David Lykken refers to as "nature *via* nurture."[64]

make them th insane but also possible

Because media representations of gang violence deny reason but not agency, it makes sense that eliciting sympathy for Ma and the criminalized, racialized poor often rationalizes "irrational" crimes (and victims' responses) as understandable and perhaps necessary reactions to difficult, dangerous environments. Race underlies the "condition" as a "permanent causal background." "Irrationality" and "senselessness" are not only "symptoms" that suggest "sociopathic tendencies" but also signifiers for racial difference and spatial disablement, such as the inner-city cultures of segregation and the war-torn cultures of Southeast Asia and Southeast Asian refugees. Ma's supporters portrayed him as a victim of violent places and violent people to depict him as sympathetic. Ma himself narrated his behavior to Judge Ho as an effect of witnessing extreme violence under the Pol Pot regime, which Ho read and trivialized as just another excuse for his unwillingness to reform: "According to this report, respondent blames his problems on his witnessing of other violence and persecution in his home, Cambodia."[65] Ma's lawyer, Jay Stansell, wrote an article on Ma's case for a collection about race, law, and psychology with the Seattle activist and educator Dori Cahn. In their essay, they also attributed Cambodian-American gang violence to Cambodia:

Children growing up in an environment where guns are the currency of dialogue, such as Cambodian children under the Khmer Rouge and in Thai refugee camps, absorbed the lessons of how to use violence. For these youth, the violence often associated with gang life may have made total sense as a response to the hostile environment in which they found themselves.[66]

To counter the accusations of irrationality and senselessness, which are simultaneously associated with gang violence and unreformability, Stansell and Cahn rationalize gang violence and mitigate youths' culpability by representing them as victims of space or as vulnerable to irreversible spatial disablement. Believed to be subjected to their natural and man-made environments, people of color are represented as products of environments that are identified as the cause, rationale, and evidence not only for a population's inability to access political and economic equality but also for its vulnerability to state-sanctioned violence.

look at systemic factors

This invented "condition" of susceptibility to spatial violence naturalized colonialism, enslavement, and genocide because it explained why in some global regions people were masters of their own (and others') environments while in other parts of the world people were subjugated by other human beings. Social theorist Denise Ferreira da Silva has named this condition "affectability." As she defines it, affectability is "the condition of being subjected to both natural (in the scientific and lay sense) conditions and to others' power."[67] People of color were not imagined as being able to actualize the principles of self-determination as if they were not guided by an interior consciousness able to analyze and rationalize; instead, they were seen as governed by instinct (outer-determined or easily affected by others) rather than guided by reason (self-determined).

justify subjugation

Space does not only explain and naturalize human beings' subordination; it was and continues to be central to engineering some of the most violent forms of exploitation. The violences of sovereignty were executed by manipulating and reinscribing space. Postcolonial theorist Achille Mbembe argues that space and race were essential to colonization.

Colonial occupation itself was a matter of seizing, delimiting, and asserting control over a physical geographical area—of writing on the ground a new set of social and spatial relations. The writing of new spatial relations (territorialization) was, ultimately, tantamount to the production of boundaries and hierarchies, zones and enclaves; the subversion of existing property arrangements; the classification of people according to different categories; resource extraction; and finally, the manufacturing of a large reservoir of cultural imaginaries. These imaginaries gave meaning to the enactment of differential rights to differing categories of people for different purposes within the same space; in brief, the exercise of sovereignty. Space was therefore the raw material of sovereignty and the violence it carried with it.[68]

Violent spatial practices were not attributed to colonial oppression but to a population's supposed inferiority.

In the contemporary era, such spatial practices enable exploitation not only in U.S. neighborhoods targeted for surveillance but also in those places that so many immigrants and refugees called home before their resettlement in the West. During the 1970s and 1980s, leading into and following the world recession, many economically vulnerable nations had to undergo structural adjustment. The World Bank and International Monetary Fund (IMF) required desperate nations to "structurally adjust" their laws, economies, and state services to make themselves more globally competitive. Structural adjustment loans required borrowing countries to agree to certain terms, such as privatizing public services, removing import restrictions, or devaluing the local currency.[69] These programs contributed to making living and working conditions both unlivable and unworkable by requiring nations to cut workers' wages and reduce government spending on welfare, health care, and social services. When the prices of raw materials dropped in the 1980s to their lowest since 1930 (partly as a result of the global recession and partly as a result of technology that created substitutes for foods such as cocoa), nations found themselves unable to make a dent in the debts they owed to the United States, Europe, and Japan.[70] As a result, already struggling nations found themselves accruing more loans to pay off old debts, and because interest rates increased each year, their debts also continued to appreciate year after year. Rather than subsidizing interest rates, decreasing the amount of money owed, or absolving debts completely, the World Bank and the IMF invested more resources in structural adjustment loans.

While transnational corporations, international investors, and domestic businesses with markets overseas prospered in nations involved in structural adjustment programs, the economies of the global South did not reap the promised benefits.[71] The structural adjustment program proposed that the required restrictions would minimize inflation rates and make local industries more efficient and competitive; proponents' reasoned that opening more sectors to foreign investment, controlling government spending, and allowing the market to dictate local spending would all help the global South

become less dependent on capital from abroad. However, structural adjustment actually made nations more economically dependent and significantly
augmented their already unpayable debts. Between 1980 and 1990, the number of people living in poverty in Latin America rose by 50 million.[72]

Capital actively maintains impoverished spaces because it depends on
the spatialization of persistent poverty for profit. To maintain and naturalize impoverished world regions, space is often read and represented as time,
as a moment along a predetermined timeline along which all nations evolve
toward becoming a "modern" nation equivalent to a European country or to
the United States. Descriptors we often use to refer to nations in the global
South reflect this way of thinking. "Newly industrialized" or "developing,"
for instance, suggest that people who live in certain areas are impoverished
and highly exploitable because their country is "not-yet" like the United
States. Reading space as a moment in time not only disconnects persistent
poverty from global capital, but also conceals that impoverished places are
violently created and maintained within the nations of the global North as
well.[73] This prevailing narrative of capital development, political philosopher
Massimiliano Tomba argues, is highly problematic because it assumes "a predetermined route in the history of all countries."[74] In actuality, when corporations directly compete with each other in the world market, they augment
their profits by "seek[ing] out or creat[ing] geographic areas with different
labour powers," places where people can be paid less and/or products can be
produced for less.[75]

Hence, while structural adjustment programs steadily undermined state-
assisted capital in the global South, technological advances modified how
products were manufactured, not only opening up new markets but also
locating new sources of cheap labor to become the new producers of surplus value. Structural adjustment undermined nations' abilities to regulate
their economies, manage their national resources, and offer public services
because the terms of these loans required borrowing countries to adopt deregulation and anti-labor policies, accurately described by political analyst
Walden Bello as "coerced competition."[76] While state control of resources
need not be romanticized, it is important to keep in mind that the IMF
and the World Bank attacked state property by making loans contingent on
adopting deregulation policies. Attacking state property in poorer nations
meant destroying the basis for communal property—or what we might refer
to as "the commons," the natural and human-made resources that should be
accessible to and free for everyone, such as water, land, and knowledge.[77]
Closing off nationally controlled natural resources and state services was a

means to terminate "communal control of the means of subsistence."[78] Turning collective property over to private ownership and privatizing public services threaten "the right to subsist."[79]

When geographically bound on privately owned land, the commons cease to be communal. Capitalists control labor through manipulating space and its use values—such as restricting indigenous access to ceremonial places, polluting drinking and fishing waters, shutting down factories, or building shopping centers. When capital manipulates space, it also disrupts or changes people's relationships to multiple spaces. As the Marxist scholar-activists known as the Midnight Notes Collective argue:

> When communal land in Nigeria is expropriated or when the policy of free housing for workers is abolished in China, there must be a matching expropriation in the United States, be it the end of a "good-paying" factory job in Youngstown, the destruction of a working class community in Maine, or the imposition of martial law in New York City's parks.[80]

Midnight Notes terms these structurally interconnected and interdependent processes that work to alienate people around the world from natural resources the "new enclosures."[81] Collective members George Caffentzis and Monty Neill explain that "capital is ever watchful to enclose any new commons that might be constituted by workers . . . to eliminate all forms of shared subsistence, from the right to land, to food subsidies, to public schooling and health care."[82] Through private property ownership and privatization policies, capital literally and figuratively "encloses" natural and necessary resources. Sometimes the resource "enclosed" is labor itself, like "export-processing zones" in Cambodia and *maquiladoras* (manufacturing plants) in Mexico. Even people whose unemployment is essential to ensure that corporations profit are subjected to enclosure; their incarceration in prisons and detention centers neutralizes political and social unrest.[83] The spatial reorganization of capital and labor not only dislocates workers from their homes and nations; it also dispossesses them of their own histories and strategies of struggle. Social movements against corporate capital and state violence are always simultaneously struggles over the control of space, over the power to access, own, use, and redefine it.

Securing Civil Rights through Interracial Violence

Attempts to rationalize Southeast Asian criminality and gang membership often attribute criminal activities, violent behaviors, and juvenile delinquency to the spaces within which Southeast Asians live (the inner city) and/or the spaces they left behind (Southeast Asia). Where people live certainly impacts people's lives, but when living in poor, predominately black urban areas becomes a primary explanation for Southeast Asian social deviancy, it naturalizes the inner city as an inherently violent space while representing refugees as out-of-place, hapless victims unfairly deposited in someone else's space. In this narrative, Asian racial difference in black residential space is described as the reason why Southeast Asian youth experience violence and the reason why they become violent themselves. Partly a consequence of simplifying race and processes of racialization to a black/white binary, such research reveals that some policy-makers and analysts cannot envision criminality without referencing black racial difference.

"Experts" on Southeast Asians as well as popular commentators represented Ma as a victim of urban spaces of color. The Associated Press attributed Ma's gang affiliation to his impoverished neighborhood and neighbors of different colors:

> In America, Kim's first home was a housing project in Seattle caught in the middle of a new war—between black and Hispanic gangs. Kim and his Cambodian American friends were different enough to become a tempting diversion in that war, with both sides taunting or beating them for sport. . . . On the streets, they grew tough, determined never to be pushed around again.[84]

Like many others, this author blamed black and Latina/o youth and space for Southeast Asian social deviancy. Unlike studies about delinquent black youth, which often blame their family structures, studies concerning socially deviant Southeast Asian youth do not hold refugee parents fully responsible for their children's wayward ways. Lykken holds black and Latina/o youth just as responsible for Southeast Asian delinquency as the youths' parents: "Not all Southeast Asian families are successful after transplantation to the United States. When the parents themselves are slow to adapt to the new culture, their children may find the lure of the peer culture irresistible."[85] In Lykken's analysis, Southeast Asian youth are already weakened by families unable to assimilate quickly and completely. Upon resettling into poverty-stricken urban areas where gang violence thrives, they fall prey to the inner city and its residents.

Likewise, Donald Kodluboy, a licensed school psychologist, declares that gang formation was geographically incompatible with Southeast Asia. Researching Southeast Asian youth in Minnesota, Kodluboy claims that gang activity was (mis)learned in the United States: "Many Asian gangs originally formed in American cities as protection or fighting gangs. The reasons for their formation in the absence of any historical or cultural basis include racial, geographic, economic and linguistic isolation as well as direct rejection by established community groups where the recent immigrants settled."[86] Lured away from mainstream American culture by the fascinations of urban "cultures of poverty" and overly susceptible to being affected (or infected) by (the "disease" of) gang violence, Southeast Asians form gangs, according to this explanation, as both an affective and instinctual response to being "rejected" and "assaulted" by their black and Latina/o peers. Although Southeast Asian youth are constructed as sympathetic victims, they are not represented as persons who have the ability to change or challenge their situations. Black and Latina/o youth, on the other hand, are imagined as able to influence and manipulate their environments and other youth, but only in irrational and immoral ways. Because they are represented as irrational agents who lack moral agency, they are not represented sympathetically, especially when in relation to Southeast Asian immigrant youth. These representations are reflective of the ways in which the discourse of sympathy has racial limits that make it difficult for people of color to access sympathy without victimhood, especially for those also considered unlawful, illegal, or illicit.[87]

Narratives that render Southeast Asians sympathetic by juxtaposing them against other impoverished groups of color lend themselves to reiterating what Eric Tang terms "refugee exceptionalism." As Tang elaborates, well-intentioned research seeking to explain Southeast Asian poverty and social deviance is sometimes invested in "rescuing" Southeast Asians from being associated with welfare or with the underclass. This type of argument, he contends, betrays researchers' investments in keeping the underclass and rhetoric about it always already black.[88] Research that takes refugee exceptionalism as its premise not only reproduces the model minority myth but also reinforces neoliberal logic that posits that poor people are poor because they don't take "personal responsibility" for not working hard enough to become socioeconomically mobile. Refugee exceptionalism rationalizes why Southeast Asians seem able to move out of the inner city and why so many African Americans and Latinas/os in the same residential spaces cannot.

For example, the following study exonerates public education in the United States from failing students of color by exalting Southeast Asian refugee children's educational achievements.

The schools across the country, even in low-resource urban areas such as those attended by the refugee children, respond remarkably well to children who come prepared and willing to learn. . . . If measured by performance on nationally standardized achievement tests, used by many education officials as the major criterion for evaluating school systems across the country, these refugee students achieved levels of learning equal to the national norms or better, particularly with regard to math and spelling. These successes indicate that their schools are succeeding in educating this group of children from diverse and disadvantaged backgrounds.[89]

For this narrative of refugee exceptionalism to absolve public school systems of their role in reproducing racial inequality, it must work through comparison. In terms of housing, job opportunities, income level, and educational access, Southeast Asians are "just like" black, Latina/o, and Indigenous Americans. When values or work ethics are named as the distinguishing characteristics that set Southeast Asians apart from other non-white groups, the comparison has the effect of saying that Southeast Asians' willingness to learn leads to educational success, while implying that other non-white groups in impoverished urban areas are less successful because they simply don't want to learn.

Along these lines, anthropologist Aihwa Ong argues that refugees from Cambodia and Laos were "subjected to a kind of ideological blackening" because they were "welfare dependent," had "high rates of teenage pregnancy," and lived in "isolation in inner-city neighborhoods."[90] However, representing nonblack racial minorities, such as Southeast Asian refugees, as imagined and managed "like" African Americans makes it seem as if nonblack racial minorities are able to overcome race in ways that African Americans cannot. Cultural studies scholar Miranda Joseph attributes this predicament to the use of analogy. As she argues, an analogy assumes there is no relationship between the terms being compared—in this case Southeast Asian refugees and inner-city African Americans.[91] Because racial identities are commonsensically conceived of as discrete, the production of racial difference and corresponding processes of racialization are also assumed to be separate and parallel, rather than relational, intersecting, and interdependent. When seen as discrete and distinct, racial/ethnic groups can appear to have "common" or "shared" struggles, which not only suggests that a cross-racial coalition would be both natural and necessary but also that the persistence of racial poverty can be partly attributed to interracial conflict.

Accordingly, when African American residents of the inner cities and their advocates rearticulate civil rights as citizenship rights, they mean to emphasize the ways in which African Americans are entitled to—and yet have been denied—the rights, recognitions, and resources given to refugees.

This tactic also represents racial categories as discrete, as if Southeast Asians and African Americans have parallel trajectories progressing unevenly due to racially allocated state aid and abandonment. For example, sociologist Letha See writes, "Blacks also see refugees as threatening decades of civil rights gains that they worked so hard to acquire. They believe that the concern for refugee families should not outweigh concern for the disadvantaged U.S. citizens who must now share housing, health care, and other benefits with foreign intruders who did not assist in building this nation."[92] Although See's informants highlight that both groups' realities are connected, they describe themselves as playing a zero sum game—that what's given to refugees is what's taken away from citizens. The zero sum game analysis, however, suggests that impoverished African Americans were supplied with rights and resources before refugee settlement and would be resupplied if refugees were relocated, even though neither has been the case.

Hence, comparisons that liken Southeast Asians to African Americans conceal the fact that remedies for Southeast Asian poverty normalize the racialized violences of segregation that keep poor African Americans economically destitute and politically disenfranchised. In other words, even when African American citizens and Southeast Asian refugees share the same spaces, their relationships to space are structured and defined much differently. In the 1990s, the Asian Law Caucus (ALC) filed lawsuits against the San Francisco Housing Authority on behalf of Vietnamese and Cambodian residents. In her analysis of the cases, comparative race theorist Helen Heran Jun argues that because there is no legal avenue to challenge the violences of racialized poverty and segregation, better housing rights for refugees could be legally secured only by demanding the right to protection from interracial (not spatial or economic) violence.[93]

> [In a press statement, the lead attorney for the ALC, Gen] Fujioka observes that all residents are entitled to safe and crime-free housing, stressing that the violence endured by Asian immigrant residents would be best eliminated by improving the overall conditions of public housing. Given that there is no legal provision to challenge racialized poverty in that manner, the only strategy available to the ALC is to demonstrate that the racial difference of Asian immigrant residents makes them specifically vulnerable to the crime and violence in the city's worst projects. The racialized warehousing of the black urban poor that produces the conditions of possibility for such violently concentrated spaces of poverty cannot be addressed by the state except through the repressive arm of incarceration. The scope of civil rights as a form of racial protection for impoverished Asian

Americans in these instances, can address the violence of black criminality but not the larger geopolitical violences of imperialist war, refugee displacement, racialized urban poverty, and racial segregation.[94]

Thus, Southeast Asians' access to better living conditions could not be argued through the right to decent housing; it could only be argued through the right to be protected from black criminality. Although racial tensions were often generated and exacerbated when refugees were resettled in poor, predominately black neighborhoods, the problem with representing Southeast Asians as having the right to be protected from racial violence is that there is no parallel narrative that assumes African Americans have the same right to be protected from violences in urban areas. Although civil rights law can address Asian immigrants' rights to protection from urban violence, it cannot address impoverished African Americans' rights to these same protections. As Jun writes,

> We can see that the Fair Housing Act mobilized by the Civil Rights movement, in this instance, operates as a legal mechanism by which Asian immigrant access to safe housing effectively means moving away from poor black residents. This equation of better housing conditions with spatial distance from black poverty is not a superficial anti-black attitude, nor a product of racial prejudice on the part of the ALC or Asian immigrants, but a systemic effect of racial segregation.[95]

Explaining further, Jun notes that the forms of spatial mobility and legal recourse available to Asians in San Francisco were not just not available to African Americans in the same neighborhoods; they were available to Southeast Asians *because* refugee neighborhoods were poor and black: "In the absence of racial epithets, black residents cannot challenge their subjection to the violence of public housing as a violation of their civil rights" whereas "[n]onblack residents in the worst public housing can make such an appeal insofar as the violent crimes they endure are likely to be accompanied by racial epithets."[96]

Civil rights law can recognize racialized spatial and economic violence as racial discrimination only if one of the consequences of that violence takes the form of interracial conflict. When racial segregation leads to within-group violence, urban violence is reduced to "black-on-black" or "Asian-on-Asian" crime, cultural pathology, or internalized racism—none of which register as "racial discrimination" in civil rights law. Hence, the need to remedy Southeast Asian poverty can only be recognizable if the state-sanctioned violences of racial segregation are not just ignored but displaced onto African Americans as well as rescripted and individualized. This not only normalizes violence against African American residents of inner cities but also holds them responsible for it, rendering law enforcement (increased state-sanctioned violence) the only solution to the everyday violences of racial segregation directed against African Americans.

It's vital that we don't misunderstand the critical task, which, as Jun reminds us, is *not* to criticize the Asian Law Caucus, other advocates for marginalized groups, or the Asian and black residents of inner cities. Assigning and allocating culpability are not what's at stake. What's at stake is figuring out the criminalized and racialized parameters of rights discourses by realizing that the ways in which a group's demands for rights and recognition can highlight an/other racialized group's ineligibility for those same rights. This is not just exclusion from rights. Rather, as Hannah Arendt articulates, "Their plight is not that they are not equal before the law, but that no law exists for them."[97] African Americans in the inner city are not eligible for civil rights not only because racism is defined in law as personal prejudice but also because inner-city spaces are criminalized. Criminalization, as I have been arguing, not only forecloses empathy but does so through producing people and places always already subject to a form of discrimination believed to be both legitimate and deserved.

Research that pathologizes *or* rationalizes inner-city violence attributes its emergence to inner-city space. On the one hand, reading "socially deviant" behavior as a "logical reaction" to dangerous environments potentially condemns impoverished communities of color to lifelong surveillance and containment. Such diagnoses imply that the spaces where gang members live need to be better controlled and better regulated because they have too much potential to produce dangerous people. On the other hand, the "irrationality" of "senseless" crimes identifies certain unlawful acts as "immoral" and "abnormal," which situates the people who commit them and the places where they take place outside the rational "rule of law," outside political and legal systems. When rendered intrinsically "affectable" or subjected to the disciplinary power-knowledge of the "condition," people of color are imagined as able only to react to (not analyze nor purposely influence) outside forces in ways that deny them reason, rationality, and ethicality—those attributes defined as "universal" and self-determining. In the United States, the way of knowing naturalized as "rationality" presumes that deliberate adherence to social norms and normative values is universal. When people's behaviors do not conform to "universal" norms and values, their conduct is rendered either irrational (as utterly unintelligible) or inescapable (due to the absence of rational options). Establishing rationality requires demonstrating that for people in certain places, abiding by social norms, heteronormative values, and/or neoliberal ethics is a luxury. Hence, representing nonnormative conduct as rational is incompatible with challenging normative thought, action, values, and ethics.

Rationality is socially, culturally, and politically constructed, and it is constructed in ways that make it all but impossible to evoke sympathy for criminalized people of color and simultaneously represent them as rational agents. As such, it is the presumption that rational thought is both universal and transparent that positions poor, criminalized persons of color absolutely outside law and justice. According to rational logic, the spaces where poor criminalized people of color live are violent for one of two reasons: because those who live there engage in irrational acts of senseless violence or because the inner city does not offer rational choices due to persistent poverty, political disenfranchisement, and chronic unemployment. In other words, the criminalized poor of color are characterized as either products of violent environments that should be heavily policed or as irrational people incapable of moral agency who need to be under police surveillance. In effect, arguments that pathologize or humanize gang members lead us to the same solutions for urban violence if "rationality" is taken for granted —more law enforcement and stricter surveillance. Either way, residents of the inner city are held responsible today for crimes they might never commit in the future.

Victims of Cultural Difference

The purported inability to act "within reason" is manifested not only by perpetrators who cannot conduct themselves in a nonviolent manner but also by victims who are supposedly complicit in these acts of violence. Such "passivity" is commonly read as an attribute of Southeast Asian or Asian cultural difference, but this assumption obfuscates the ways in which the violent reorganization of capital and labor disempowers impoverished populations. Passivity (or what looks like it according to "rational" forms of action) may be a strategy of survival or resistance for various immigrant and diasporic communities and for people who cannot or choose not to leave their homelands. These spatially disoriented and politically disempowered communities are exposed to circumstances that engender new economic and political vulnerabilities as well as exacerbate preexisting ones. Yet the language of "the condition" ostensibly describes why Southeast Asian gangs targeted · "their own," and in so doing, misreads this situation as a product of "cultural difference" rather than seeing this "difference" as produced in part by the "new enclosures" of spatial containment.

Whether attributed to traditional habits or to dangerous environments, "cultural difference" both normalizes and abnormalizes the violent acts committed by Southeast Asian gang members. Cultural difference was deployed to construct the violences committed by Southeast Asians as normative within their respective cultures but deviant and foreign to American liberal culture. In a typical example, New York City police detective William Oldham likened Vietnamese gang members to "vicious predators" who "preyed on their fellow Vietnamese immigrants in unparalleled rates."[98] Regarding them neither as "fellow" Americans nor as human beings, Oldham pitied (but did not identify or feel empathy with) "the Vietnamese [as] probably one of the most victimized immigrant populations in the City of New York."[99] Along these lines, in A Law Enforcement Source Book of Asian Crime and Cultures, Douglas Daye considers how and why the Vietnamese could target "their own":

> Law enforcement personnel often wonder at the brutal way some Vietnamese home burglars abuse and torture other Vietnamese. Quite simply, because we don't understand the Vietnamese mindset, many ask what kind of an idea of humanity and of human compassion—or the lack of it—can they have? How can they be so brutal to countrymen who have shared many of the same hardships of their parents or themselves?[100]

His answer is the "Vietnamese village mentality," which he literally locates and contains in the cultures of rural Viet Nam.[101] He explains that in rural Viet Nam,

> One is not just a "Vietnamese." Rather, one belongs to a particular extended family lineage in a specific village, in a specific delta or highland, near specific mountains or a river, in the north or south. It is of that specific place and of that specific group that one is a member. And it is from that family and that village that one gets one's identity, one's sense of self.[102]

Characterized as parochial and provincial, gang members have no empathy for their victims because they would not identify with them, feeling neither loyalty nor connection. According to Daye, the "village mentality" explains Vietnamese violence against other Vietnamese because one's identity and sense of community are not tied to being Vietnamese but rather grounded in belonging to a place.

Elaborating on what he sees as Vietnamese gang members' "village mentality," Daye reasons that Vietnamese morals are the inverse of American values:

> One need not worry about the degree of pain, violence, or pleading of one's victims if they are immorally selfish, for such wealthy (and thus immoral) people do not deserve the compassion that one extends to one's fellow villagers. Therefore, one ought to and can be as vicious as one needs to be to get (and redistribute) wealth as quickly and easily as possible.[103]

By rationalizing violence as logical and normative for Vietnamese culture, Daye identifies culture as a disabling "condition," as the abnormality that threatens to become sociopathology in the United States.

We can say much about the ways in which Daye comes to this conclusion by fixing culture (literally to a "specific" place) as stable and unchanging, and we might comment on how his account has no place for Vietnamese who might have been raised in urban areas in Viet Nam or for Vietnamese Americans raised in the United States. Indeed, he uses an array of problematic assumptions about Viet Nam and Vietnamese refugees to demonize the "Vietnamese mindset." Furthermore, Daye is not just demonizing Vietnamese culture and implying that in the United States there is no parallel —that violence directed against one's own culture, race, religion, or ethnicity does not happen here. He is also using cultural difference as a signifier for a "mindset" he characterizes as an irrational worldview that privileges the downward redistribution of wealth, condemns the unnecessarily wealthy, repudiates greed as immoral, and encourages community accountability and policing. By using these values to make gang violence intelligible, he encourages not only the repudiation of gang members but also the rejection of any values that pose a threat to global capitalism and the American empire that protects and extends it.

Various institutions reproduced the notion that violence within Southeast Asian communities must have been imported because it was so unimaginable and so foreign that nothing like it could exist in the United States. Home invasions in particular illustrate discourses of racial, ethnic, and cultural profiling that target both criminals and victims as irrational actors, as democratically disabled. The employment of the "village mentality" trope constructs cultural difference as a foundational condition of abnormality to explain the sociopathic behavior of Vietnamese gangs. This condition has also been extended to Southeast Asian victims of gang crime, manifesting as a different "social disability" seen to affect their commitment to the American "rule of law" and the state agents who enforce it. San Jose police Sergeant Douglas Zwemke testified that Vietnamese culture predisposed refugees to be victims of gang violence:

> The victims of the robberies are often their own worst enemies. The cultural habit of hoarding gold and money at home is common, and Vietnamese gangsters prey on these habits. Home invasions often go unreported or under-reported and are difficult to investigate and prosecute. Distrust of police and victim/witness intimidation frustrate these investigations.[104]

Although victims acted lawfully, because their alternate forms of wealth accumulation are not technically "illegal," they were also portrayed as insufficiently law-abiding because "cultural difference" prevents Southeast Asians from recognizing the virtue of liberalism's rational institutions.

Home invasions were among the more prevalent and remarked-upon crimes committed by Southeast Asian gangs. Contrary to its common usage, the term "home invasion" does not refer to a specific crime. If caught, perpetrators would be charged with burglary, robbery, assault, and/or kidnapping. The use of "home invasion" became much more common when it began to be used to evoke and refer to violent robberies committed by Southeast Asian gangs. "Invasions" worked metonymically and metaphorically across both spatial scales and sign systems, drawing upon and foreshadowing other kinds of "invasions" that had also been or would later be associated with Asia or Asians, such as unwanted immigration "invading" the financial health and cultural stability of America ("yellow peril"), or non-native species "invading" and endangering local ecologies (Asian carp),[105] or deadly parasitic and viral diseases that "invade" the body (malaria, SARS).

Rhetoric about home invasions also drew upon and preceded the anxious discourses that figured the movement of Asian labor and Asian capital as encroaching, ever-present threats to the economic stability of the nation —threats from outside and within, from below and above. Asian organized crime and Southeast Asian home invasions embodied the anxieties of globalization, casting Southeast Asians in the United States in the role of the minions (who defeated the United States) for organized crime in (communist) China and (collective capitalist) Japan. During a 1992 U.S. Senate hearing on Asian organized crime, Delaware Senator William V. Roth Jr. declared that emerging Asian organized crime groups "cannot be viewed simply as a domestic problem, but rather must be recognized and confronted as an international problem. Asian criminal groups personify a major new threat confronting law enforcement around the globe."[106]

"They Feared Their Own Families More than the Gang Members"

U.S. refugee policy with Southeast Asia, as with Cuba, has long invested in disrupting familial ties. Both the 1980 Refugee Act and the 1987 Amerasian Homecoming Act enabled and facilitated the immigration of unaccompanied minors and families with absent fathers; these unaccompanied children were the ones imagined to be responsible for gang violence. As Oldham testified,

> [I]n regard to the Vietnamese gangs, these people came here—they have no family. . . . They spent 2 or 3 years being institutionalized in relocation camps overseas, and they come here and they end up in foster homes, some of which aren't quite up to standards. They end up waifs, and they are recruited by the street gangs. They really have nowhere else to go sometimes.[107]

The legislation that enabled unaccompanied minors to immigrate to the United States was part of the state's attempt at altruism in response to pressures by the American public to "rescue" the American children born to Southeast Asian mothers during the Viet Nam War.[108] The need to rescue American children from Southeast Asia emerged in part because of rumors that the Vietnamese had abandoned mixed-race children,[109] rumors that made it seem as though children's abandonment was due to Southeast Asians' cultural predisposition toward racial prejudice rather than to the sexual irresponsibility of American military men.

As victims of gang violence, Southeast Asian parents often shoulder the blame for the "epidemic" of gang violence because they are not the solution to it. Represented as passive victims "paralyzed" by cultural differences, Southeast Asian parents are conceived of as easy targets for the victimizers they had raised or abandoned. Inasmuch as struggles over parental authority and adolescent autonomy within refugee families are exacerbated and complicated by social and class differences, they are often oversimplified as inevitable consequences of "cultural conflict." Figured as the battle between the new world and the old, American versus Asian, modernity against tradition, and West over East, generational conflict has been imagined as solely responsible for distorting gendered roles and undermining patriarchal authority within refugee households, functioning as the "symbolic conflict between nativism and assimilation."[110] As Lisa Lowe argues, "The reduction of the cultural politics of racialized ethnic groups, like Asian Americans, to first-generation/second-generation struggles displaces social differences into a privatized familial opposition."[111] Accordingly, the National Crime

Prevention Council takes the position that both gang crime and police mistrust can be traced to the power imbalances within refugee families: "Often refugee children learn English more quickly than adults and therefore control the communication with the rest of the world. Many adults feel they have lost control of everything in their lives."[112] In this way, Southeast Asian refugee parents are portrayed as "impotent," as already left behind by their assimilated, Americanized, self-sufficient children. Pastor Sadudee Harichaikul of the Visalia Lahu Baptist Church told the Fresno (CA) Bee, "Parents don't know what or how to do [discipline]. . . . In our culture, sometimes we hit the children with sticks, but in America, we cannot do that. Children threaten to call the police."[113] According to the pastor, children's empowerment is facilitated through choosing subjection (to the state) over imposed obedience (to and by the family or tradition), which ironically then creates the conditions for juvenile delinquency and state surveillance.

With their cultural difference being represented as an obstacle to rational action, Southeast Asians gain agency only through assimilation, Americanization, and the unconditional acceptance of the U.S. "rule of law." For poor people of color, following the "rule of law" includes unqualified compliance with law enforcement. Testifying for the President's Commission on Asian Organized Crime in 1984, Lieutenant Kenneth Adair of Garden Grove, California, held refugees' prior experiences as solely responsible for their current (irrational and traumatized) state of mind, saying "these people have lived in an atmosphere of fear and intimidation and corruption for such a period of time [in Southeast Asia] that they are unwilling to take the chance on law enforcement to provide those things necessary to keep them safe."[114] In a teaching manual for law enforcement to learn how to earn refugees' trust, the National Crime Prevention Council offers instructions to Southeast Asian refugees, including encouraging them to integrate police surveillance into their community events and daily lives: "When you hold cultural activities, invite law enforcement. Send a letter and follow up in person. Consider giving law enforcement a few minutes to speak at your event."[115] Distrust of U.S. state officials is assumed to be part of the Southeast Asian's cultural baggage, a survival mechanism left over from government-sanctioned abuse in their respective countries of origin.

Being wary of law enforcement is never considered to be a distrust that might emerge, wholly or partially, from the corruption or brutality of law enforcement. In the 2007 report prepared for the United Nations Committee on the Elimination of Racial Discrimination, researchers found more than enough evidence to conclude that the U.S. Department of Justice is incapable of systematically prosecuting "race-based policing and abuse" because of the "high standard of intent imposed by legislation" and the "limited resources devoted to investigation and prosecution of law enforcement misconduct."[116] Already difficult to prove and prosecute, investigations "are often conducted by the very same law enforcement agencies which employ the offending officers, or by civilian review agencies with little or no authority to discipline officers."[117]

The diagnosis of cultural difference as a disabling condition is repeatedly used against refugees by the state to perpetuate a range of violences. In a 2003 issue of the FBI Law Enforcement Bulletin, Sergeant Richard Straka of the Saint Paul, Minnesota, police department provided a law enforcement perspective on issues of refugee-civilian trust in regards to rape, kidnapping, and forced prostitution by Hmong gangs. Unsurprisingly, the cultural, communal, and familial retributions for a woman who is raped are represented as more violent and more emotionally injurious than the gang rape itself. As "damaged" persons, Straka writes, "they [Hmong rape victims of Hmong gangs] feared their own families more than the gang members."[118] Locating and situating sexual violence in Laos and Thailand refugee camps, Straka reads these sites as harboring a "condition" from which rape as a culturally and spatially specific pathology arises. In doing so, he characterizes the United States as a place of (sexual) freedom and implies that proper assimilation (and proper regulation) would preclude rape. In this manner, Hmong culture is imagined as culturally unable ("disabled") and socially unwilling ("sociopathic") to protect its young women from its men of all ages. Hmong culture is represented as lacking moral agency: "The Hmong community is not seeing this, they are not acknowledging it."[119] Hmong culture is also represented as complicit and predisposed to sexual violence in general: "The pimps are Hmong who usually only offer the girls to other Hmong, often older members of the community."[120] Young Hmong men who form gangs are represented as perversely unassimilated. Neither "traditionally" Hmong nor "properly" American, they are characterized as using their displacement and subsequent immigration as an opportunity to distort Hmong cultural beliefs in presumably un-American ways: "The gang members also used this belief [that sex before marriage is shameful] to their advantage. They told the victims that they were no good to their families and that the gang was now their family."[121]

Furthermore, victims are once again understood as both passive and complicit in their victimization. In this case, Hmong rape victims are portrayed as lacking rational, sexual, and moral agency: "Some of the victims stayed with the gang members even after being raped."[122] This is why Straka urges other police officers to "not question [the victim's] judgment in allowing herself to become a victim or not reporting the incident in a timely manner."[123] Straka avoids "blaming the victim" narratives only by "blaming" Hmong cultural difference for rape victims' forced prostitution, which he also interprets as victims' passivity toward their sexual violation.[124] In contrast, Straka quotes a local journalist, whose attempts to depathologize Hmong culture include this disturbing suggestion: "I'm not saying these guys are all innocent angels. They're not. They're gang members, but forcible rape, to me, is out of the question. The girls themselves were gang members too."[125] Refusing to repudiate or reject gang members as "inhuman" in defense of Hmong culture, the unnamed journalist relies on problematic assumptions regarding female gang members' presumably deviant sexuality and social devaluation.

In effect, sexual violence against female gang members cannot be recognized as rape. In other words, rape against some women is rendered illegible. A young woman's membership in a gang is read as her consent; her body cannot be violated because as a gang member she has entered a "sexual contract" with the gang that makes her body communal property.[126] Without victims, there is no crime—and the serious accusations against Hmong culture become groundless. This journalist does not challenge the premise that some women cannot be raped but instead revises the criteria for determining which bodies are "rape-able," offering criminal status and social devaluation as more suitable indicators than Hmong cultural difference of sexual violability. Whether or not Hmong women are understood as "rape-able" because of cultural difference or social deviancy, they are rendered passive (and thus irrational) and devalued (as less than human, they cannot be violated). As such, while refugees are urged to call the police, it is not clear that a victim's report would be considered to be or prosecuted as a crime.

Always Already Unsympathetic

On October 25, 1999, before he won his case against indefinite detention, Ma was released under INS supervision. Fourteen months later he fought with a "female companion" and was arrested for assault and domestic violence. The charges were soon dismissed, but the INS reincarcerated him anyway. In the letter ordering Ma to return to INS custody, George L. Morones, the assistant district director in charge of detention and removal, wrote:

> You have not been convicted of the crime, however no conviction is required. . . . It is clear however, that the manifestation of temper was the pure product of self-indulgence. It can neither be explained nor excused . . .

your uncontrolled rage imperiled others beyond your immediate companion. . . . The most charitable interpretation of the event is that your violent
temper impaired your ability to foresee that consequence. I believe it more
likely though that you simply have no regard for public safety, or the well-
being of others. Your actions make it clear that you are either unwilling
or unable to subordinate your own desires and impulses to the peace and
good order of society.[127]

Ma's parole was revoked as "a matter of discretion."[128] No conviction was
required because Ma was an object of, not merely subject to, law or justice.
Morones acted as Ma's arresting officer, judge, and jury; his decision was
founded only on his evaluation of Ma's moral character. This detention was
lawful, despite the lack of a trial, because Morones had decided that Ma's actions resembled a crime without his ever committing one. Because of his status—as ex-gang member, as criminal alien—Ma was subject to punishment
for the potential (if not actualized) consequences that his actions could have,
but did not lead to. Ineligible for legal prosecution or protection, he does not
escape moral judgment, social banishment, or lawful isolation.

In order for sympathy to be evoked for Ma, he would need to be represented as "undeserving" of his punishment and "unfairly" locked up; his "innocence" would need to be emphasized to highlight Morones' unjust decision. But Ma's unnamed female companion was cited as the only evidence
for Morones' decision to reincarcerate Ma. To represent Ma as innocent dictates calling her accusations into question. The charges were dropped, but
her allegations nevertheless led to the revocation of Ma's conditional and
contingent "freedom." Ma is most sympathetic if we can displace what Morones interprets as irrational agency onto Ma's unnamed companion, if she
can be scripted as someone who overreacted and over-exaggerated, who be-
haved vengefully before thinking rationally. However, when reported crimes
are not prosecuted, we should not automatically assume that the charges
are false or groundless. In this case, not pursuing prosecutions may also be
indicative of the devaluation of Ma's unnamed female companion because
crimes against bodies already devalued are often illegible. If we see her as
more than evidence for Ma's false or future crimes, dropped charges may tell
us something about her as well as Ma. Perhaps her body, too, is unprotected
by law; perhaps she, too, was an unsympathetic victim of an unrecognizable
—and so an unprosecutable—crime.

As both the perpetrators and victims of home invasions, sexual assaults,
and other gang-related violence, Southeast Asians are rendered "disabled"
and their culture is rendered "disabling," incapable of fostering liberal

agency. In this logic, passivity is not intelligible or recognized as an expression of agency because law enforcement and other state agents assume that a self-possessed subject would always desire the rational, active choice: to call the police, to appeal to the state for protection. Rational agency is figured as ("freely") choosing state regulation, as acting in accordance with state dictates of moral and legal being. Hence, Southeast Asians are portrayed as either irrational perpetrators or passive victims. The state is portrayed as the only solution to cultural and community violence, and state violence is not portrayed at all.

Indefinite House Arrest

Southeast Asian-on-Southeast Asian crime is represented in ways that pathologize culture and communities while also presenting Americanization and assimilation as the "cure," as the sign that the disability of culture has been "overcome." Turning "the refugee" into an "American" is one of the important preemptive strategies for "defense" and "security." As New Hampshire Senator Warren B. Rudman emphasized in a 1991 Senate hearing on Asian organized crime, the problem was specifically "Asian" not "Asian-American" behavior: "It should be stressed that the prevalence of Asian organized criminal activity is no reflection on the U.S. Asian community itself: on the contrary, the members of this hardworking and upstanding Asian citizenry are more often than not likely to be the prey of this violent behavior."[129] As Rudman's comments illustrate, being "properly" law-abiding is the precondition for becoming American, and Americanization is the prerequisite for legal recognition.

Not-yet-American refugees of the Viet Nam War are conscripted subjects of "freedom" who attest to the rightness and righteousness of the United States and its "rule of law." For refugees, freedom is not an entitlement but a "gift." As transnational feminist Mimi Nguyen theorizes, "the gift of freedom" is constitutively violent because it binds the refugee in a relation of debt and obligation.[130] When refugees accept the "gift of freedom," they "enter into an economy of indebtedness that is the concession or negation of one's desires or directions. Thus is the gift freighted with asymmetry and non-equivalence, with the dispensation of power *over time*, because the gift cannot be returned straightaway lest its significance be undone."[131] The "gift of freedom" formally resolves (or postpones) "the inalienability problem" for Southeast Asian refugees transformed by neoliberalism and multiculturalism into law-abiding Asian American U.S. citizens. When they are thus drafted into personhood, the conceptual impossibility of (re)conferring personhood to those previously ineligible is resolved by narrating inalienability and its necessary denial as a geographic affliction. This geographic affliction is characterized as originating from and bound to (non-Western) space, so that imperial wars "take place" between places of "freedom" and spaces of "unfreedom." In this way, ineligibility to personhood becomes not a U.S. state-produced category for the living non-being but the way of being in an elsewhere place.

Ma did not see his freedom as a "gift." In the Supreme Court case that determined the indefinite detention of civilian noncitizens unconstitutional, Justice Scalia dissented. Scalia insisted on the constitutionality of using criminal punishments against civilian noncitizens, emphasizing that for noncitizens, freedom was not a protected, inalienable right. Hence, according to Scalia, Ma should be subject to life imprisonment for any violation, regardless of kind or degree. During oral arguments, Scalia asked Ma's lawyer, Jay Stansell, the following questions to illustrate his arguments and reframe indefinite detention.

> QUESTION: "Mr. Stansell, what if— these people are deportable because of committing felonies, right? What if the punishment for the felony were life in prison? That, I assume, would not be unconstitutional?"
>
> MR. STANSELL: "That's correct, Your Honor."
>
> QUESTION: "Then why is it unconstitutional to say to an immigrant, if you commit a felony, we're not going to put you in prison for life, but we are simply not going to let you back into the general populace, and we will deport you if you can find a place to be deported to, but otherwise you will be held under house arrest, not punitive, but you will not be allowed into the general population?
>
> "Why is that lesser punishment [indefinite detention as a lesser punishment than life imprisonment], if you consider it that, although it really isn't punishment, it's—you know, that was a deal. Why is that lesser sanction unconstitutional, whereas sending the felon to jail for life and punitive treatment for life would not be unconstitutional?"[132]

Scalia proposed that indefinite detention could be characterized as U.S. "house arrest," rather than as life imprisonment. In this reframing, indefinite detention "really isn't punishment" for a crime but simply the consequence noncitizens should expect for breaking the "deal." "Released" into INS custody (usually after serving their criminal sentences), no-longer-criminal aliens were sent to live in the spaces of social death, "doing dead time,"[133] which was construed by Scalia as neither indefinite detention nor punishment but simply living in a space of unfreedom, not enslaved nor in-carcerated but indefinitely and deservedly unfree.

Worse Than Criminal Law

Ma's status and identities were much more important to justifying his deten-tion and eventual deportation than the actual crime for which he was con-victed. As a noncitizen, he had already "given up" his right to rights by break-ing the "rule of law," which renders irrelevant the fact that the crime took place in 1995 and was not considered an "aggravated felony" at the time.[134] Ma was convicted in 1996, the year that crimes considered "aggravated felo-nies" were redefined by two new immigration laws, the Antiterrorism and Effective Death Penalty Act (AEDPA) and the Illegal Immigration Reform and Immigrant Responsibility Act (IIRIRA). The IIRIRA was retroactive, targeting thousands such as Ma and thousands unlike him for deportation. Many had immigrated as infants or very young children and had no memo-ries of the nations from which they emigrated. Many had committed gang-associated or ganglike crimes as teenagers and pleaded guilty or no contest because doing so was easier and cheaper than a trial, and, at the time, they had no reason to fear indefinite detention or deportation. They had not imagined that a few years later Congress would redefine a number of crimes as "aggravated" felonies. They did not foresee that the AEDPA would affix seventeen more aggravated felonies to the Immigration and Nationality Act. They could not have anticipated that the IIRIRA would add four more to the list of deportable crimes nor that all these new provisions would be retroac-tive and legally uncontestable.[135] They had not expected to become perma-nently criminal, irredeemably dangerous, and imminently deportable long after they had served their time, long after they had been released into the general populace, as if they were just like everybody else.

But they were not just like everyone else because these new laws con-cocted "criminal aliens" out of people who had at any time committed a crime. Unlike earlier immigration laws, and even unlike most criminal law at the federal and state levels, the IIRIRA did not make an effort to distinguish the dangerous from the desperate or the career criminal from the juvenile delinquent. After 1996, murder and tax evasion, aggravated assault and joy riding, drug-trafficking and petty shoplifting all became deportable crimes that rendered the convicted ineligible for an immigration hearing to argue against his or her mandatory and permanent removal. As in situations in-volving gang membership, the details of the criminal act are less important than the conviction itself. Indeed, the suggestion of guilt can be enough to justify detention or deportation; noncitizens are presumed guilty if they cannot prove they are innocent or if their proven innocence is doubted.[136] Because practically any crime, regardless of type or severity, is ineligible for judicial review, "criminal aliens" are absolutely subjected to "the rule of law" yet completely outside legal recognition. For "criminal aliens," justice is non-applicable in every respect.

As criminal lawyers have noted, the punishments for committing an "aggravated felony" by a noncitizen are almost always far worse than the punishment for the same crime committed by a citizen under criminal law.[137] Because it is people's noncitizenship status, not their crimes, that marks them as undeserving of sympathy and second chances, noncitizens are also defined as being far beyond the presumed ethical obligations of the U.S. government and its citizenry.[138] Because freedom is understood as a "gift," freedom is easily revoked. Any transgression—large or small—is an inexcusable act of ingratitude deserving of detention or deportation. The logic of the 1996 immigration laws presumes that criminality for certain human beings is an interior attribute, inherent or irreversible, and in either case fixed. For noncitizens, it is irrelevant if they are law abiding for the rest of their lives because for people imagined as without the "ability" or "capacity" for reform, rehabilitation can never really be "real."

the act doesn't matter

The IIRIRA and the AEDPA make more sense when we realize that they targeted immigrants of color from cultures and world regions deemed "affectable." As such, neither law needed to differentiate serious felonies from petty misdemeanors because the legislation did not purport to reassign more appropriate punishments to crimes committed and convicted in the past. Like gang enhancement sentencing, these laws intended to punish and prevent the future crimes that immigrants were imagined as likely to commit—crimes premised upon and justified by the attribution of "affectability," as a contagion or condition carried by people who come from places where race, cultural difference, persistent poverty, and criminality cannot be disentangled. The 1996 laws are the legal means for "detecting" the abnormal, the immoral, and the criminal. They target races and world regions, developing nations, and non-Western cultures because "affectability" is assigned to places that have become signifiers for atavistic time, for different moments in human progress, for people and places still "developing."

justification

future crime

Hence, certain geographies are read as "disabling," and certain bodies and certain minds are interpreted as "lacking" the ability or the capacity to "overcome" poverty, racism, and cultural difference, as too easily affected by less-than-fortunate circumstances, as too emotionally and irrationally reactive. When the state marks human beings in this way—as ineligible for

blame their abilities

ɛrsonhood both naturally and necessarily—life incarceration and indefi-
ite deportation are not considered exceptionally severe punishments but
rather preemptive measures and methods of social protection. This is not the
kind of racism that activists and academics are used to fighting because it is
a racism "whose function is not so much the prejudice or the defense of one
group" but a racism whose function is "the detection of all those *within* a
group who may be the carriers of a danger to it," which "permits the screen-
ing of every individual within a given society."[139] Immigration laws such as
the AEDPA and the IIRIRA are methods of early detection and procedures
for prescreening, functioning like many other aggressive treatments that
seek to "eliminate the problem wherever it exists."[140]

3

Grafting Terror onto Illegality

In his September 2001 speech to O'Hare International Airport workers in Chicago, President George W. Bush proclaimed,

> We're a nation based upon fabulous values.
>
> We're also a nation that is adjusting to a new type of war. . . . We face a brand of evil, the likes of which we haven't seen in a long time in the world. These are people who strike and hide, people who know no borders, people who are—people who depend upon others. And make no mistake about it, the new war is not only against the evildoers, themselves; the new war is against those who harbor them and finance them and feed them.[1]

The post-9/11 moment asked Americans to risk their lives as well as others' lives in a "new type of war" waged against the "evildoers" of the world. Although Bush intended for his audience to equate "evildoers" with "terrorists," he did so with descriptors that could easily refer to gang members ("people who strike and hide"), undocumented immigrants ("people who know no borders"), the disabled or mentally ill ("people who depend upon others"), and their allies ("people who harbor them and finance them and feed them"). The "terrorist" was a new kind of composite figure, and like previous menaces, this figure drew upon and "reassembled" the body of existing dangers to bring into being a "new enemy."[2]

This chapter investigates how the "new enemy," imagined to be "people who know no borders," was juridically, discursively, and relationally produced during the war on terror. I examine the way in which races, nations, and religions associated with or suspected to harbor "terrorist" intentions are rendered unlawful in origin and illegal in status. Unlike the racialized threats discussed in the previous chapters, suspected terrorists and any non-Western place where they may reside are rendered not only ineligible for personhood but disentitled to life. In these cases social death becomes much more than a killing abstraction; it becomes the premise and the precondition for actual death.

During the war on terror, "illegality" was a particularly salient incarnation of social death as the basis for literal death because the state depends on the notion of "illegality" to naturalize ineligibility to legal personhood, to justify the status of rightlessness as a biopolitical necessity, and to neutralize popular and potential dissent. Yet because "illegality" in immigration discourses has been racially reified as "Latina/o," the need to incorporate the Arab and Muslim "suspected terrorist" within the racial vocabulary of the national imaginary destabilized and repurposed (abruptly but not absolutely) the gendered racial signifiers for "illegality," noncitizenship, and non-belonging. Discourses of terrorism overlapped, unsettled, and resecured racialized imaginings of undocumented immigration as Latina/o, as well as racist narratives of Latinas/os in general, as economic and cultural threats. These ruptures altered the epistemological frame, or the evaluative structure, that has rendered undeserving the figure of the undocumented immigrant and the real world Latina/o bodies that signify it. Those Latinas/os (legal or not) who were not marked as possessing the "background-body" of "terrorism" within U.S. borders were extended the "opportunity" to earn social value for themselves, their families, and their communities by participating in the war on terror as soldiers and supporters.

This shift offered limited and costly possibilities for "rehabilitation" to a few, on a case-by-case basis, while denying redemption for the rest. In a very literal way, expedited naturalization for those who serve the U.S. military recuperated a select group of Latinas/os. And although still repudiated in reality, undocumented Latinas/os were also symbolically recuperated, positioned as the loyal noncitizen counterpart to the suspected terrorist. In this way, as queer studies scholar Jasbir K. Puar contends, "the terrorist and the person to be domesticated—the patriot—are not distant, oppositional entities, but 'close cousins.'"[3] In this instance, both the undocumented patriot and the illegal terrorist are recruited relationally to conceal the violences that U.S. systems of value direct toward its devalued and disposable others for the purpose of silencing the dead of all nations and nationalities. Because the dead can force us all to reckon with the violences that produced them, the ever-present haunting of these restless ghosts will always be the most salient threat to the United States.

Under Surveillance and Suspicion

Because the national demand for so much death risks citizens' lives when invoking the right to kill others, the demand must be rationalized as more than political, more than economic, and more than social and cultural. Not many will answer a call to likely death unless those othered politics, religions, or economies appear to jeopardize life itself. For states that govern through biopower, that threat to human existence is manufactured to manage and be managed in everyday life. Unlike disciplinary power, Michel Foucault explains, biopower is a "power of regularization," a power that is about "making live and letting die."[4] In these instances, racism is the "basic mechanism," the technology of biopower that justifies and naturalizes why the state makes some live and leaves others to die.[5] Race, region, and religion, in contemporary discourses of terrorism, interchangeably stand in for the "other" that threatens human life itself, functioning as the "more than" subtext that legitimates the call to arms. These othered threats become fundamental, immutable, and biological through appearing to establish, in Moustafa Bayoumi's words, a "blood relationship to Islam."[6] Hypostatizing the threat of another way of life, racism transforms the threatening politics of another worldview into the world's always threatening other.

Violent and unforgiving in its means and intentions, the war on terror far exceeded the biopolitical day-to-day objectives of regulating and regularizing populations in the United States by not only seeking control over life but also demanding domination through death. Beyond letting die and making live, the war on terror insisted that it was the United States' right to determine who may survive and who *must* die, to exert the power to let live and *make* die. For a state that regulates its population through biopower, racism is "the precondition that makes killing acceptable," but when a state secures its sovereignty through necropower, killing does not need to be justified because what a population finds acceptable is irrelevant.[7] "Necropower" and "necropolitics," postcolonial theorist Achille Mbembe explains, "account for the various ways in which, in our contemporary world, weapons are deployed in the interest of maximum destruction of persons and the creation of *death-worlds*, new and unique forms of social existence in which vast populations are subjected to conditions of life conferring upon them the status of *living dead*."[8]

Justifying the creation of death-worlds, the Bush administration constructed the Middle East as an area where "the condition" of "evildoing" was hidden and latent, posing permanent and unpredictable threats to civilization. Afghanistan and Iraq were constructed as terrorist "hideouts" or places with "hidden" weapons of mass destruction, and this presumption of guilt assumed the existence of unseen evidence that may not, in fact, have existed. In other words, Iraq and Afghanistan would be presumed guilty even if proven innocent because the requirements for exoneration were also the terms of indictment: How does one provide tangible proof that terrorists are not hidden? How can one provide concrete evidence of the nonexistence of weapons of mass destruction? If such threats are assumed to be concealed, then the absence of evidence can also be proof of concealment.

Because terrorism was represented as a "condition" (of "evil") that did not just threaten human bodies but threatened human life itself, the environments conceived of as conducive to harboring and propagating terrorism were likened to a disease so dangerous or a species so prolific that not just the bodies but all the surrounding areas needed to be quarantined and burned. Bush constructed terrorism as contractible, as not only affecting but infecting the world: "Its goal is remaking the world—and imposing its radical beliefs on people everywhere."[9] He charged the United States with the responsibility for eradicating terrorism through aggressive, nonselective intervention: "The only way to defeat terrorism as a threat to our way of life is to stop it, eliminate it, and destroy it where it grows."[10] Whether war on terror metaphors drew from epidemiology or ecology, the "solution" always pointed toward obliteration by any means necessary. In this limiting framework, inevitable casualties were not accidental; they were instrumental. To eradicate "terrorism," entire nations and surrounding areas needed to be made into death worlds. The war on terror not only racialized disposability; it also spatialized death. The language of invasion changed the scale of war. U.S. intervention became prevention, obscuring its purposeful invasion of the Middle East. In this context, the Bush administration's ultimatums can appear appropriate: "No free nation can be neutral in the fight between civilization and chaos."[11] Bush demanded that every nation make its "choice," but no nation was given the choice not to choose. By marketing the war on terror as the world's war, any group the United States identifies as "terrorist" is invasive no matter where it resides or where it might materialize.

The language of invasion also invokes discourses of immigration in the United States, particularly discourses of Latina/o undocumented immigration. Media scholar and anthropologist Leo Chavez's analyses of the "Latino Threat Narrative" illustrate that the narrative of invasion has typified the ways in which Mexican immigration have been depicted for more than three decades (since the late 1970s).[12] Along similar lines, media scholar Otto Santa Ana posits that during the Proposition 187 campaign in California, "immigration as invasion was the least obscure anti-immigrant metaphor in general use."[13] As Santa Ana further argues, "the war metaphor used during the Proposition 187 campaign stresses a violent aggression against America. This metaphor patently ignores the nation's entire immigration experience, which always has been the search for employment and freedom by unarmed and peaceful individuals."[14]

Following September 11, undocumented Mexican immigration was not the only imagined threat immigration posed to the nation. Even legal immigration was delinked from deservingness. Legal immigrants faced heightened scrutiny as both legal and illegal immigration were increasingly associated with the "terrorist" that no one had noticed. But the reason no one had noticed was not simply due to the inefficiency of the INS; rather, it was because illegality, like criminality, is also unrecognizable in popular discourse without a body of color. Specific racial and/or ethnic groups are more legible than others as "illegal" according to both region and historical moment, such as the Chinese in the late nineteenth century and more recently, immigrants from Mexico and Central America.

Anxieties over undocumented immigration following September 11 generated a new kind of crisis over "illegal" immigration. Because Latina/o bodies have rendered the status of illegality recognizable, differently racialized unauthorized immigrants unsettled this racial coupling, producing considerable anxiety over not being able to distinguish "illegal" immigrants from "fraudulent" foreigners. These anxieties worked to simultaneously create and legitimate a racially profiled threat to national security. As the *Los Angeles Times* reported,

> Most or all [of the hijackers] appear to have come in legally, on the kinds of temporary visas routinely granted each year to millions of foreign tourists, merchants, students and others.
>
> Nothing in the backgrounds of these middle-class men from Saudi Arabia, Egypt and elsewhere apparently aroused suspicion among State

Department consular officers who review visa applications. And, once here, the 19 hijackers-to-be didn't have to fret much about checkpoints and police stops, even after some of their visas expired and they became illegal immigrants.

The suicide attacks that killed 6,000 or more have brutally exposed shortcomings in airline security and intelligence gathering. But the strikes also highlighted another vulnerability: the nation's visa-granting and immigration regimen.[15]

According to the *Los Angeles Times*, the hijackers were not easy to monitor because they were educated, middle-class persons performing the "model minority": "At least 16 of the 19 suspected hijackers who commandeered American jetliners entered the United States with legal visas. . . . Once in the United States, the men simply blended in, even as some of their visas apparently expired."[16] Slipping from legal to undocumented status drew on already present anxieties because "legal" status could no longer be counted on to confer the moral virtues associated with family reunification, the consumer ethos ascribed to tourism, or the work ethic that students and professionals are presumed to have. As the *Washington Post* reported shortly after the attacks, "Over the past decade, terrorists have posed as students, slipped across the lightly patrolled Canadian border, used false passports and presented themselves as tourists to enter the United States and plot deadly acts."[17] Ethnic studies scholar Junaid Rana contends that post-9/11 constructions of illegality construed undocumented immigrants as "duplicitous." As he writes, "Using fake, stolen, and mistaken identities confounds systems of surveillance that cannot clearly differentiate bodies that might bear a close resemblance."[18] As in references to terrorist "hideouts" in the global South or to "hidden" weapons of "mass destruction," the men "blended in"—and the INS did not know where to look.[19]

Such perceptions of concealment, fraud, and invasion also worked to naturalize enduring and emergent notions of Arab and Muslim noncitizenship and illegality. In a follow-up to the 9/11 Commission's report on "terrorist travel," Janice Kephart, a lawyer for the commission, focused on flaws in U.S. immigration laws.

What requires emphasis is the ease with which terrorists have moved through U.S. border security and obtained significant immigration benefits such as naturalization. . . . Once within U.S. borders, terrorists seek to stay. Doing so with the appearance of legality helps to ensure long-term operational stability. At the 9/11 Commission we called this practice embedding.[20]

Throughout her report, Kephart ascribes illegal status to suspected terrorists even though the report details all the legal means that enable them to reside in the United States. In doing so, she both disregards noncitizens' legal status by insisting that they possess only the "appearance of legality" and symbolically revokes naturalized citizen suspects of their U.S. citizenship. Thus, she also maintains the mutually exclusive binary between "suspected terrorist" and "U.S. citizen" by labeling all suspects, regardless of status, "illegal," or in Puar's words, not legal or illegal but "*un*-legal."[21]

Emphasizing "illegality" worked to deprive Arab and Muslim noncitizens of their rights (rights that undocumented Latina/o immigrants already did not have). Generally, the state does not necessarily have to comply with laws presumably meant to protect people from blatant abuses of state power, especially if such persons are ineligible to personhood. The same laws that render undocumented immigrants ineligible for personhood were used to disenfranchise noncitizens suspected of terrorist activities or sympathies. Almost all detainees have been Arab or Muslim; likewise, half of the "foreign terrorist organizations" identified by the secretary of state in 1999 were either Arab or Muslim.[22] The primary use of the Antiterrorism and Effective Death Penalty Act (AEDPA) of 1996 has been to restrict Arab and Muslim immigration even though the act was passed in response to domestic terrorism —the Oklahoma City bombing in 1995.[23]

Identifying Arabs and Muslims as "illegal" didn't just justify racial profiling; it positioned them in a category that already faced legalized racial profiling. The U.S. Supreme Court does not consider "selective immigration enforcement"—such as racial profiling—unconstitutional on the grounds that "unlawful" or "illegal" immigrants do not have a constitutional right to use "selective enforcement" as defense against deportation.[24] Even before the Patriot Act was passed, the attorney general had absolute authority to enforce immigration laws, and immigration agencies could already prolong detention indefinitely.[25] Already existing immigration law permitted all proceedings and information regarding noncitizen detentions to be kept secret from the U.S. public.[26] Laws directed against the "illegal," "unlawful," and "unlegal" within immigrant groups worked explicitly to deprive noncitizens of legal personhood.

Performing Patriotism

The biological subtext for the war on terror underlay many of President Bush's speeches, which consistently insinuated that racial and religious profiling globally and domestically was regrettably necessary. Although the message was hard to ignore, it was rarely expressed explicitly. Part of the way in which it was concealed was through describing "terrorists" with language that invoked race, national origin, and religion while describing "Americans" in cultural and legal terms through referencing multicultural citizenship. Cultural critic Jodi Melamed's analysis of the Patriot Act reveals how U.S. citizenship recuperates racial, ethnic, and religious groups who have been targeted as "terrorist suspects."[27] Melamed argues that an opening section of the Patriot Act entitled "Sense of Congress Condemning Discrimination against Arab and/or Muslim Americans" functions as a "multiculturalist gesture of protection for patriotic 'Arab Americans,' 'Muslim Americans,' and 'Americans from South Asia' [that] rhetorically excuses the racializing violence that the act enables—namely, the stripping of civil and human rights from nonpatriotic or non-American Arabs, Muslims, and South Asians."[28] The act also enables the recuperation of Muslim Americans and Americans of Arab and South Asian descent. As Mahmood Mamdani puts the matter simply but accurately, such "culture talk" works to differentiate "Good Muslims" from "Bad Muslims."[29] While the Patriot Act discriminates against noncitizens on the basis of race, nationality, and religion, it also explicitly extends symbolic protection to Americans who are simultaneously racially profiled and nontargeted. Thus, in effect, the act reads like a disclaimer of, as well as an apology for, recent and future acts of legal and social misrecognition.

Discourses of multiculturalism not only pressured targeted immigrant groups to demonstrate that they were U.S. patriots but also managed dissent among racially and religiously profiled U.S. citizens and loyal legal residents. In her ethnography of South Asian Muslim youth, Sunaina Maira contends that multiculturalism enables youth to criticize state policies without criticizing the state. Calling this practice "dissenting citizenship," Maira argues that it betrays an investment in the state rather than a radical departure from it: "Dissenting citizenship is harnessed to multicultural citizenship by the state, for multiculturalism was one of the political and rhetorical strategies used after 9/11, as well as before, to absorb Arab, South Asian, and Muslim Americans into a discourse of difference and belonging to the 'pluralistic' and tolerant nation-state."[30] Noncitizen groups racially profiled as "suspected terrorists," on the other hand, are required and thus recruited to represent themselves as "docile patriots." Analyzing Sikh organizing post 9/11, Puar and Amit Rai explain that to construct themselves as misrecognized or falsely profiled, Sikh communities were called upon not only to "educate" Americans about religious and ethnic differences but to perform the "banal pluralism of docile patriotism," emphasizing "Sikh commitments to American life" by validating heteronormativity and middle-class domesticity.[31] Under the guise of multiculturalism, citizenship can manage dissent while docile patriotism works to transform racial profiling into misrecognition, making Arabs, Muslims, and/or South Asians responsible for alleviating the state-sanctioned and vigilante violences of racial profiling.

But U.S. multiculturalism could not incorporate those whose bodies were the real world referents for the ontologized figure of the terrorist.[32] The National Security Entry-Exit Registration System, established in June 2002, specifically targeted men from mostly "friendly" nations in the Middle East for special registration. Unlike "docile patriots," men targeted for "special registration" were not misrecognized by law because special registration targeted them. This gendered racial profiling program claimed to enable the Department of Homeland Security to monitor where foreign nationals lived and what they did; people selected for interviews needed to reregister at least annually and faced the possibility of endless detention.[33] Bayoumi argues that the program is particularly troubling because insofar as special registration is based on geography, "it makes descent or inheritability of Islam (and gender) the defining criterion."[34] The legal production of racialized suspicion, Bayoumi asserts, demands that noncitizens prove their U.S. loyalty by actively disavowing the legally constructed and popularly imagined "Muslim-as-terrorist-figure."[35] As he notes, "special registration" treated people "as if they were guilty of a crime and had to prove their innocence."[36] Because terrorism in the United States was associated with Islam and signified by both Arab/Muslim bodies and nations in the Middle East following as well as predating 9/11, being suspected of terrorism because of one's race, ethnicity, and/or religion became a de facto status crime that could be enforced through immigration law and justified through the ascription of illegality. The passive act of being recognized as a potential terrorist rendered one rightless because it was not only criminal to look suspiciously Arab and/or Muslim; it was also criminal not to actively, emphatically, publicly, repeatedly, and insistently reiterate that one was not a terrorist.

Hidden Victims and Unsung Heroes

Tapping into an already present discourse of multiracial multiculturalism, the administration worked to reassemble an American identity that was multiracial yet basically American, essentialized over and against the bodies that visually signified the "terrorist threat." As Leti Volpp contends,

> Post September 11, a national identity has consolidated that is both strongly patriotic and multiracial. . . . This expansion of who is welcomed

as American has occurred through its opposition to the new construction, the putative terrorist who "looks Middle Eastern." Other people of color have become "American" through the process of endorsing racial profiling.[37]

In this section, I consider the ways in which the repurposing of "illegality" worked to incompletely and insincerely rehabilitate undocumented Latinas/os when juxtaposed against the administration's construction of anti-American terrorism.

As "terrorism" was increasingly fused with "illegality," different narratives and images emerged to symbolically recuperate undocumented Latinas/os. Representations of undocumented Latina/o immigrants reassured the nation that the "American way of life" still circulated as a worldwide symbol of freedom. As people who were willing to live in America and were ineligible for almost all rights and protections, undocumented Latinas/os affirmed that living in the United States even without rights was better than living in other nations "ravaged by poverty or political instability."[38] Undocumented Latina/o settlement did not activate the same anxieties and resentments of the previous decade. In fact, the very activities represented as economically and culturally threatening in the 1990s were largely renarrated during this era as evidence for the "universality" of the "American Dream" when written about in relation to September 11. As the *New York Times* reported just days after September 11, undocumented Latina/o immigrants "came to America to escape poverty, repression and war," and they "made lives in mostly humble jobs."[39] U.S. citizen patriots could read about undocumented immigrants and remind themselves that for most of the world, living in America was worth the sacrifices that others were expected and compelled to make. Recoding undocumented Latina/o immigrants also functioned to critique the INS for focusing on the wrong population. Undocumented Latinas/os were symbolically "rehabilitated" (even if only partially and provisionally) because they had been recognized as the wrong primary targets of the INS—because they were the people that transformed the question "Why do they hate us?" to "How *could* they hate us?"[40]

Undocumented Latina/o immigrants verified that America's promise of freedom and democracy was so desirable that even those who could never access it still wanted to live in a place where others could. Sympathetic representations of undocumented Latinas/os in the immediate wake of September 11 did not just recode already prevalent national narratives; they also reinvented them in ways that notably mitigated the racial hysteria over undocumented Latinas and children that had preoccupied the national imaginary in the 1980s and 1990s. In the wake of September 11, immigrants who crossed the border without authorization could be represented as highly (though ironically) patriotic. As journalist Elizabeth Llorente stated, "Many of the day laborers along Columbia Avenue in North Bergen, New Jersey, as well as others interviewed in other towns, said they were determined to stay, to ride out the hard times. Many of the men—who also had U.S. flags on their shirts and caps—said they would fight in Afghanistan if they could enlist in the military."[41] Being determined to stay and work as undocumented is not usually characterized as admirable in news media, but the decision becomes honorable and courageous in the shadow of September 11. These Latino day laborers literally wrapped themselves in U.S. flags, waiting for the opportunity to be unmarked as disposable "illegal" bodies and remade into American patriots willing to sacrifice their lives for their country of residence.

Machismo and the Military

The Bush administration organized the chaos of 9/11 by providing a national narrative that connected patriotism to nativism and terrorism to illegality. Recoding illegal status as both Latina/o and Arab/Muslim and repurposing Latina/o racial difference as a signifier for both undocumented immigration and militarized multiculturalism required revising and reinventing how undocumented Latinas/os were both publicly represented and productively managed. Representing post-9/11 national identity as diverse and multiracial helped blur the blatant racial line that divides who serves in the military and whom the military serves. This multiracial, multicultural American identity attempted to conceal the racialized dimensions of the war on terror even as it highlighted the war's biological undertones. Noncitizen U.S. soldiers—80 percent of whom are persons of color[42]—answer a call to duty for a country that has not claimed them as its own. In 2002, approximately 37 percent of noncitizens who joined the military were Latina/o, 23 percent were Asian or Pacific Islander, and 20 percent were black.[43] Although not drafted for service, noncitizens were conscripted into service by their legal nonpersonhood. As deportable, they were already disposable. Since the end of the draft in 1973, the all-volunteer U.S. military has not been able to attract young U.S. citizens to enlist, compelling the military to recruit outside U.S. borders. At the Iraq War's inception, U.S. military recruiters even crossed the Mexican border to sign up recruits—in excursions euphemistically characterized by military media as a few individuals' "overzealousness."[44]

The U.S. military has also focused on those whom the United States has disenfranchised within its borders. Like African Americans, young Latinas/os have been selectively targeted for aggressive recruitment. According to Jorge Mariscal, "The *Army Times* reported that 'Hispanics' constituted 22 percent of the military recruiting 'market,' almost double their numbers in the population."[45] The Hispanic Access Initiative (HAI), described as "affirmative action" to help "diversify" the military's officer ranks,[46] created military partnerships with colleges and high schools—even middle and elementary schools—with large Latina/o student populations in a manner akin to the establishment of a military presence at historically black colleges and universities. Similarly, the 2001 revision of the Solomon Amendment,[47] which cuts an entire university's federal funding if any of its subdivisions deny access to military recruiters, seems more about securing soldiers of any rank at any cost than about ensuring equal representation in the military's relatively privileged positions.[48] While constituting only 10 percent of the military, more than 25 percent of the army infantry and more than 20 percent of the Marine Corps infantry is of Latina/o descent.[49]

The overrepresentation of Latinas/os in the military's infantry ranks has been attributed to and naturalized as Latina/o cultural difference—a difference colloquially and sometimes disdainfully referred to in the United States as "macho." Marine recruiter Gunnery Sergeant Jorge Montes explains that Marine recruitment in predominantly Latina/o high schools and Latina/o communities sells the military through an "aggressive, testosterone-heavy image."[50] Representing Latino U.S. soldiers as unable to resist the adrenaline rush of honorable, freely chosen disposability, Montes claims that "even recruits who score out of the infantry choose it anyway. . . . There is a certain pride in being in the front lines at the tip of the spear."[51] "Machismo" thus functions as an abnormal "condition," a perversion of masculinity signified by and thought to originate within Latina/o cultural difference. As a result, masculine "pride"—not poverty, disposability, or racism—becomes the reason why too many Latinas/os are at the tip of the spear. To be "macho" is read as compulsively choosing to die even when given the choice to lessen the odds. In this way, being "macho" is rendered a cultural difference that naturalizes Latina/o overrepresentation among the dead.

Labeling Latinas/os as "macho" displaces the necropolitics of the war on terror onto (supposedly improperly gendered and perversely over-sexed) Latina/o cultures and conceals how the necropolitical works through the biopolitical in its use of racial difference to determine who is disposable and who is killed for whom. To be on the "front lines" is to be in a zone of disposability that separates the lawless civilized from the death-worlds they were creating. For those living with little or no rights, the possibility of dying on the front lines is transformed into an "opportunity" for legal recognition.

Between September 2001 and April 2011, U.S. Citizenship and Immigration Services naturalized 68,974 members of the military.[52] In July 2002, Bush issued an executive order that not only expedited the process of attaining naturalized citizenship for active duty soldiers but also waived the residence requirement and naturalization fees for soldiers serving during military hostilities.[53] Margaret Stock, a law professor at the U.S. Military Academy at West Point, contends that the executive order applies to undocumented as well as legal immigrants.[54] A 2004 investigation by journalist Bruce Finley, for instance, found that the U.S. military lists 16,031 members whose citizenship is "unknown."[55] Even though undocumented immigrants cannot legally enlist in the U.S. military, they are not exactly deterred from joining. In some cases, the military even helps undocumented U.S. soldiers attain U.S. citizenship. The military helped Private Juan Escalante, an undocumented Mexican immigrant, begin the process of naturalization; however, at the same time, an immigration judge ordered the deportation of his parents, brother, and sister.[56] For undocumented Latina/o immigrants such as Escalante, embracing the possibility of patriotic death becomes the method to demonstrate one's deservingness of legal personhood.[57]

Citizenship for the Dead

For noncitizens, naturalized citizenship has two particularly important, practical functions: You cannot be deported, and your family members can immigrate legally. Posthumous citizenship, however, only sometimes enables the latter. In fact, I would argue that posthumous citizenship has more purpose and function for the state than for family members of the dead. For the state, noncitizen soldiers are just as valuable, perhaps even more so, in death than in life. As Sharon Holland explains, the dead are central to nation building because "their 'desires' *not* their 'bodies' are exhumed for use by the state."[58] In death, the noncitizen U.S. soldier becomes the perfect naturalized U.S. citizen because "the dead are the ultimate 'docile bodies.'"[59] U.S. citizenship claims ownership over noncitizen soldiers' bodies in order to exhume and use their desires, militarizing soldiers' past yearnings and romanticizing soldiers' (lack of) choices. For example, José Antonio Gutierrez, who was both an undocumented immigrant from Guatemala and the second U.S. soldier killed in the war, was represented by mainstream and military media as unselfishly choosing military service over higher education.[60] This portrayal of Gutierrez was consistent across news reports: He joined the Marines because he "wanted to give the United States what the United States gave to him. He came with nothing. This country gave him everything."[61] News stories represented him as wanting to "give" (not pay back) everything to the nation, but they failed to add that the nation did, in fact, take everything he had to give, including the rights to tell his story. In contrast, Heidi Specogna's documentary *The Short Life of José Antonio Gutierrez* offers a competing representation. According to the film's narrative, Gutierrez reluctantly joined the U.S. military because he needed to become a more competitive college applicant and wanted to obtain U.S. citizenship.[62]

In another example, a deceased soldier's father was recruited to speak for his son and on behalf of the nation. Columbian-born noncitizen U.S. soldier Diego Rincon died overseas while on active duty. Diego Rincon's father, Jorge Rincon, was portrayed as the representative (father) figure for speeding up the naturalization process for noncitizen soldiers. Through Jorge Rincon, naturalized U.S. citizenship was characterized not just as a reward for dying during combat but as the culmination of a father's dream: legal recognition for his son. Jorge Rincon also was portrayed as passionately and unconditionally supporting the United States and its military. For example, a *Washington Post* story reported that "at Diego's enlistment ceremony in January 2002, his father was so moved that he approached a sergeant and asked whether he could sign up, too."[63] According to news narratives, Jorge Rincon's enthusiasm was not tempered by his son's death. Upon learning that his son received posthumous U.S. citizenship, Rincon said, "I'm proud for Diego and proud to be in this country and proud that my son was in the United States Army."[64] In the same article, Rincon continued with "the only thing that keeps me going now is to make sure that he's buried as an American. . . . That will be my dream come true."[65] Jorge Rincon's "American Dream" was not social or economic mobility; it was not property ownership or educational opportunities for his son. It was not even political membership for himself. His America Dream was to bury his son on American soil as an American citizen—a dream indicative of the fabulous values of this nation.

As Holland theorizes, it is actually not the biological menace (whether suspected terrorist, illegal alien, or criminal) that represents the nation's most threatening enemy. Rather, it is the voice of our dead: "Here the dead are the most intimate 'enemy' of the changing and growing nation. Should they rise and speak for themselves, the state would lose all right to their borrowed and/or stolen language."[66] Rincon, Gutierrez, and other noncitizen U.S. soldiers were devalued and disposable agents of "freedom," not the intended recipients. Far from a "reward," posthumous citizenship is a technology of necropower, another means by which the state retains and legitimates its sovereignty through controlling the dead. U.S. Citizenship and Immigration Services reported that between August 2002 and April 2011, 132 members of the military had been granted posthumous citizenship.[67] Posthumous citizenship is not just symbolic belonging; it allows the state to claim the rights to these individuals' stories as American stories, making sure to silence or censor what they might have to say otherwise.[68]

Rearticulating Race and Rights?

Latina/o activists and their allies were recruited into an anti-terrorist discourse that validated the racist logic foundational to draconian immigration laws deemed necessary for capturing potential terrorists. It is this foundational logic—a logic that hinges upon biopower's premise of making live— that explained not only why the policing functions of the INS would become the responsibility of Immigration Customs and Enforcement (ICE) but also why ICE needed to be the largest agency with the most discretionary power in the Department of Homeland Security, which in itself marked a radical shift from the underfunding of the INS. In December 2005, the House of Representatives passed the Border Protection, Anti-terrorism, and Illegal Immigration Control Act, also known as HR 4437.[69] The legislation made no distinctions among undocumented populations as either deserving or undeserving, either docile or dangerous, nor did it differentiate undocumented immigrants by intent, race, religion, or nation of origin. Rather, it grafted "terrorism" onto already existing discourses of "illegality." Although controlling "terrorism" was its stated intention, mothers, workers, and students would be the inevitable casualties of any immigration legislation passed during the war on terror—not accidental casualties but instrumental ones.

In just over a decade, national sentiments regarding the Latina/o family shifted from contempt (during the Proposition 187 campaign in 1994) to compassion (during the Immigrant Rights marches in 2006). Yet from 1994 to 2006, the Latina/o family had not significantly changed; it was still mixed-status, transnational, and disproportionately poor. From 1994 to 2006, undocumented immigrants were still employed in the jobs that some Americans would never do and that poor Americans of color envied. Instead, what had changed was the political context, and this in turn shifted how value was determined and distributed to bodies and lives. This shift enabled immigration activists to center on and to celebrate the previous decade's demonized Latina/o family, foregrounding the importance of family life and hard work, countering anti-immigrant rhetoric that so often criminalized Latinas/os' family and work life through stories about "anchor babies" and stealing jobs.

While not the primary objects of U.S. value, they were also not necessarily its not-valued others. For undocumented Latina/o immigrants, this moment not only disrupted the signs and signifiers of illegality from Latina/o to Latina/o and Arab/Muslim; it also recast Latina/o illegality. Latina/o settlement was not about invasion or contamination when represented in the wake of September 11; it was evidence of the American Dream's worldwide appeal. In other words, undocumented Latinas/os were conferred social value as an unintentional by-product of universalizing the "American way of life." Patriotic processes of value and valorization rendered Americans, America, and the "American way of life" absolutely, universally, and transparently valuable through the equally absolute not-value of the "terrorist." This negative resource for American value became the violent grounds of possibility that would enable undocumented Latina/o immigrants and noncitizen soldiers of color to be represented as socially valuable.

Because they were not seen as the immediate nor primary threat after September 11, undocumented Latina/o immigrants could be reinterpreted not necessarily as deserving, but also as not absolutely undeserving. These ideological maneuvers were made possible because other racial and ethnic groups— namely, ("un-legal") immigrants from the Middle East—appeared to pose new and more immediate "threats" to national security. Consequently, national concerns about undocumented Latina/o immigration were not just momentarily displaced but also temporarily rearticulated. Unauthorized border crossing was provisionally recoded: It did not represent a threat to American culture and the American family but rather was representative of the universal appeal of the American Dream itself. This rearticulation made viable, and perhaps even necessary, the activation of both labor and family as the organizing themes of the Immigrant Rights demonstrations in 2006.

But the *need* for action in 2006 was not because undocumented Latina/o immigrants were sometimes characterized in the 9/11 aftermath in socially valuable terms of work and family, resolution and sacrifice. "Illegal alien" (like gang member or criminal alien) invokes images of, but is not a fixed signifier for, Latina/o. Different racial and ethnic groups have been associated with "illegality" throughout U.S. history, but what has remained consistent from the late nineteenth-century Chinese Exclusion Act to the present-day Patriot Act is the legally recognized nonpersonhood of the racialized "illegal alien." Thus, the *need* for a movement in 2006 can be traced to the destabilization of the signs and signifiers of "illegality," which unhinged but never detached Latina/o as its present-day primary racial signifier. To represent Middle Eastern immigrants as not only "suspects of terrorism" but also as "illegal" justified and made essential the intensification of immigration restrictions and exclusions. In other words, while "Latina/o" might have been repurposed and rearticulated, the "illegal alien" was not. In fact, because "the terrorist" was grafted onto the "illegal alien," the figure of the "illegal alien" (and the legal status category it represented) only became all the more threatening and unnerving, all the more in need of surveillance and restriction.

The "illegal alien" is the signifier, which should concern us because it signifies persons fundamentally unentitled to rights, and it refers to a category of nonpersonhood that institutes discrimination. The laws that have made undocumented Latina/o families legally vulnerable and highly exploitable are the same laws that empowered the federal government to racially profile and divest "suspected terrorists" of everything and anything resembling "rights" because to be "unlawful" is to be ineligible for personhood, as noncitizens "suspected" of "terrorism" know all too well.

Immigrant Rights versus Civil Rights

In 2002, Elvira Arellano was arrested during a sweep of Chicago's O'Hare International Airport for using a false Social Security number. Implemented after and in response to September 11, "Operation Tarmac" was designed to find and deport unauthorized airport workers. On the day she was ordered to report to immigration in 2006, she defied her deportation orders and took sanctuary at Chicago's Adalberto United Methodist Church with the help of her good friend and fellow immigrant rights activist, Emma Lozano, and Lozano's husband, the Reverend Walter "Slim" Coleman, also a local activist. While trying to work with her very few and very unlikely legal options, Arellano and Lozano founded La Familia Latina Unida (the United Latino Family), an organization that lobbied Congress to recognize the citizenship rights of 3 million U.S. citizen children who faced the "decision" to be separated from one or both of their parents or to lose everything else in their lives. Arellano's 7-year-old U.S. citizen son, Saul, was one of those children. Saul was Arellano's primary motivation for seeking sanctuary. As she stated, "my son is a U.S. citizen. . . . He doesn't want me to go anywhere, so I'm going

>>   115

to stay with him."[1] Her courage was inspiring and reinvigorating not only for immigrant rights activists but also for religious leaders and their congregations. Because she refused to return to Mexico and publicly decried the vast injustices that U.S. immigration law imposes on mixed-status families, she was credited with sparking the New Sanctuary Movement and named by *Time* magazine as one of the "People Who Mattered in 2006."[2] Unfortunately, all her work did not matter enough to protect her from deportation in 2007. Once back in Mexico, she began organizing on behalf of the Central American undocumented populations who resided in Mexico.

Arellano's decision to take a steadfast stand against the injustices of immigration law reminded many of African American civil rights icon Rosa Parks. U.S. Representative Bobby Rush, a founding member of the Illinois Black Panther Party and a member of the Congressional Black Caucus, met Arellano at a memorial service for Parks and made the comparison.[3] Soon after, some activists began referring to Arellano as our very own "Rosita Parks."[4] Arellano also cited Parks as one of her inspirations, telling reporters, "I'm strong, I've learned from Rosa Parks—I'm not going to the back of the bus. The law is wrong."[5]

Yet some found the comparison of Arellano to Parks unsettling and the premise for the likeness fundamentally flawed. Mary Mitchell, an African American columnist for the *Chicago Sun-Times*, was among those who were most outraged and outspoken. As she expressed with conviction, "Elvira Arellano is definitely no Rosa Parks."[6] The columnist critiqued Arellano for likening herself, an undocumented immigrant rights activist, to Parks, a civil rights activist for U.S. citizens. As Mitchell wrote,

Despite the rhetoric, the 31-year-old Arellano doesn't seem to know much about black Americans' struggle for civil rights.

Parks didn't refuse to go to the back of the bus. She refused to give up her seat to a white man who couldn't find a seat in the so-called "white section." As onerous as the Jim Crow laws were, Parks didn't break them. That's why she could calmly go to the police station and sit in jail until her husband came to bail her out.

Because Parks wasn't a lawbreaker, the local NAACP decided to use her as a test case to challenge the Jim Crow laws. Her righteous cause drew widespread support and launched the civil rights movement in earnest.[7]

Whereas Rush likened Arellano to Parks on the basis of each woman's actions, Mitchell denounced the comparison on the basis of each woman's legal status. For Mitchell, Arellano had no right to challenge U.S. law at all because *dumb af*

her unauthorized immigration status marked her permanently and irrefutably as a "law-breaker," as "illegal" in presence and for being, In Mitchell's view, it mattered that Elvira Arellano and Rosa Parks had different relationships to U.S. law; in fact, on some level, she considered this difference to be all that mattered. Mitchell saw the legitimacy of Parks' action as dependent on the legitimacy of her legal status as a law-abiding citizen.

respectability politics playing out

Because undocumented immigrants are marked as indelibly "illegal" across various institutions, mobilizing support for undocumented immigrants' rights requires negotiating accusations of criminal intent. Mitchell also wrote that she could not feel sympathetic toward Arellano because she disagreed with the means by which Arellano contested immigration laws.[8] Because being an "illegal alien" is essentially a de facto status crime, undocumented immigrants' "illegal" status renders their law-abiding actions irrelevant. At best, "illegal" status complicates representing undocumented immigrants as moral, ethical, and "deserving." Mitchell believed that Arellano should have reported to immigration authorities rather than seek sanctuary. Speculating that Arellano would have received more public sympathy if she had taken that route, Mitchell wrote that Arellano should have "marched into the immigration office and showed America exactly what the present immigration laws really mean: That a single mother can be separated from her child; that husbands can be snatched from their wives; that working-class families can be torn apart simply because America has waited far too long to craft a fair and reasonable immigration policy."[9] While Arellano would have been deported immediately if she had challenged immigration law in this way, for Mitchell, such self-sacrifice on Arellano's part was necessary just to warrant public sympathy. As she wrote, "Maybe then more of us would respect her stance."[10] Mitchell is not unaware of how much Arellano stood to lose. However, because Mitchell's definition of morality cannot be disentangled from her commitment to the "rule of law," she cannot apprehend the irony that for Arellano, following the "rule of law" would have meant complying with deportation orders, thereby freeing herself from the obligation to follow the U.S. "rule of law."

wanted her to suffer even more to prove her point

wtf makes it hard to empathize

dumbass

For both Mitchell and Arellano, "family rights" needed no explanation to serve as a political tactic to garner support and sympathy for undocumented immigrants. By appealing to the needs of family members, immigrant rights advocates and their sympathizers attempt to lessen the perception of undocumented immigrants' criminal culpability by emphasizing their commendable commitments to their families. In fact, both undocumented Latinas/os and un(der)employed African American citizens are required to provide evidence that their intimate relationships are proper embodiments of

sympathy through family

should about ↑ than families

heteronormativity and respectable domesticity. This, then, narrows the focus of rights-based struggles, making them seem synonymous with securing family rights within U.S. law. Moreover, the focus on family rights can sometimes distract us from critiquing the structural conditions of global capital and neoliberal reforms that create, perpetuate, and aggravate hyperexploitability and legal vulnerability. Global capital and the U.S. state threaten not only the conventional gendered roles within families but also family members' very ability to survive, thereby generating the need for less-than-ideal familial relationships and less-than-legal work opportunities and business ventures.

In this chapter I revisit the master narrative of black and Latina/o conflict, analyzing the stories news media told about the 2006 immigrant rights marches. Although media representations of the contemporary battle for immigrant rights were reflective of Arellano's and Mitchell's complex definitions and competing deployments of "civil rights," the news media represented the movement primarily in racial and relational terms. The movement was positioned as both enabled by and in conflict with the African American struggle for civil rights in the 1950s–1970s. This particular juxtaposition cannot help but characterize undocumented immigrants as always already and unquestionably criminal because the African American struggle for civil rights in the United States revolved around and relied upon respecting the rights of personhood that U.S. citizenship supposedly already recognizes. In this way, immigrant rights as civil rights was articulated as a racial controversy and enmeshed within relationally racialized discourses of criminality, illegality, respectability, and heteronormativity.

By superimposing a U.S.-centric and race-based framework for understanding "rights" and comprehending "movements," mainstream news media obfuscated not only undocumented immigrants' transnational struggle to protect, provide for, and reside with their families, but also U.S. minorities' diverse histories of social activism from the 1950s to the 1970s. In particular, media erased the history of African American social activisms that situated struggles against racial discrimination in the United States as part of that era's global struggle for sovereignty, freedom, and independence. In representing the immigrant rights movement racially and relationally, I argue, media erased the international tenets or the "worldliness" of both historical and contemporary rights-based movements while leaving intact and primary an uncomplicated master narrative of black-Latina/o conflict and competition in the United States. Remembering other histories is important for understanding how and why undocumented Latinas/os and the African American working poor are structurally positioned as economic competitors

↳pit against each other

and political allies. This context can help us to avoid debating which group is more deserving of rights that are sure to be denied—even if conferred.

Creating Criminals and Globalizing the Prison Regime

When used as a political tactic, claiming deservingness through demonstrating respectability assumes that we can make a clear distinction between people of color who are criminal and people of color who are respectable, but this distinction is far from being fixed or stable. Global capital capitalizes on local and global processes of racialization and criminalization to produce "illegal" persons as well as spaces of lawlessness, or what Denise Ferreira da Silva terms "zones of illegality."[11] These zones of illegality are essentially "death-worlds" governed through lawlessness, places where corrupt law enforcement officials abuse the laws by which they are supposed to abide, leaving residents heavily policed and yet absolutely unprotected.[12]

Both within and beyond the borders of the United States, indigent and indigenous populations of color are literally made into criminals. This ensures that the poorest people will remain legally vulnerable and hyperexploitable because, as criminals, they are denied not only rights but also compassion. For the last half century, economic restructuring has exacerbated poverty for the poor of color in the United States and abroad. Poor people of color were also increasingly targeted for deportation, regulation, and incarceration as federal laws and international trade agreements further pathologized and criminalized their various methods of coping with their increasingly insurmountable obstacles and setbacks, such as working in underground economies or self-medicating with nonprescription street drugs.

In the early 1980s, the world faced a recession that began to undermine the gains secured by social movements across the globe. In the United States, organized labor began to lose more battles against corporate capital, and the hourly wages of 80 percent of the U.S. workforce declined.[13] Asserting that the high wages of U.S. workers impeded corporate competitiveness, U.S. corporations complemented their assault on labor unions by moving production sites to the global South and increasing their foreign investments.[14] During the recession, the Reagan administration reversed the hard won gains of previous decades by implementing neoliberal reforms in the United States and by supporting structural adjustment programs in the global South. According to political analyst Walden F. Bello, the Reagan administration effectively dismantled the "activist state" of nations in the global South and global North.[15]

The recession in the 1980s was difficult for all but the wealthiest classes in the United States. President Ronald Reagan's tax "reforms" from 1981 to 1983 facilitated the upward redistribution of wealth: The tax share of the wealthiest 1 percent dropped 14 percent while the poorest 10 percent of the population saw their share rise by 28 percent.[16] Unemployment rose from 4.8 percent in 1973 to 10 percent in 1981–1982 and was further exacerbated by the steep cost-of-living increase of 133 percent from 1972 to 1982.[17]

For low-income African American households, the recession intensified and accelerated the effects of deindustrialization that had begun decades earlier. Urban historian Thomas Sugrue paints a bleak picture of deindustrialization's national impact on African Americans who lived in cities such as Chicago, New York, Cleveland, Gary, Philadelphia, Pittsburgh, Saint Louis, Camden, Baltimore, and Newark. As Sugrue notes, in those cities' urban areas, the poverty rate for black residents ranged from 25 to 40 percent because of a massive loss in manufacturing jobs coupled with a major growth in the poorly paid service industry.[18] Between 1970 and 1980, the male nonemployment rate in low-income black neighborhoods rose from 25.9 percent to 40.7 percent.[19] In Los Angeles alone, black women's employment in manufacturing declined by 37 percent in durable goods and by 114 percent in nondurable goods.[20] By the end of the Republican era in 1992, the United States was the most "unequal nation of all modern nations," with a poverty rate of almost 50 percent for children of color.[21]

In the 1980s, the criminalization of victimless illicit activities associated with poverty, race, and urban space redirected state funds from developing social welfare programs to expanding institutions of social protection.[22] As professor of law and public policy Michael Tonry writes, "Arrests of Blacks for violent crimes have not increased since 1980, but the percentage of Blacks sent to prison has increased starkly."[23] New mandatory sentencing laws that criminalized and imprisoned drug users were disproportionately enforced in poor neighborhoods of color hit hardest by the world recession. This rise in incarceration rates can be directly attributed to the "war on drugs." From 1982 to 1999, the number of prisoners sent to prison for drug violations increased 975 percent.[24] In the 1980s, however, similar victimless crimes in the inner cities were colorfully repackaged as the not-so-innocent recreational activity that inevitably leads to violent crimes. When African Americans were 90 percent of those found guilty of distributing crack cocaine, for instance, Congress not only mandated prison sentences for possessing and selling it but also mandated that the punishments were 100 times harsher than the sentences for possessing and selling its powder counterpart, primarily because powder cocaine was associated with a more affluent clientele.[25] Following a similar logic, most states lessened the criminal punishments for marijuana in the 1960s and 1970s because white teenagers had begun using it.[26] The rapid rise of the incarcerated minority population in the United States greatly expanded the number of state and private prisons and helped strengthen related industries, such as businesses that depended on prisoners for cheap labor.

Needless to say, increasing incarceration rates in the United States do not necessarily indicate that more crimes are being committed. Instead, they often result from the fact that more and more activities are either repackaged as much more dangerous than comparable suburban delinquencies or redefined as illegal. Criminal laws in the United States are expanded and extended every year at the local, state, and federal levels. The vast majority of these laws either criminalize the recreational activities of the poor of color, such as using specific street drugs, or create harsher penalties for crimes already on the books, such as gang enhancement charges or mandatory domestic violence sentencing. According to the Bureau of Justice Statistics, drug offenders and public-order offenders (which include those who break immigration laws) accounted for 87 percent of the growth in the federal inmate population between 1995 and 2003.[27] Although African Americans constitute only 13 percent of the U.S. population, in 2005 black men accounted for 40 percent of state and federal male inmates who had been sentenced for more than one year.[28]

The pervasiveness of law-and-order ways of knowing accompanied by discipline-and-punish strategies of subjection can be attributed to what ethnic studies scholar Dylan Rodríguez calls the "prison regime." For the state, criminalization and its regulation are central practices of governmentality because they are vital for legitimating the state's authority. As Rodríguez argues,

> The multiple technologies of power inaugurated and spun outward by the prison regime enable the material practice of state power, inscribing its self-narrated dominion, authority, and (moral) legitimacy to coerce: *the ascendancy and authority of the state must be enacted, ritualized, and signified through the prison regime—and massively performed on target bodies —to become "real."*[29]

A prison is more than an institution or an apparatus. As Rodríguez explains, a prison is "a dynamic state-mediated practice of domination and control."[30] And as the neoliberal state increasingly intervened on behalf of capital to strengthen the United States' position within the global economy, such practices were imposed on other nations as well.

Mirror struggle for Af. Am. and Global South

While the middle classes of the United States were beginning to recover, though not prosper, in the 1990s, living conditions only worsened in the global South in no small part due to the U.S. state's "free trade agreements." These agreements bolstered the economy in the United States, and they facilitated the expansion of global capital and extended the reach of multinational corporations. Just months after implementing the Dominican Republic–Central American Free Trade Agreement (DR-CAFTA) in 2006,

Pursuit of ↑ cheap labor

more than 6,500 workers in the United States lost their jobs because companies relocated some of their production to Central America. (Every member of Congress representing the districts where these U.S. jobs were lost supported DR-CAFTA.[31]) However, even when job loss in the United States can be traced to corporate flight, decent work opportunities in the global South

Global South not benefitting either

are not inversely proportionate to job loss in the global North. In only two years, 22 textile companies left the nations participating in DR-CAFTA (the Dominican Republic, El Salvador, Honduras, Costa Rica, Nicaragua, and Guatemala), resulting in 50,000 jobs lost in the textile industry.[32] As more and more corporations set up shop overseas, not only are less jobs available to people living in the United States, but more people are put out of business

exactly

in the global South as well because they cannot compete with multinational corporations. In the Dominican Republic, 84 percent of the 400,000 small and medium businesses cannot compete at all in the globalized market because they lack the basic technology.[33] In Nicaragua, seven *maquila* (manufacturing) plants opened after DR-CAFTA in 2007, creating 1,993 jobs, but Nicaragua also lost 4,000 jobs during the same time period because other businesses had to close or relocate.[34] Local businesses need state intervention often in the form of subsidies or loans in order to be able to compete on the "equal" terms dictated under "free trade" agreements, but only the United States is able to offset the costs of production. In 2007, it cost $9.40 for a U.S. farmer to produce 100 pounds of rice, but it cost only $8.45 for a farmer in the Sébaco Valley of Nicaragua to produce the same product. While it may seem as though Nicaragua would be able to profit from exporting rice, this competitive advantage is undermined by U.S. subsidies that en-

not "free"

able 100 pounds of U.S. rice to be sold in Nicaragua at $7.65.[35] Under "free trade" Nicaragua can no longer increase its import tariffs on rice and must eliminate its tariffs on all agricultural products (including rice) by 2025.[36] Because rice is a food staple in Nicaragua, people will become dependent on the rice imported from the United States at the same time that rice growers

[handwritten margin note: Global econ. domination]

in Nicaragua will be steadily pushed out of the local market because locally grown rice will not be able to compete with the cheaper rice imported from the United States. By 2025, U.S. rice can be sold at a much higher price because Nicaraguans will already be dependent on import rice, which will be not only duty-free, but without local competition the United States government will no longer need to subsidize U.S. rice farmers as well.

DR-CAFTA's predecessor, the North American Free Trade Agreement (NAFTA) implemented in 1994, also did not fulfill its promise to stabilize farmers' incomes in participating countries—Mexico, Canada, and the United States. Like DR-CAFTA, NAFTA benefited only large agribusinesses. For small Canadian farmers, bankruptcies and delinquent loans were five times higher in 2001 than pre-NAFTA. In the United States, 33,000 small farms ceased to exist altogether.[37] But for ConAgra, the largest supplier of agricultural chemicals and fertilizers in North America and the second largest supplier to grocery stores (under product names such as Butterball, Hunt's, Healthy Choice, and Peter Pan Peanut Butter), profits increased 189 percent from $143 million to $413 million between 1993 and 2000.[38] Under NAFTA, Mexico's already alarming 52 percent poverty rate escalated to 69 percent in only two years.[39] NAFTA displaced approximately 15 million farmers by undoing eighty years of land reform in Mexico.[40] As a result, small landholders were unable to make a living, and unemployment and underemployment in Mexico's urban centers were also inevitably exacerbated. Consequently, more and more people were compelled to migrate beyond Mexico's borders.

[handwritten margin note: forced to migrate b/c of US intervention]

U.S. advocates for both NAFTA and DR-CAFTA claimed that undocumented immigration in the United States would decrease with the formalization of free trade because multinational corporations would not only provide jobs in Mexico, the Caribbean, and Central America but also promise incentives for people to remain in their countries of origin. But since the implementation of NAFTA, the undocumented immigrant population increased dramatically, from 2.2 million before NAFTA to 11 million in 2005.[41] Following DR-CAFTA in 2006, the undocumented population increased to 11.9 million by 2008.[42] Although the increase was not as drastic, it's worth noting that undocumented immigrants from Latin American nations other than Mexico increased more than 40 percent from 1.8 million in 2000 (before DR-CAFTA) to 2.6 million in 2008.[43] Many undocumented immigrants cite NAFTA or DR-CAFTA as their reason for migrating; they felt coerced into crossing national borders because their living conditions after free trade necessitated their doing so. In fact, the coercion was so powerfully felt that in Oaxaca, Mexico, indigenous communities are organizing around the right to not migrate, demanding "*el derecho de no migrar.*"[44] As Rufino Dominguez,

[handwritten margin note: opposite happened!]

[handwritten margin note: don't want to leave their home]

head of the Oaxacan Institute for the Care of Migrants, said, "There are no jobs here, and NAFTA made the price of corn so low that it's not economically possible to plant a crop anymore. . . . We come to the U.S. to work because we can't get a price for our product at home. There's no alternative."[45] These populations have been denied the right to stay home.

For the people of Mexico, Central America, and the Dominican Republic who did not migrate, the North and Central American free trade agreements made lives difficult beyond the devastating effects of weakening their agricultural economies. NAFTA and DR-CAFTA also required participating nations to protect U.S. intellectual property rights. DR-CAFTA, in fact, offers pharmaceutical companies more protections than both laws in the United States and the World Trade Organization's multilateral agreement on Trade-Related Aspects of Intellectual Property.[46] DR-CAFTA's intellectual property regulations provide drug companies monopoly protection, making it all but criminal for organizations to offer affordable, generic medicine. Thus, DR-CAFTA greatly constrained health care systems in the global South.[47] In Guatemala, many affordable generics had to be withdrawn from the market altogether, and many new generics have been barred from even entering, which makes the cost of necessary medicine exorbitant for common but fatal conditions such as cancer, HIV/AIDS, hypertension, stroke, pneumonia, cardiac disease, and diabetes. For example, 100 milliliters of insulin made by Sanofi Aventis under the brand-name Lantus costs $50.31, while Drogueria Pisa de Guatemala locally manufactures a generic that costs only $5.95 per 100 milliliters. Because Lantus is protected until 2016, Guatemalans buying insulin will have to pay the higher price, which amounts to 846 percent more than the local equivalent manufactured by Drogueria Pisa de Guatemala.[48] Before the implementation of DR-CAFTA, pharmaceutical companies rarely bothered to obtain patents in Guatemala because such little profit was expected, but under DR-CAFTA, brand-name drugs can be "data-protected" for five or fifteen years, thereby drastically reducing or altogether removing their competition.[49]

Abiding by U.S. intellectual property rights as dictated by NAFTA and DR-CAFTA required nations to radically restructure their legal systems as well, resulting not only in more working poor, unemployed, homeless, and landless but also in creating and increasing so-called "criminal" populations. Money-making activities that were not illegal or criminal before NAFTA and DR-CAFTA were redefined as illegal under the legal reforms that were required by the trade agreements to protect the interests of multinational corporations. NAFTA and DR-CAFTA subjected member countries to the World Intellectual Property Organization (WIPO) Copyright Treaty. Among its many generalized restrictions, the treaty revised international copyright laws to protect the profit potential of advanced information technology by, for instance, redefining computer programs as "literature" and therefore rendering them subject to the copyright laws that protect artists and musicians. As George Caffentzis explains, the WIPO Copyright Treaty imposed "privatized 'intellectual property rights' on formerly colonized or socialist countries where patents, copyrights and licenses did not have much legitimacy."[50] Many people living in participating countries depended on piracy to make a living, but under DR-CAFTA, vendors and purchasers of pirated copies and counterfeit commodities, such as CDs, DVDs, clothes, and shoes, not only were under stricter surveillance but also faced imprisonment and fines.[51] DR-CAFTA imposed thirteen new laws in El Salvador criminalizing informal economies, which immediately made 20,000 people's means for making a living subject to prison sentences.[52] Under El Salvador's new intellectual property rights laws, people producing knock-offs could be sent to prison for four to six years, and those convicted of violating "technological measures" could be imprisoned for two to four years.[53]

As the culture of crime and punishment continues to extend far beyond prison walls and as the definition of "property rights" continues to attack both physical "commons" (water and land) and virtual "commons" (information via the internet), the poor of color within and beyond the U.S.-Mexico border are increasingly pathologized and criminalized, especially during and following moments of economic decline. Arguably, the intensified criminalization of these classes not only tells us that those most vulnerable are hurt the most during widespread economic hardship but also suggests that multinational corporations and neoliberal states have a monetary interest in increasing the number of people whose ways of coping economically (such as in informal economies) and emotionally (such as through unregulated self-medication) leave them with few sympathizers, as well as with an increasingly urgent need for more allies.

Hence, the victims of immigration law, free trade agreements, deindustrialization, and the prison regime are not always as respectable as they need to be imagined. Many of the people within and beyond U.S. borders who are most vulnerable are those who work (whether voluntarily or out of necessity) in unregulated, noncapitalist, or nonmarket economies, which incorporate not only counterfeit clothiers, indigenous fisherpersons, and subsistence farmers but also digital bootleggers, pop culture pirates, prostitutes, drug dealers, gang members, freedom fighters, and undocumented immigrants working for wages. The men and women whose means of living and working are criminalized are among the most legally vulnerable populations, whether they are citizens or immigrants, whether they are black, Latina/o, Asian, Arab, or indigenous. The same structures of capital exploitation that create differentially disadvantaged populations also create surplus populations that cannot be incorporated into the "legal" economy at all precisely because the (assumed) legal economy runs on the illegal corporate practices that are absolutely dependent on indigent populations' coerced participation. This population is marked as socially and often sexually deviant precisely because they make a living—and they make their lives worth living—outside legal and lawful boundaries.

"Fighting Back with the Family"

The pressures to perform respectability and repudiate criminality need to be read in relation to neoliberal states' past and present role in facilitating and extending global capital's violences on both sides of and beyond the U.S.-Mexico border.[54] Compelled to negotiate their respective exclusions and exploitations through relationally racialized and gendered discourses of criminality, illegality, and respectability, African Americans and Latinas/os in the United States are required to disavow the "deviants" within and in relation to their communities, to focus on those who have, as Cathy Cohen puts it, an "uncomplicated status—in terms of moral codes."[55] Consequently, such rhetoric implies that aggrieved communities deserve social resources, political rights, or steady employment because they, too, hold dear the normative American values, corporate morals, and neoliberal ethics that sustain and maintain racial/ethnic exclusion, gender stratification, sexual regulation, and middle-class privilege. As Cohen contends, such issues pressure activists "to engage in a calculus of human worth," according to which some lives would be "designated as more important and worth saving."[56] Aspiring to attain respectability demands disavowing those labeled as criminal, immoral, deviant, and illegal. But the meanings and definitions of criminal, immoral, deviant, and illegal appear to be commonsensical and incontestable only because they are continually being devised, redefined, reinvented, and repackaged.

By multiplying the racialized ranks of the chronically unemployed and widening the ever-increasing racialized spaces of persistent poverty, capital engenders conditions that often require so-called "illegal" persons and people within the spaces of illegality to violate U.S. ideals of family, domesticity, and respectability. Limited work options and untimely job losses destabilize gendered domestic duties and disrupt child-rearing responsibilities. As theorist of race and sexuality studies Roderick Ferguson aptly articulates, "Nonwhite populations were racialized such that gender and sexual transgressions were not incidental to the production of nonwhite labor, but constitutive of it."[57] In the racialized spaces of social death, intimate relationships and living arrangements don't often conform to idealized understandings of respectable domesticity.[58] When lives are governed by racialized and gendered exploitation and violence, people must be creative with what they have and what they forego, which includes not only material things but also time, relationships, dreams, and ideals. Capital's ever-increasing drive for profit makes it hard for people to attain and/or maintain the comfortable lifestyles characteristic of the American Dream.

Consider, for instance, women of color who not only work outside the home but also across national borders, who often by necessity live within intimate relations and living arrangements formed outside the sanctity of nuclear families bound by marital law and family rights.[59] Arellano's choice to take sanctuary in order to keep her son in the United States was used to characterize her as a "bad mother." As one reporter wrote: "In the last four months Arellano herself has missed her son's parent-teacher conferences, the opening of Mel Gibson's film 'Apocalypto,' and has gained 10 pounds from being limited to her small apartment above the church."[60] Arellano's inability to go to parent-teacher conferences or take her son to parks often served to portray her as uncaring and opportunistic, and thus to emphasize that her "illegal" status was to be expected and deserved. The perception and production of racialized gender and sexual deviancy inspire new laws and policies that aim to regulate and regularize people of color, such as racial segregation, Americanization programs, and exclusionary immigration acts.[61]

Historically and currently, academic research has participated in blaming the violences of racialized poverty in urban and rural areas on nonnormative family structures, inappropriately gendered employment patterns, and nontraditional child-rearing relationships that emerge in response to and because of racialized exploitation. Anthropologist Oscar Lewis' "Culture of Poverty" thesis, published in the mid-1960s, sought to explain poverty and criminality in Mexican and Puerto Rican communities by reasoning that Mexican and Puerto Rican families not only failed to properly socialize children but also taught them the wrong values and thereby ruined their chances for achieving socioeconomic success. Lewis hypothesized that poor families passed down dysfunctional values inherent in their cultures with the effect of reproducing poverty and criminality over generations. Hence, he saw poverty as created and perpetuated by the relationships between and among family members of Latina/o cultures.[62] To respond to research such as Lewis', activists and academics in the 1960s would politically mobilize the family. As Chicana/o queer studies scholar Richard T. Rodríguez notes, *la*

POC families not acting "properly"

don't have the resources to live like a "Good American"

not always married

not acting like "good mom"

wtf does that matter

not good mom, so deserves deportation

academia part of the problem

pathologized

familia de raza worked to counter "the racist terms in which Mexican and Mexican American communities were pathologically rendered."[63] In other words, when prominent scholars, such as Lewis, pathologized the family of color, this tactic elicited defensive responses that sometimes lead to revaluing practices that, Rodríguez warns, are susceptible to romanticizing and idealizing the private-propertied nuclear family of color.[64] In his rereading of Chicano nationalist politics through queering "la familia," Rodríguez argues that "machismo" did not only refer to male traits but was recast in the service of cultural nationalism during the Chicano Movement to mobilize Chicano activism.[65] Demands for political, social, legal, educational, and economic rights were often, and to this day continue to be, articulated as "family rights."[66]

Like Lewis, Assistant Secretary of Labor Daniel Patrick Moynihan took heteronormativity as an assumed universal value and social good. Adapting and applying Lewis' research to African American families, Moynihan's 1965 report blamed single black mothers for poverty within African American communities. According to the report, too much independence (evidenced by raising children on their own) made black women more likely to be too dependent on state assistance.[67] Moynihan held African American single mothers responsible for emasculating fatherless sons, who then supposedly become unable and unwilling to work productively in legal economies. He recommended that young African American men be remasculated by U.S. institutions such as the military, and he prescribed marriage for their mothers.[68] Research like Lewis' and Moynihan's (from which public policy was created and legitimated) generated an unsettling atmosphere for scholars and activists of color and one that the discipline of ethnic studies has inherited. Critiques of "the family" of color, as a patriarchal or homophobic institution, then and now risk being aligned with conservative politics. As historian Melinda Chateauvert writes, "To problematize 'the Black family,' scholars feared that evidence of sexuality and gender nonconformity would weaken claims of respectability and citizenship."[69] Because racial poverty has been and continues to be attributed to gender and sexual "deviancy," activists and academics are pressured to disavow nonheteronormativity in order to discredit blame-the-victim narratives and recuperate respectability so that social value for pathologized communities of color can be reclaimed.

Hence, respectability operates as a mode of discipline. It is an unachievable prerequisite for the conferral of rights and dignity that functions to align paid and unpaid workers with the regulating institutions and ideologies that keep them economically exploitable and legally vulnerable. As Ferguson argues, "sexuality [is] a mode of racialized governmentality and power."[70] For

an unreadable standard

working poor populations of color, the U.S. economy makes it all but impos-sible (and even impracticable and inadvisable) to assimilate to middle-class ideals of heteronormativity.[71] And yet these groups' claims to rights acquire legitimacy only by conforming to those U.S. heteronormative "morals" and "standards of living" that, ironically, have been defined over and against their very communities and their communities' survival strategies. Because we inherit such limitations when demanding that rights be recognized, many are justifiably wary of media, politics, and scholarship that critique already pathologized working poor families of color for not being more politically progressive. We see this limitation perhaps most clearly when two sympa-thetic but rightless groups, such as unemployed African Americans and un-documented Latinas/os, are positioned and represented as vying for rights, resources, and recognition. Because neither population has been conferred full social membership and political participation in the United States, the emerging debates and discourses regarding citizenship and immigration consistently center on "respectability" as both a shorthand for "deserving-ness" and proof for a population's humanity. This strategy, however, demands the disavowal of all persons of color whose intimate relationships do not conform to U.S. notions of family and domesticity, all those whose bodies and/or behaviors rearrange, rather than reinforce, the meanings and the being of race, sex, and gender. *Only people who "behave" deserve sympathy*

have to meet goals that were made to oppose them in first place

proving your worth as a human being

Respectable Representations

To be represented as entitled to civil rights and deserving of legal recogni-tion, working poor African Americans and undocumented Latinas/os must demonstrate that they are deserving and/or in need of U.S. citizenship and its rights and privileges. For these marginalized groups, connections to hetero-sexual nuclear families are crucial to illustrate respectability and deserving-ness. As scholar of transnational feminism M. Jacqui Alexander argues, "loy-alty to the nation as citizen is perennially colonized within reproduction and heterosexuality."[72] Sexual practices and gendered identities that fall outside accepted and expected norms are interpreted not only as threats to "the fam-ily" but also as evidence of what Alexander calls "irresponsible citizenship."[73] Impoverished African Americans and undocumented Latinas/os need to perform sexual normativity to construct themselves as moral agents deserv-ing of rights, recognition, and resources.

Because the deportation of a father or mother so explicitly infringes on the rights of all family members, reframing immigrant rights as family rights enables supporters to recast U.S. citizen spouses and children as the injured

deportation makes it impossible to have the proper family

parties, de-emphasizing undocumented immigrants' "illegal" status and in-eligibility to rights. As Arellano declared, "It's wrong to split up families. I'm fighting for my son, not for myself."[74] For Arellano, La Familia Latina Unida, and the religious leaders and congregations involved in the New Sanctuary Movement, "family" (as traditionally defined and constituted) followed its own "rule of law." Frank Johnson, a retired pastor, explains simply that "there is a law of love that trumps some laws that exist on the books if there is in-justice. That's why we're doing this."[75] Under the "law of love," the rights of a family to stay together trump the right of the United States to regulate its borders. Reasoning along similar lines, Lutheran Reverend Alexia Salvatierra explained, "We want to make visible these families' status not as faceless bor-der jumpers but as children of God. . . . And when they are ripped apart by raids and deportations, they become the suffering 'strangers within your gates' that the Bible tells us to aid."[76] In other words, giving a face to "faceless border jumpers" challenged not only the "illegal" in "illegal alien" but also challenged the "alien" by making "immigrants visible in a new way, not as criminals, but as children of God, like the rest of us."[77] Although "like the rest of us" is deployed to humanize undocumented immigrants, it does so by rendering the violences of law invisible. The phrase implies that dehu-manization is the unfortunate result of people's prejudicial perceptions; thus, dehumanization appears deceivingly easy to ameliorate as we need merely to make undocumented immigrants "visible in a new way."

In addition to religious values and ethics, family rights can also assemble compelling arguments by drawing upon international law to bypass U.S. law altogether. When supporters cite family rights as human rights, they repre-sent U.S. immigration law as more invested in rules and regulation than jus-tice, more concerned with trivial matters of policy and procedure than with the actual people affected by them. To condemn U.S. deportation policy, the nonprofit organization Human Rights Watch declared, "The right to found a family includes the right to 'live together.'"[78] At the same time, not acknowl-edging the very fine line this strategy walks in appealing to "family values" runs the risk of trivializing the limits and dangers of family rights discourse because it risks intensifying an already naturalized conservative position. If immigrants' countries of origin are not denigrated when "family rights" are rendered absolute and above the law, anti-immigrant activists merely need to point out that a family's unity is not dependent on living in the United States. As columnist for the *Pittsburgh Tribune-Review* Dimitri Vassilaros asked, "is there even one American standing in the way of an alien family leaving intact to return to its country of origin? Deportation threatens unity only when a foreigner would rather be here illegally than back home preserving his family. Many Americans believe in traditional family values. It's too bad more illegals don't."[79] Accusing undocumented parents of poor parenting practices invites—in fact, requires—repudiation, but to do so necessitates that allies and advocates produce evidence of migrants' "traditional family values." These condescending statements impugn migrants' moral fiber, but at the same time they fully and publicly support the core argument that undocumented immigrants' advocates make *against* deportation: that family unity is more important than the law. While immigrants' advocates argue that the law should protect family unity above all else, their adversaries argue that immigrants should prioritize their family's unity over fighting against immigration law. By concealing the forces of transnational capital that fragment families, anti-immigration activists suggest that there is only one morally correct reaction to deportation orders: comply and take the entire family back, regardless of any members' U.S. citizenship status.

The argument aptly illustrates the impossibility for undocumented immigrants to follow "the rule of law" in their country of residence (the United States) because their status, their *presence*, is illegal and therefore always already in violation of the "rule of law." According to this logic, undocumented immigrants can follow U.S. law only if they leave the country, which means they can abide by U.S. law only when it no longer applies to them. In other words, to prove they are law-abiding, undocumented immigrants must reinforce the laws that mark them as always already criminal. This status of impossibility could really be countered only with equally absolute rules and inflexible laws, such as "divine law" to override the "rule of law," or "human rights" to challenge "U.S. citizens' rights." Because undocumented immigrants are often refused recognition as people with the right to demand rights and just treatment, they must frame their demands outside the arbitrary and absolute confines of U.S. law by drawing on different moral rubrics that could confer the right to demand rights such as labor rights, human rights, or the "natural" rights of nuclear families. Little else could be read as directly opposed to U.S. society's "rule of law" than the ethical obligations of international law coupled with the moral authority of a mother's love.

The Disadvantages of U.S. Citizenship

Sympathetic journalists often draw upon family ties to refute explicit and implicit accusations of delinquency, deviancy, or deception.[80] Under U.S. antiterrorist and immigration laws, Arellano and others in her position are legally defined as irrefutably criminal. She is unable to legally challenge the charges and is left only with the ability to evoke a potentially sympathetic public's emotional attachment to motherhood, children, and family. However, this is wholly dependent upon the presumed mutual exclusivity of family and criminality, positioning family as diametrically opposed to criminality (rather than, for instance, law-abiding as opposed to criminality). Arellano's image as mother produces a disturbing, uncomfortable disconnection with her label as a criminal *only* if a sympathetic public equates those other legally vulnerable (and just as problematic) categories of "the criminal" and "the terrorist" with its own racist imaginings of men of color. Arellano's statements—"I am not a criminal. I have nothing to be ashamed of. We are workers, mothers, human beings. We should be able to be proud of who we are,"[81] and "I am a mom and a worker. I am not a terrorist"[82]—can be effective only if "criminal" and "terrorist" are absolutely irreconcilable with mom, worker, and human being. In this way, immigration rights activists unintentionally reify other legally vulnerable, legally constructed categories.

On the other hand, news media often undermine immigrants' demands for rights by recasting men of color from "criminal" and "terrorist" to family men, evoking the same dichotomy that renders family and criminality mutually exclusive. Accordingly, undocumented immigrants, as workers who "steal jobs" or depreciate wages, are scripted as compromising the "natural" rights of U.S. citizen fathers of color to provide for their families. By employing the narrative of racial emasculation in its coverage of the immigrant rights movement, mainstream media have portrayed impoverished U.S. citizen men of color as being in direct competition with undocumented Latina/o immigrants for decent wages and job opportunities in ways that serve to undermine social activism and naturalize capitalist value practices. Juxtaposing immigrant rights against the high unemployment rates of U.S. citizens of color risks romanticizing men of color as the sole and ideal financial provider needed to support families of color. This narrates the desire for decent wages not only as a privilege of citizenship but also as a gendered entitlement, a family necessity, and the young man of color's due inheritance.

Much of the so-called conflict between African Americans and Latinas/os has been articulated through narratives of castration, emasculation, and impotence. For example, the *Christian Science Monitor* reported that "in cities where almost half of the young black men are unemployed, a debate is raging over whether Latinas/os—undocumented and not—are elbowing aside blacks for jobs in stores, restaurants, hotels, manufacturing plants, and elsewhere."[83] In this quotation, Latinas/os are represented as bullying their way to employment, "elbowing aside" young African American men to be the first pick of employers. Not only does this suggest that Latinas/os have a stronger desire to work and are better at utilizing their human capital than

African Americans, it also positions Latinas/os as the contemporary agents of the emasculation of African Americans who are left behind, as one article states, to "watch Hispanics flex their political muscle."[84] Using similar standards of respectability (and its investments in gender and sexual norms), such articles reproach young African American men for not working hard enough and often suggest that they do not have the right values to compete against immigrants successfully.

In ways that are akin to model minority discourse, these narratives discipline unemployed young African American men by applauding hardworking, uncomplaining undocumented Latinas/os for doing whatever it takes to feed their families, which almost always means accepting highly underpaid and insecure wage labor —a precarious situation that is further exacerbated by employers' unspoken yet ever-present threat of deportation. Undocumented immigrants, as Monisha Das Gupta reminds us, "serve a number of critical functions. They not only supply the cheap, exploitable labor that forms the foundation of a service economy but also serve as bodies that the state uses as ideological projects."[85] For example, an April 2006 *Boston Globe* story contrasted Latina/o immigrants, who are construed as responsibly "just feeding their families," with young African American men, who are characterized as socially "deviant," shunning education. The story paraphrases James Banks, an African American store manager in Lynn, Massachusetts, saying he "doesn't blame the immigrants: They're just feeding their families. Banks, 36, says the fault lies with a generation of young African-American men who would rather 'walk their sneakers up and down the street' then step up on a stage to collect high school diplomas."[86] Located on "the street" as opposed to in a home, workplace, church, or school, these young men are portrayed as disconnected from familial stability and disinterested in decent work. Unlike hard-working immigrants, the article implies, young African Americans are not as committed to family and community. As such, they not only will not participate in the reproduction, development, or progress of African America but will themselves allow immigration to effectively castrate an entire generation. As Banks said, "'Immigration is going to set the black community back 25 years, because they'll let it.'"[87] One of many that chastises the black poor for not being as self-sacrificing as undocumented Latinas/os, this article is a typical example of the ways in which the news media blame the high rates of black unemployment on (the perception of) African Americans' personal problems or character flaws rather than on the structural conditions that make both groups hyperexploitable.

Supporting neoliberal ideologies, these stories erase the workings of global capital by exaggerating the importance of personal qualities such as ambition and motivation. In this narrative, Latina/o immigrants function as the "model minority" of the working poor, putting family first, working hard, and doing whatever it takes to get ahead, while impoverished African American young men are depicted as wayward, unmotivated drifters waiting for the U.S. government to solve their problems or refusing to take advantage of the many opportunities available to them.[88] Like the Asian American model minority myth, the compelling story of hardworking, disenfranchised, uncomplaining Latinas/os disciplines their supposedly more "privileged" citizen of color counterparts. To put this another way, "model minorities" can be conceived of as populations whose legal vulnerability makes them exploitable as well as ensures that they cannot complain.[89] Asian American studies scholar Victor Bascara explains that the model minority narrative functions in American culture to mobilize racial/ethnic difference in the service of U.S. imperialism, where "members of that minority are a testament to the success of the incorporative capacities of the United States, politically, economically, and culturally."[90] When such "model minorities" are juxtaposed against un(der)employed young African American men, U.S. citizenship rights appear to be both an already achieved goal and an underutilized asset of African Americans' human capital, at the same time that the fact that poor African Americans are politically disenfranchised and legally vulnerable too is dismissed.

The news narrative of black-Latina/o conflict, however, explains employer preference for undocumented workers as the result of racial bias and cultural stereotypes, which we can see when stories use language such as "there is a hidden code that black people are lazy" or "immigrants have a reputation for working harder, which gives them a leg up."[91] When black and Latina/o informants are interviewed to make these claims, news stories give the impression that Latinas/os perpetuate anti-black racism and vice versa.

> Some Hispanics say African-Americans treat them with hostility and disparage them with slurs, even though blacks know the sting of racism all too well. They say many blacks are jealous of their progress and resent the fact that whites, who dominate the business sector, look increasingly to Hispanics to fill work forces. Blacks say employers favor immigrants because they work for less money.[92]

As in this example, the black-Latina/o conflict narrative often trivializes or omits the role of employers altogether and instead places the blame on both groups by representing blacks and Latinas/os as perpetuating stereotypes about each other.

Yet when these dynamics are acknowledged as socially constructed and politically unproductive, the news media oversimplify interracial coalition-building, offering only facile analyses and commonsense explanations such as having a "common ground" or "similar struggles."[93] In actuality, the struggles of the black and Latina/o working poor are interdependent and linked, but they are neither common nor similar. This is important to underscore because the current arrangement of global capital and neoliberal states use the racial, class, and immigration status hierarchies of the United States in ways that can sometimes make employment for black and Latina/o communities seem inversely proportionate, which gives the false impression that increasing political power for immigrants would decrease the political power of African Americans.

[handwritten margin notes: not the same, but connected; think that only one group can succeed]

Caught within such capitalist logics, African Americans' entitlement to employment and related resources is depicted as a finite quantity, being depleted by Latina/o competition. The following example from *Newsday* makes it seem as though immigrants' demands for rights hurt African Americans' chances for decent jobs and living wages.

As Congress debates immigration reform mostly without strong input from black leaders, many African-Americans worry that competition from low-wage immigrants is making it harder for economically-disadvantaged black Americans to find work.

A generation ago, area residents with little education could rely on unskilled jobs to earn a living—unloading trucks, washing dishes, mopping floors or painting houses.

Now, those without high school diplomas are facing stiff competition for low-skilled jobs from undocumented workers, which helps fuel the immigration debate.[94]

By conflating support for undocumented Latinas/os with disregard for African American citizens, journalists not-so-subtly suggest that anti-Latina/o nativism is an inevitable by-product of compassion for African American citizens. When reporters framed the immigrant rights movement in terms of black unemployment and underemployment, they not only overexaggerated Latina/o immigrants' successes but also downplayed the "struggle" in social justice struggles. By emphasizing that groups receive rights from the government (rather than demand them), journalists equate rights with government handouts for which people wait in line. In this analogy, Latinas/os seem to be cutting in line for the right to work. This kind of coverage also racializes underpaid service economy jobs as black, normalizing unskilled, low-wage

[handwritten margin notes: only one group can have sympathy; make rights seem like a privilege that have to wait for]

work as a property of African Americans, even as a "privilege" that citizenship fails to protect.

When journalists represent undocumented waged workers as "privileged" by representing state abandonment as "worse than," rather than integral to, capital exploitation, they naturalize and even unwittingly advocate for gendered, intranational, and international wage differentials that are necessary for competing capitals to accumulate surplus value.[95] The U.S.-Mexico border is central to maintaining poverty on both sides. International wage differentials would not be profitable for competing capitals if all workers were able to cross national borders freely. To ensure international wage differentials, the border functions politically to regulate different populations' mobility between and within nations. As political philosopher Massimiliano Tomba explains,

> Sovereignty, rights of citizenship and control of the borders operate economically in order to delineate different wage areas that can be preserved only by reducing to a minimum the movements of labour power from one area to the other. The chains of valorisation cross a multiplicity of wage areas, national and intranational, using those differentials profitably.[96]

By "violating the borders," Tomba writes, the migrant worker "tends to disrupt the division of labour and national differentials of wages."[97] Both legal and undocumented immigrants of color can potentially benefit from the wage differential maintained between their countries of origin and the United States because just as capital pays less for the same job in different countries, workers can presumably earn more for the same amount of work in the United States. By keeping nonnormative relationships and living arrangements, transnational workers spend less on the costs of social reproduction to maximize the value of their labor power, increasing how much they can send home to the families many had to leave behind in their countries of origin.

When we assume that the United States is always the destination for immigration and never the origin of emigration, we run the risk of obscuring how forced immobility is just as necessary as coerced emigration to maintain capital profitability. Poor African Americans are not just disadvantaged in the U.S. economy. They are also disadvantaged within the global job market. As scholar-activist Clarence Lusane asserts,

In this era, job competition takes place on a global scale. Governments around the world, including the United States, have made it clear that they no longer have full employment as a goal. U.S. workers are not only competing with their next door neighbor for that potential new job, but with 700 million people around the world who are unemployed and beholden to the vicissitudes of capital.[98]

The vast majority of inner-city African Americans can compete for that potential new job only if it is located in the United States (exacerbated by the fact that the United States is one of the few nations where the ability to speak other languages is stigmatized).[99] Unlike immigrants of color, if the poorest African Americans were to migrate, they would not profit from the international wage differentials that competing capitals maintain between nations. Put another way, if African Americans were to work unskilled jobs in Mexico and send wages back to their families in the United States, they would likely aggravate rather than alleviate their families' impoverished conditions.[100] Nonemployed and unemployed African Americans are unable to benefit economically from international wage differentials in part because they are essentially denied the right to migrate; they are denied the rights of socioeconomic and spatial mobility,[101] and, thus, like undocumented immigrants, denied "the right to subsist."

[handwritten margin notes: "Would be going from high → low wage area" and "—would be making even less, no incentive to migrate"]

[handwritten: "No upward mobility"]

Civil Rights for Citizens Only

The misrepresentation of African Americans and Latinas/os as constantly and inevitably in conflict provided the explanatory framework for news stories that debated whether the immigrant rights movement could be likened to the civil rights movement. This comparison was narrated through and organized by analogics, a narrative, which Miranda Joseph argues, "presupposes . . . the autonomy" of each group, "thus erasing the prior history and current dynamics" that have formed each community in relation to each other."[102] Analogics work to frame these groups and these historical moments as discrete and disconnected, and in doing so, they "work in concert with binary oppositions."[103]

[handwritten margin note: "not looking at the broader context"]

Disassociating the immigrant rights movement from the civil rights movement was a rhetorical tactic used to criminalize undocumented immigrants and to represent the movement itself as not a "true" rights movement. To establish this disassociation, many reporters and writers portrayed the U.S. history of civil rights as African Americans' private intellectual property. Mitchell, for instance, argued that Arellano's "blatant exploitation of Parks' legacy undermine[d] the fragile coalition between some blacks and Hispanics that has formed around the immigration issue."[104] Framing the immigration

[handwritten margin note: "exclusive to them"]

debate over the use of "civil rights" frames the black-Latina/o relationship as one of debt and ingratitude, as more about respect than about rights.

Positioning African Americans as the gatekeepers of civil rights history, the media discredited and trivialized the immigrant rights movement by representing civil rights as rights that African Americans had to pay for (with their bodies and their lives) and had to earn (through civil rights protests). Often these sentiments were expressed bitterly; as Mitchell articulated, "instead of thanking blacks for paving the way, other groups have walked across black backs without so much as a 'thank you for your sacrifices.' . . . The benefits that so many other groups—women included—now enjoy were purchased with black blood, sweat and tears."[105]

Following this logic, the news media suggested that to protect the civil rights of African Americans, the federal government must legislate and enforce discrimination against Latina/o immigrants unauthorized to work in the United States. Ronald Walters, director of the African-American Leadership Institute at the University of Maryland, expressed this concern in a *Newsday* story.

> "I don't think the African-American leadership wants to buy into criticism of immigrant workers. . . . Because if you point to the fact that there is low-wage competition, you run the risk of getting into bed with people who are criticizing the immigrants rather than criticizing the system that is bringing them in."[106]

As Walters's apprehension suggests, reading immigrant rights, labor rights, or civil rights as simply racial issues not only encourages anti-immigrant nativism but also misrepresents African Americans as the source of anti-Latina/o resentments.

Beyond Rights as Properties of Personhood

When people are presumed entitled to protection, rights are naturalized as properties of personhood. But for populations ineligible for personhood, those same "inalienable" rights can be called into question or even outright denied, thereby compelling people to prove they are indeed deserving. In his work on the social psychology of justice, scholar Norman T. Feather suggests that we consider the subtle distinctions between "entitlement" and "deservingness" to explain why only some demands for justice seem subject to evaluation. Entitlement, he writes, is grounded within a group's "socially recognized rights."[107] Deservingness, on the other hand, "pertains to the *evaluative* structure of actions and their outcomes."[108] In other words, deservingness and entitlement have different frames of reference, which determine how legitimacy and credibility are assigned. Thus, when a group's rights are presumed to be entitlements, discussions about injustice can focus on whether people's rights have been respected. But when a group's rights are not socially recognized, discussions revolve around whether or not the aggrieved group even deserves to speak out against discrimination or exploitation, which effectively subverts or forecloses any dialogue about the actual injustices. Such debates concentrate on the deservingness of the population itself, as well as on whether or not the injured group should be allowed to voice grievances against unjust treatment. In so doing, they avoid discussing appropriate remedies or penalties to address the injustices. As a result, the fact that certain institutions and individuals have assumed they have the power to discriminate or exploit disempowered others is rarely called into question or up for debate.

Feather's analytical distinction between deservingness and entitlement is useful for thinking about why some groups' rights are automatically recognized while others have to demonstrate they deserve them. At the same, though, this distinction needs to be slightly nuanced to account for the ways in which the entitlement to rights in the United States has been racialized as white and legally protected as such.[109] Ironically, calling upon African Americans to claim ownership of "civil rights" (both the term and the history) requires African Americans to emphasize that their entitlement to rights was earned. Therefore, black entitlement to rights is essentially renarrated or re-presented as premised upon deservingness, rather than taken for granted like white entitlement to rights and personhood. In the following example, the *New York Times* constructed African Americans' rights not as "socially recognized rights" but as rights that were earned through mass suffering and social protest.

> But despite some sympathy for the nation's illegal immigrants, many black professionals, academics and blue-collar workers feel increasingly uneasy as they watch Hispanics flex their political muscle while assuming the mantle of a seminal black struggle for justice.
>
> Some blacks bristle at the comparison between the civil rights movement and the immigrant demonstrations, pointing out that black protesters in the 1960s were American citizens and had endured centuries of enslavement, rapes, lynchings and discrimination before they started marching.
>
> Others worry about the plight of low-skilled black workers, who sometimes compete with immigrants for entry-level jobs.

And some fear the unfinished business of the civil rights movement will fall to the wayside as America turns its attention to a newly energized Hispanic minority with growing political and economic clout.[110]

Because the journalist's informants are expected to recount civil rights history in relation to immigrants' demonstrations, they are already positioned to remember and rehearse black entitlement to rights as deserved because it was earned.[111]

only citizens have rights

Representing rights as a property of U.S. citizenship, even when those rights are denied, functions to construct the struggle for political inclusion as a right of citizenship rather than as a response to its denial. When the right to demand rights is imagined as an attribute or a property of U.S. citizenship, it emphasizes the "law" and "legal recognition" as the appropriate means for achieving social justice. This positions the state as the guarantor and administrator of justice even though it is the state that engendered the conditions conducive to violence and exploitation in the first place by either denying or refusing to recognize marginalized groups' rights to personhood. Moreover, the legal recognition of a population's personhood is thereby cast as the end point of struggle, whereas an aggrieved group's humanity is the *premise* of resistance, not its goal.

migrants don't even have the right to demand rights

giving back what they stole to begin w/

eg low bar

Furthermore, when U.S. citizenship is assumed to be a prerequisite for civil rights, African American activisms are detached from their *own* histories as part of the 1950s–1970s *global struggle for personhood*, decolonization, and sovereignty. As ethnic studies and queer studies scholar Chandan Reddy elaborates, the move to represent civil rights as only for citizens' is

wasn't isolated; were fighting for global freedom

> a current neoconservative ideology that exclusively highlights legal redress in order to efface rhetorically the *worldliness* of the civil rights movement, turning that movement into an *American* exceptionalist drama of the nation's repeated betrayal of black equality. In this latter ideology and rhetorical argument, that betrayal typically has been manifested and imagined as a contest between "immigrants" and "African Americans" for social mobility in civil society.[112]

As Reddy notes, locating civil rights history as part of the American exceptionalist drama scripts both that particular historical moment (1950s–1970s) and our own (in the early decades of the twenty-first century) as related incidents of state betrayal. The failure to confer civil rights and the threat to grant immigrant rights are both represented as evidence for the state's failure to protect its African American citizens, which undercuts competing interpretations of social movement history that see civil rights and immigrant rights as allied struggles.

If we recognize that the United States was not the only site of social justice struggles and that legal recognition was not the only goal of the 1960s rights movements, we can set aside the notion that rights are contingent (with citizenship as the prerequisite) and conditional (with deservingness as the proviso). Throughout the 1950s, 1960s, and 1970s, movement leaders both inspired and were inspired by the movements for social justice and national independence worldwide. In fact, juxtaposing the immigrant rights movement with other forms and fronts of black social activism in the 1960s could avoid framing the contemporary moment in racial and relational terms as "us or them" or in Mitchell's terms of "debt" and "disrespect."

For instance, the Revolutionary Action Movement (RAM), formed in 1962, developed a theory of "revolutionary Black internationalism," which, according to culture and labor historian Robin D. G. Kelley, "argued that the battle between Western imperialism and the Third World—more so than the battle between labor and capital—represented the most fundamental contradiction" of that era.[113] RAM articulated the urban uprisings in the United States as part of "an international rebellion against imperialism."[114] This global perspective did not replace black nationalism; it deployed black nationalism differently. As Kelley puts it, the members of RAM were "internationalists before they were nationalists."[115]

By placing a critique of neocolonialism and imperialism at the center of their theory, RAM militants never agonized over whether to support reactionary black regimes in Africa or the Caribbean. They flatly rejected unconditional racial unity and developed a nationalism built on a broader concept of revolutionary Third World solidarity.[116]

If we read the contemporary immigrant rights movement as part of the still-ongoing international rebellion against imperialism, rather than as an emergent movement solely against U.S. immigration and deportation law, we can explain the ways in which the contemporary struggles of both groups in the United States are linked not only to one another but also beyond the U.S.-Mexico border. The Oaxacan struggles over the right to stay home, or "el derecho de no migrar," are connected to undocumented immigrants' struggles for rights in the United States, and both, in turn, are linked to the struggles of working poor African Americans for whom the futility of international migration ensures persistent poverty. All these racialized populations are rendered essentially rightless and ineligible for personhood —they all must struggle for the right to subsist.

Unthinkable?

Defining subjugation as the state's refusal to protect rights already recognized by law supports and sanctions the state's monopoly on violence. As Dylan Rodríguez explained for us earlier in the chapter, the state acquires legitimacy and authority through sanctioning violence and formalizing disempowerment. This makes the state an ineffective and ill-chosen ally in the fight for human rights. As a result, "human rights" loses its potential for mobilizing populations to demand structural changes. As state-enforced and administered, human rights cannot adequately address injustice. This is because, Randall Williams argues, the concept of human rights has been limited to law, which means it "can be posed only within the question of the improper/proper application of law."[117] Complying with the "rule of law" will always legitimate the state's authority to create and enforce law; doing so, however, will not ensure that justice, empowerment, or equality will be the result.

Moreover, we also expect less of struggle, especially political struggle, if a movement's legitimacy hinges on its constituents' deservingness as rights-bearing, law-abiding subjects because this focus pressures community leaders and committed activists to concentrate their efforts on lobbying the state to enforce its unfulfilled promises of privilege and protection. For this reason, it would be productive to follow the example of RAM activists to search beyond U.S. law and U.S. borders for alternatives to racialized "rights-based" and U.S.-centric struggles. Inspirational, though not perfect, movements have arisen worldwide in response to neoliberal reforms, and they often originate from spaces criminalized by the United States. For instance, in cyber-space, the hacker group known as "Anonymous" uncovers evidence of the abuse of corporate and state power. More of a global collective than an identifiable group of individuals, Anonymous uses the Internet to publish corporate crime as well as corporate and state officials' efforts around the world to impede social activism through censorship. In Argentina, workers displaced by privatization, structural adjustment, and capital flight took control of abandoned factories and created worker-run cooperatives.[118] Under Hugo Chávez, Venezuela threw out its constitution and created a new one. These actions are unthinkable in the United States because they are largely

[handwritten: can't radically change the status quo w/ out being seen w criminal?]

criminalized and to some degree even categorized as "terrorist" or akin to treason. Furthermore, confronting the state is not without consequences. For instance, RAM's incisive protests resulted not only in their being named one of the lead "extremist groups" but also in their members being targeted by Counter Intelligence Programs (COINTELPRO).[119] Targeted members' homes were raided, and they were framed for allegedly planning to commit crimes. The unthinkability of direct confrontation with the state also hindered RAM's ability to build a solid community base.

This does not mean that contemporary rights-based movements in United States are devoid of hope and potential. Oftentimes activists have to negotiate uncomfortable contradictions inherent to struggles over rights and recognition, but these contradictions are not always evident when buried beneath media master scripts of racial conflict and competition. For instance, when the black-Latina/o master narrative is imposed on representations of contemporary social movements, not only are the international tenets of African American social activism in the 1950s–1970s erased, so, too, is the work of young undocumented adults. The focus on family rights and civil rights draws attention to Arellano and Mitchell, and because the black-Latina/o divide is often spoken about and naturalized in terms of uneducated citizens competing with undocumented immigrants for low-wage, unskilled work, people who don't fit these identity and status categories are largely left out. U.S. immigration policy has also created a U.S.-educated and socially (but not economically or politically) integrated undocumented population for whom legal status is not as easily connected to nationality as most coverage of immigrant rights demonstrations lead us to believe. Each year that the Development, Relief, and Education for Minors Act (known as the DREAM Act) fails to get through Congress, the promise of citizenship is foreclosed to countless young adults, producing a highly educated population of people we might consider "undocumented Americans." These youth and young adults are relegated to the realms of social death, perhaps permanently so. Social relations influenced by race and legal status expressed themselves differently for young DREAM activists, whose countries of origin can be traced to Latin America, Asia, the Caribbean, the Middle East, and Africa. Young undocumented activists have been organizing protests around the nation for years. When engaged in acts of civil disobedience, these activists publicly disclose their undocumented status, unsettling witnesses' perceptions and prejudices of undocumented immigrants.

Like RAM members in the 1960s, today's young undocumented activists who engage in unthinkable politics are all too aware that there is much at stake in daring to critique the state. The state targets their families for deportation when their voices become too loud, their criticisms too astute, their whispers too influential. What these youth have learned is that unthinkability is not merely synonymous with impracticality but that state violence, whether enacted or inherited, makes certain ways of knowing and methods for mobilizing unthinkable. Upon voicing the injustices undocumented people must live with in the United States, many young activists find themselves and/or their family members in deportation proceedings. These young adults are not reckless; rather, they risk so much because they realize that there are few alternatives if they want meaningful change.

One statement, which circulated briefly and locally in 2011 during the Georgia 7 sit-in, explained why these young activists do what for many would be unthinkable.[120] In this sit-in, seven undocumented high school and college activists from around the country went to Georgia to protest the state's new anti-undocumented immigrant act, which denied undocumented students admission to the top public colleges in Georgia. These activists, like others around the nation, knowingly and willingly risked deportation to make these issues public. Connecting their actions not to civil rights struggles per se but to a history of activism that demanded and desired more than political incorporation and national belonging, the activists saw themselves not as drawing upon but as continuing the legacy of those who dared to demand not only a new world but a new way of perceiving and interacting with the world.

> We recognize that throughout history the only time things have changed is when those affected have stood up and put themselves at risk. I am doing this action to stand up and say I am no longer afraid of being undocumented.
>
> We are here putting our futures at risk to ask if you will make a choice to stand with us? We are making a choice to stand up for our communities and we will not back down until they are no longer suffering. Laws that do nothing but damage our communities are wrong. As undocumented youth we will not tolerate the most vulnerable in our communities being attacked. It is our responsibility to protect them.[121]

Although these national actions have occurred in response to the increasing attacks on undocumented youths' access to higher education, the statement reflects the activists' commitment to much more than education and political incorporation. In fact, despite being racialized and rightless, these undocumented youth activists still see themselves as empowered agents of social change who have a responsibility to protect "the most vulnerabl[e] [their] communities," including those for whom the DREAM act can[not] even be a dream.

Decentering the state as sole authority over legitimate power and recognized personhood requires being willing to be critical of what makes us vulnerable to state violences *and* what makes us susceptible to the state's seductions, what makes most avenues for social change not only unthinkable but criminal. For most, this is the assurance that when democracy prevails, political membership ensues, but in the spaces of social death, the state makes no attempt to offer such promises. Without the expectation of rights and recognition, we start from the reality of social death rather than the promise of a better life. As I demonstrated in this chapter, the space of social death is not a location of pure politics free from racism and heteropatriarchy. On the contrary, the space of social death is a desperate space, overwrought with and overdetermined by the ideological contradictions of ineligible personhood. The alternative actions, politics, and ways of knowing that emerge from or are inspired by social death are not without fault. They do, however, have a different relationship to fear and failure because they have a different relationship to rights and personhood.

As Derrick Bell argues, a racial realist approach realizes that victory is not connected to winning but to struggling despite guaranteed failure. When ~~shouldn't think they'll / fail~~ guaranteed failure is the predicted result of struggle, an aggrieved group's allies and adversaries will seem to want the same course of action —to put the struggle on hold, to wait, to give up. In the spaces of social death, any and every option is unthinkable, not because of impracticality or the U.S. public's reluctance to change but because of the threat and promise of state violence. We are disciplined to not think the unthinkable when we learn about the risk of incarceration or deportation or when our families are held hostage. ~~hopeful~~ And yet the space of social death is always graced with hope, courage, and/ or youthful idealism, where those who decide to take responsibility for the unprotected are always looking for and stepping on the pressure points that can barely manage the contradictions that their very presence, their very being inspires.

Conclusion

Racialized Hauntings of the Devalued Dead

This story is about a road that never ends. It begins with a car crash.
—Rubén Martínez, performance, April 22, 2000

Wreck in the Road

On March 24, 2000, my cousin Brandon Jesse Martinez died in a car accident in San Diego, California.[1] He was nineteen. When Brandon was alive, he frustrated teachers, counselors, employers, and even his friends and family. He took drugs sometimes, drank sometimes, and sometimes slept all day. He liked low-rider car culture and Tupac Shakur. He was quick witted and too clever, thoughtful and impulsive, well intentioned as well as reckless. His teachers thought he was "lazy" and a "troublemaker"; he proved them right by never graduating from high school. He lied on job applications and didn't pay his bills on time. He believed that one day he would go to prison even though he never planned to commit a criminal offense. He didn't donate his free time to religious or social activism. Instead, he smoked a lot, drank a lot, and joked a lot. These were the memories Brandon left me, his parents, his sister, and the others who loved him. They made it hard to share stories about him that didn't also characterize him as a "bad kid," a "deviant subject," or an "unproductive citizen."

Our conflicting memories and feelings about Brandon's "deviance" evoked deeply felt tensions at the memorial service and the gatherings afterward as we struggled but failed to ascribe value to Brandon's life and life choices. We were nostalgic for the days of his childhood, and we were very upset over losing his future and the person that he would never become. Our most recent memories—his teenage and young adult years—were shared in fragments with obvious omissions. For some of us, his death became the pretext for teaching moral lessons. Don't drink and drive. Go to school. Listen to your parents. Pray. These lessons attributed meaning and purpose to Brandon's death. His death could be instructive for his friends and cousins because for those he left behind "it was not too late." But these lessons also taught us to devalue his life because they were dependent upon understanding Brandon as an example never to emulate or imitate. His life was narrated as important because he provided us with a constructive model to evaluate, judge, and reject. The first line of a poem written by his sister Trisha Martinez echoed loudly, persistently, and honestly in the space of his haunting: "You just don't know how much he meant."[2] In many ways, we didn't because we didn't know how to valorize the choices we warned him not to make or how to value the life we told him not to live. How could we explain to others and ourselves "how much he meant" when his most legible asset was his death?

We couldn't translate his value into language. We couldn't talk about Brandon as valuable not only because he was marked as "deviant," "illegal," and "criminal" by his race and ethnicity but also because he did not perform masculinity in proper, respectable ways to redeem, reform, or counter his (racialized) "deviancy." Even if we had attempted to circumvent the devaluing processes of race and gender by citing other readily recognizable signs and signifiers of value, such as legality, heteronormativity, American citizenship, higher education, affluence, morality, or respectability, we still would not have had evidence to portray him as a productive, worthy, and responsible citizen. Ascribing (readily recognizable) value to the racially devalued *requires* recuperating what registers as "deviant" and "disreputable" in order to reinterpret those devalued beliefs, behaviors, and bodies as misrecognized versions of normativity. Value is ascribed through explicitly or implicitly disavowing relationships to the already devalued and disciplined categories of deviance and nonnormativity.

As Lindon Barrett reminds us, the "object" of value needs an "other" of value as its "negative resource."[3] The act of ascribing legible, intelligible, and normative value is inherently violent and relationally devaluing. To represent Brandon as the "object" of value, we would need to represent ourselves as the devalued "other." On some level, the *violence* of Brandon's death was perversely and disconcertingly a source of value for us because it valorized the life choices that each of us made but he did not. It naturalized how and why he died while simultaneously reaffirming our social worth and societal value. His violent death validated the rightness of our choices and the righteousness of our behaviors, thereby illustrating Barrett's insight that "relativities of value [are] ratios of violence."[4]

Examining how "value" and its normative criteria are naturalized and universalized enables us to uncover and unsettle the heteropatriarchal, legal, and neoliberal investments that dominant and oppositional discourses share in rendering the value of nonnormativity illegible. We could not disentangle the various intersecting, differential, contingent, and relational processes of valuation and devaluation. The choices we made to become valuable members of society validated U.S. society's exclusionary methods for assigning social value. These methods also assign not-value, fixing the other's devaluation, necessitating the violent invalidation of Brandon and his life decisions. Although he was disciplined by many of us many times, we never disowned, abandoned, or rejected him. His absence left us raw and uncertain because the ready-made reasons for his death were hurtful and heartbreaking rather than healing. Hence, the empty space he left behind in each of us *necessarily destabilized* the binaries and hierarchies of value that formed the foundations for each of our lives. Brandon was profoundly valued, but we could not tell you why. Still empty, the space of his absence holds ruptural possibilities, where we must reckon with what has always been unthinkable.[5]

Drinking Suspected

When Brandon died in a car crash with his two friends, Vanvilay Khounborinh and William Christopher Jones, news media coverage of their accident criminalized them and the racial masculinities that they each embodied. They became part of the pre-existing news narrative that devalued their lives when they were alive. As Isabel Molina-Guzmán reminds us, "news media draw upon routine professional practices and socially available and widely circulated narratives to tell their stories . . . stories that perform beyond the function of information."[6] To apprehend how such widely circulated narratives about criminalized men of color function beyond disseminating information, it is productive to also examine the inundation of stories about white men and women in positions of power. Ruby C. Tapia argues that such news stories are never inconsequential because the media not only honor the memory of public figures but also "pass on" social values, "immortaliz[ing] ideologies of patriarchal capitalism and White supremacy."[7] Tapia encourages us to read the erasure of "non-spectacularized lives" in relation to or against "hypervisible *whiteness*, along with its haunting figures and social consequences."[8] These representations aid in constructing the "norms of gender, sexuality, and domestic space" that Nayan Shah contends are necessary to prove one's "worthiness" of political rights and social resources.[9] This means that these stories also form and inform the representational and narrative violences that make discipline and punishment of the racialized unreformed seem natural and necessary.

For these reasons, the print media's erasure of the nonspectacular lives and devalued deaths of Brandon, Vanvilay, and William Christopher might best be understood through a comparison with the haunting figures and social consequences of white masculinity. By juxtaposing the *San Diego Union-Tribune's* representations of Brandon's accident with those of the fatal accident of San Diego Padres outfielder Michael Darr, we learn that the "facts" of people's behaviors have little significance for determining whose deaths are tragic and whose deaths are deserved. The detailed descriptions of these drunk-driving accidents provide us the short-cut ideological codes used for deciding which human lives are valuable and which ones are worthless. In effect, the articles about Michael Darr evoke public sympathy by representing his embodiment of heterosexual, white masculinity as socially valuable and by depicting his friends' and family's grief as a universal experience. In contrast, the article about Brandon, Vanvilay, and William Christopher activates racial anxieties over criminalized youth and young men of color.

On March 25, 2000, the *San Diego Union-Tribune* printed an article about Brandon's car accident entitled, "Three Men Killed When Speeding Car Hits Trees; a Fourth Walks Away," with the subtitle, "Drinking Suspected; Auto Was Traveling without Headlights."[10] Joe Hughes, who often reports on local crimes and drunk-driving accidents for the *San Diego Union-Tribune*, described Vanvilay's driving as reckless and irresponsible joyriding and reported that witnesses corroborated police officers' suspicions that the car was "speeding and may have been racing other cars."[11] Vanvilay was driving Brandon's 1984 Mustang, which was not a racing car and, in fact, was not even a car that ran very well. (In San Diego, "racing" alludes to a racialized car culture predominately practiced by young Asian men in high school.[12])

It did not seem to matter to police, witnesses, or the reporter whether or not the examiner's report would reveal alcohol in Vanvilay's blood; even if he was not legally intoxicated, he was definitively represented as driving reck-lessly and (if not, then as if) drunk. The accident was framed as inevitable and deserved through construing their "illegal" behaviors (underage drink-ing and driving) as a daily pattern, connoting both immorality and criminal-ity. As Hughes reported, "In addition [to detectives learning that the four had been drinking that evening], alcoholic containers and mixing beverages were found in the car's mangled remains."[13]

In contrast, even after it was confirmed that Michael Darr's blood-alcohol level was ".03 above the legal limit [of .08]," the Highway Patrol officer on duty still doubted that Darr's accident was the result of drunk-driving. The officer said: "Did alcohol play a role? . . . It may have. We described the cause as inattention. He was driving in the flow of traffic. He was not speeding. He was not weaving."[14] Despite the facts that Darr was intoxicated and not wear-ing a seat belt, he was still portrayed as a good driver on the night of his fatal accident ("not speeding" and "not weaving"). The same *Union-Tribune* story quoted Padres second baseman Damian Jackson, who tried to distance the drunk driver from drunk-driving.

> "I can't justify the amount of beer that he had," Jackson said. "But I believe that alcohol was not a factor.
>
> "Mike had the tendency to pay attention to other things while he was driving, just like myself. He'd be changing a radio station, or putting CDs in while driving. Carelessness like that I think had something to do with getting off track and trying to overcompensate."[15]

Even though Darr had been drinking and driving, the cause of his death was attributed neither to intoxication nor to reckless driving but rather to "inattention," "carelessness," or "trying to overcompensate."

Sports writers, not local crime reporters, covered Darr's accident, which is important because sport has become a crucial site for securing "the cen-tral and dominant cultural position of White masculinity."[16] Because white men are no longer perceived as athletically dominant, Kyle W. Kusz contends that sport "enables the fabrication of a crisis narrative about the precarious and vulnerable cultural position of White males."[17] As "America's national pastime," baseball in particular has been "associated with whiteness in the West."[18] Darr's death, thus, was also empathically representative of the "tragic" position of white men in contemporary U.S. society.[19]

When alive, Darr received little media attention because he was only a fourth outfielder, but in death Darr was transformed into a would-have-been-great ballplayer.

Darr, 25, was the Padres' minor league Player of the Year in 1997 and again in 2000, when he shared the award with Jeremy Owens. He ran faster than the average ballplayer, threw farther and harder than the average outfielder and as a minor leaguer posted on-base and batting averages well above the norm.[20] In death, Darr can be *idealized*. The various news articles about Darr's life and death drew upon testimonies by his trainer, manager, and colleagues (not his wife or family), who idealized him as well as the population he represented. As Dana Nelson has argued, "national manhood" as an imagined white fraternity works effectively with "absent or dead men."[21] As a relatively young white athlete, Darr symbolized (an innocent) white male victimization; his death activated these anxieties while his professional, fraternal relationships told the *shared* story of loss. As one *Union-Tribune* story reported, "[Manager Bruce] Bochy said he told the players: 'Let's make every day count, with our family, our friends and what we do on the field. Do it for Mike's sake. . . . We all should count our blessings. Every one of us. Really, it could have been any one of us.'"[22] In other words, Darr's death not only mobilized national manhood ("Do it for Mike's sake"), it also mobilized an imagined white fraternity[23] over and against the absent bodies of women and the abject bodies of racialized others such as Brandon, Vanvilay, and William Christopher.

This is most evident when we compare how the two accidents were represented to *Union-Tribune* readers. While sports writer Tom Krasovic often quoted the Padres, all of whom continually invoked fraternal belonging ("Every one of us. Really, it could have been any one of us"), sports writer Nick Canepa directly facilitated public identification with the Padres so readers could figuratively experience Darr's death as a member of the Padres fraternity.

> What can you say?
> You get the call early in the morning, just before heading over to the Padres complex to examine the rites of spring. It is a terrible, terrible thing. Darr was married (Natalie) and was the father of two sons.
> What can you say?
> You can say nothing. You can say you're sorry. It never seems as if it's enough. Because it isn't enough.[24]

The articles that reported on the Padres' reactions to losing Darr tell us that losing a loved one is a universal experience—"a terrible, terrible thing" that happens to "every one of us."[25] But this "universal" experience is not invoked in the article about Brandon.

In Hughes' article, not only are first- and second-person pronouns and referents ("we," "you," "every one," "our," and "us") never used, but the terms employed to refer to Brandon and his friends detach them from their *own* personal connections to communities, friends, and families as if they were already merely another statistic. With language such as "the four had been drinking," "three men died," and a "fourth occupant walked," the article does not encourage readers to empathize with the car-crash victims nor with those who survived them.

On the other hand, people of all colors and genders are encouraged, if not expected, to identify with Darr's family and empathize with his fraternity. We can all relate to losing a loved one, but the "universal" experience of sudden loss and unexpected death is represented through a particular and specific dead body—a body reconstructed and idealized to mobilize the interests and investments of an imagined white fraternity to secure its cultural, political, social, and economic dominance.[26] Perhaps the most illustrative example of the (particular) Padres fraternity as representative of the (universal) American nation was when manager Bruce Bochy associated the tragedy of Darr's death to the tragedies of September 11, 2001, by saying "I think we experienced as a club something akin to what the nation felt after 9-11."[27]

The social value of particular lives and specific deaths such as Michael Darr's continue to be "immortalized" through familial relations as well. When the Padres played their last game at Qualcomm Stadium on September 28, 2003, players Phil Nevin and Gary Matthews Jr. took turns carrying Mike Darr Jr. onto the field with the theme song from the movie *Field of Dreams* playing in the background. Fittingly, *Field of Dreams* is a movie about the living ghosts of fathers and baseball players—hence, a movie not so subtly "conjuring" Darr Sr. to participate in the postgame ceremony.

> The sight of [Padres third baseman Ken] Caminiti and Darr's son on Nevin's shoulder were also the moments that seemed to strike the strongest chord with the fans staying long into the evening.
>
> "The reaction of the fans was very special," said Matthews. "They remember. I think they'll always remember. It's easier for me to deal with now. Seeing Junior is a positive thing. I don't feel sad anymore."[28]

While "seeing Junior" felt healing for Matthews, what evoked tears from the fans was the sight of Darr Jr. growing up without a father. In this way, the social value of Darr Sr. is reproduced and passed on not just through but also because of his familial relations.[29] But not all familial relations can script social and human value onto the dead. It is telling but not surprising that in the death and funeral notices, my aunt and uncle connected Brandon to the same nationally sanctioned and sanctified institutions—family and sports— that ascribed social value to Michael Darr. The notices they published about Brandon's death read: "Beloved by all who knew him, he left a large family and many friends behind. Brandon was active in youth sports and played baseball in Mira Mesa."[30]

Because racialized deviancy is rendered as gender and sexual nonnormativity, much of our efforts to be included within the populations deemed worthy, deserving, and valuable are spent trying to conform to those norms of gender, sexuality, and domesticity considered "universally American" and crystallized as the "national family." Sport affiliations and family relations are ideological codes for normative (socially valuable) masculinity as evidenced through the narrative strategies employed by the Union-Tribune sports writers to rework Darr as the "idealized" victim of social change. But these codes work only incompletely for Brandon because ascribing societal value to the devalued dead requires narrating their lives through the same ideals, morals, and ethics that disciplined them while they were alive.

Mourning without Words

The very different depictions of deaths by drunk driving presented by the San Diego Union-Tribune communicated whether or not the dead deserved to be mourned. Oftentimes, "official" accounts of death and dying such as news stories or police records do not acknowledge particular racialized tragedies in terms of collective loss. In fact, the deaths of Brandon, Vanvilay, and William Christopher were represented by the journalist as not-losses and not-tragedies through what Diana Taylor calls a "performance of explicit non-caring."[31] Not only was public sympathy for them not evoked, it was explicitly refused. This refusal compels us to juxtapose the limited "official" archive of the written, recorded accounts of their deaths with the ephemeral performances of their friends' and relatives' mourning, their explicit performances of love, care, and grief beyond words.

Privileging "anecdotal and ephemeral evidence," as José Esteban Muñoz explains, "grants entrance and access to those who have been locked out of official histories and, for that matter, 'material reality.' Evidence's limit becomes clearly visible when we attempt to describe and imagine contemporary identities that do not fit into a single pre-established archive of evidence."[32] Brandon's friends and relatives created what Ann Cvetkovich calls "an archive of feeling," an archive constituted by the lived experiences of mourning and loss, ephemeral evidence that is now anecdotal.[33] It is an archive of the felt traces and sticky residue their deaths left behind in everyone's chests. These feelings were temporarily incarnated and took various visual forms: a road-side memorial, T-shirts, and the wrecked car. Witnesses would be left with fleeting imprints etched somewhere in their memories, raw material their unconscious might use for dreams. When the story about the value of lives cannot be told, the visual can be an alternative mode of expression. It is akin to the way in which Karla Holloway examines performances of mourning as central to African American culture. Holloway argues that "visual excess expressed a story that African America otherwise had difficulty illustrating —that these were lives of importance and substance, or that these were indi-viduals, no matter their failings or the degree to which their lives were qui-etly lived, who were loved."[34]

In this archive, value is ascribed to Brandon, Vanvilay, and William Christopher through their friends' and relatives' public mourning and their performances of explicit caring, profound pain, and deeply felt depression, desperation, and despair. I situate these ephemeral traces alongside the news article to illustrate how people ascribe value to the devalued through visual languages. While the official, limited archive of Brandon's death functioned primarily to repudiate him, this "archive of feeling" documented a different way to measure value. Unlike the news article, there was no attempt to make this grief universal, and, in fact, the particular and specific was all that mat-tered. His name was Brandon. He died in this car on this road. The fam-ily and friends of Brandon, Vanvilay, and William Christopher created their own publics to witness their grief. In doing so, they resisted the erasure of their loved ones and made a statement: These were valuable young men and they are missed. Their audiences were not given the opportunity to ask why.

Soon after the crash on the median of Calle Cristobal, friends and rela-tives erected a roadside memorial, overflowing with flowers, brightly lit by candles and replete with personal messages, mementos, tributes, and items the deceased might need, such as rosaries, oranges, water, boxes of their fa-vorite cigarettes, and cans of menudo. Brandon's sister, Trisha, attached her poem to the site's tree, the memorial's center, reminding us all of the need for alternative meaning-making at the base, or the core, of the tragedy: "You just don't know." Noticeable from both sides of the road, the makeshift memorial mourned and remembered Brandon, Vanvilay, and William Christopher, but it also functioned to reactivate the "scenario" of their deaths, forcing road-side spectators to become witnesses and participants.[35] According to Diana Taylor, a "scenario places spectators within its frame, implicating us in its ethics and politics."[36] This particular memorial was staged in such a way that pedestrians and drivers would have to actively and consciously not notice it. Because the memorial was on the median of Calle Cristobal, people who wanted to contribute to it had to run across the road that claimed the young men's lives. It was not a safe crossing, but the peril protected the site from intentional and accidental vandalism.

One of the young men's best friends, Shawn Essary, who had declined to go out with them that night, created 400 T-shirts and fifty caps in their memory. In his design, three open roses are connected by thorny vines, symbols of love and death connected by the pointed pains of suffering, violence, and redemption (see figure 1). The shirts bear their pictures, birthdays, and death-day, and all the clothing is boldly underscored by "R.I.P." (see figure 2). Worn in public by the young men's family members and friends long after the funerals were over, the clothing unerased our racialized dead as our "other/ed" bodies, helping Brandon, Vanvilay, and William Christopher transgress another border, the one between the living and the dead.

The roadside memorial and clothing were especially important in enabling friends of Brandon, Vanvilay, and William Christopher to participate directly in honoring their dead with dignity. Their friends had limited resources to express their grief and no control over the mourning rituals or funeral preparations and needed to negotiate the pain of losing three people all at once. Fusing three distinct religious and cultural backgrounds, they held their ceremonies in the middle of the road: It happened *here*. They used their bodies to display the communal tombstone that they would have written, walking around in silent protest: Our chests hurt *here* where Brandon, Vanvilay, and William Christopher Rest In Peace. They carried their grief heavy on their backs, like living altars with so much symbolism: I got your back.

The visual performance of explicit caring also was vital for my aunt and uncle, Christine and Jesse Martinez Jr., who made brief appearances on the news and gave speeches at high schools. Saving the car in its wrecked form, they towed it to and erected it on several San Diego high school campuses. Their activism in encouraging teenagers not to drink and drive narrated Brandon's death as illogical and preventable, as tragic and avoidable. Rather than warning people *of* young men like Brandon, Vanvilay, and William Christopher, they cautioned young adults *like* Brandon, Vanvilay, and William Christopher. They recognized that one's life circumstances can be unforgiving but never have to be all-determining. Directing their rage and intense sadness into anti-drinking-and-driving activism ensured that Brandon's death had a purpose. They refused to let him die in vain, speaking their story and leaving behind his name like an echo. Here is the car, and this was

Brandon Martinez
Oct. 30, 1980

Chris Jones
Jul. 5, 1980

Van Khounborinh
Aug. 30, 1979

R.I.P.
March,24,2000

R.I.P.
Brandon, Chris, Van

Fig. 1 (*top*): front of T-shirt; fig. 2 (*bottom*): back of T-shirt (Photos by David Coyoca)

his name. Perhaps at the next party their teenage audiences would attend, fleeting imprints of a wrecked car and a parent's tears might be resurrected, a reminder and a remainder: Hand over the keys.

This "archive of feeling" evidenced the human, familial, and social value of Brandon, Vanvilay, and William Christopher as their friends and family publicized their private pain. They were important alternative representations that helped us to mourn and work against his absolute erasure. But his picture on a T-shirt, a poem by his sister, the red box of cigarettes he smoked, and a lonely funeral card were not enough pieces of his lost life to reassemble into a proper eulogy to tell *you* why he mattered, to tell you why you have lost out, too, because the life he led and the future he would have had were your loss, too. I began to forget what his voice sounded like and couldn't remember the exact brown of his eyes. The emotive power of this archive of feeling also was limited precisely because it relied upon feeling; it was dependent upon grief and survival guilt. And it was all we had to ascribe value to Brandon; how much we hurt was evidence of how much he was valued.

Driven and Disciplined

What we wanted to tell you was why Brandon was a valuable human being who did not deserve to die so young, and lacking a narrative that could convince others why Brandon mattered hurt us all. When he died, it seemed as if he did not hold the attitudes, values, desires, or work ethics that would have eventually enabled him to have a decent paying job that could take care of a future wife and future children in a nice suburban neighborhood. This "American Dream" framed how our middle-class, mixed-race families grieved. Because our parents, aunts, and uncles wanted this dream and this future for their children, Brandon was narrated as a bad example to follow but a good lesson to learn. We either devalued his life by demonizing the same "deviant" qualities we missed and mourned, or we unduly disciplined ourselves for not diverting his "delinquency" early enough.

We all wanted a better life for Brandon, but no one could guarantee it, and so his death also became understood and talked about as everyone else's private failures and the incomprehensible "will of God."[37] I found myself wanting to argue with my family that the "inevitability" of Brandon's death could not be attributed solely to his decisions, the choices his parents made, the personal moments when we each failed him, or God's will. Brandon could not be completely blamed for his decisions because there were so many options he never had and so many second chances he was never given. How could Brandon, his parents, or his friends and other relatives be held accountable for making the "wrong" choices when the "right" opportunities never arose?

Weren't most resources withheld from Brandon, Vanvilay, and William Christopher? Economic restructuring and capital flight eradicated the blue-collar jobs that these young men did not have to go to the next morning.[38] Poorly funded schools in segregated communities provided them with inadequate educations to attend a four-year college.[39] Gang profiling marked them as potential criminals and gang members by law enforcement.[40] The widespread exploitation of both professional and unskilled immigrants makes it more profitable for companies to hire immigrants than to train the racialized working class.[41] The long history of U.S. militarism and imperialism in Asia, Latin America, Mexico, and Africa makes it more profitable for companies to relocate to countries economically devastated from structural adjustment policies because it is more profitable to exploit, abuse, and dehumanize racialized women and children in the global South than it is to pay decent salaries, provide insurance, and follow health and safety regulations at home.[42]

Brandon, Vanvilay, and William Christopher were surplus labor, not needed then, but presumably always already desperate enough to take a job. What they did in the meantime was live with their parents and sleep late in the morning. They drank beer while everyone else was sleeping and talked about dreaming their way out of their respective depressions, about how one day there would be a day when their lives would be different. Socializing over a few beers can be imagined as either an innocent, harmless recreational activity (e.g., after a long day at work) or an indicator of criminality. Which one is evoked depends on the color of your skin, your gender, your age, your drinking company, where you live, where you drink, and whether you have a job to go to the next day. Brandon, Vanvilay, and William Christopher were a racially mixed group of unemployed and insecurely underemployed young men of color (Chicano, Laotian, and African American, respectively) who were fostering their homosocial relationships with each other in a predominately middle-class suburban neighborhood. The recreational practices they shared as well as the individual work activities they lacked marked them all as "lazy" and "immoral," potentially "criminal," and always "illegal." When they died, their lives were not on the way to middle-class status, marriage, property ownership, or white-collar careers, and their (in)activities already fit a media and law enforcement profile that criminalizes racial masculinities —especially when embodied by Latino, Southeast Asian, and African American young men.[43] Read and represented as irresponsible and reckless, their social practices are rendered deviant, understood as needing discipline by the military or requiring punishment by and containment within the prison industrial complex. Could Brandon, Vanvilay, and William Christopher really be blamed for not making better decisions when the only institutions recruiting them were prison or the military?[44]

I thought that if I explained the ways in which racialized economic hierarchies governed Brandon's life, I could give my family a different story for why he died that did not center his or their personal failures. I felt compelled to make sense of how structural conditions can constrain people's lives.

Brandon was a born and raised, English-only speaking American citizen; he was a high school dropout who came from a middle-class family that lived in a middle-class neighborhood. No one in my family would have been convinced that he was destined for tragedy, and no one would have believed that his life choices were so limited, that he could choose only between "bad" and "worse." And because I did not have concrete evidence or cousinly intuition that Brandon *wanted* the options that would have made it possible for him to have a higher education, job stability, and a decent salary, even I didn't believe the story I spun for myself, though telling it made me feel better most of the time. In other moments, the subtext unsettled me because it conveyed that some people are not afforded the opportunity to become "better people" or to make "better decisions"; it implied that some people are fated to die too young. I had to take away his agency to represent him as a victim manipulated by his own desires; I had to ignore his decision to not make decisions and erase his talent for choosing nonoptions.

Before Brandon died, the story of racial exclusion and racial exploitation always seemed so sensible. For me, its primary purpose is to evoke sympathy for the people that many Americans are quick to devalue. This is not an easy task even though it seems as if it should be. To evoke public sympathy, we need to appeal to U.S. norms and values; doing so, however, requires obfuscating all the evidence that might suggest a person or population deserves devaluation if evaluated by those norms. This means re-presenting young men of color who lead unsympathetic lives—gang members, drug users, or risk-takers—as latent law-abiding, hard-working, family-oriented men who have been "unfairly" excluded from the resources and opportunities that would lead to responsible, normative choices.[45] If we concede that economic opportunities will not necessarily integrate marginalized men of color into legal and moral economies, we run the risk of unwittingly validating conservative policies. In other words, the subtext is unsettling because for racial exclusion to work as a sympathetic narrative, it needs to draw upon the neoliberal ideologies that legitimate global capitalism, naturalize inequality, and stigmatize nonnormativity.

Roderick Ferguson argues that contemporary capital requires the people of color whom it recruits and/or renders redundant to transgress the normative prescriptions of gender and sexuality that the state works to legally universalize.[46] In the era of American neoliberalism, the state pathologizes or pities racially marked gender and sexual transgressions, and it celebrates racialized normativity exemplified by U.S. multiculturalism.[47] To reiterate Foucault's interpretation of neoliberalism, the particularly American history of liberal democracy created the context for the distinct character of American neoliberalism. As Foucault argues, "the generalization of the economic form of the market beyond monetary exchanges functions in American neo-liberalism as a principle of intelligibility and a principle of decipherment of social relationships and individual behavior."[48] In other words, as deciphered and interpreted through American neoliberalism, human value registers as human capital, and social worth is evaluated from the perspectives of "real" and "speculative" markets. We can attribute value by recounting a person's useful and unique assets, talents, skills, and investments, and we can speculate about a person's future value: What can we expect this person to contribute to U.S. society in the future?

When he died, Brandon's value was entirely noneconomic. From what we knew, he didn't have (and so he couldn't capitalize on) a rare talent in high demand; his education was not a low-risk investment that promised a high return. In fact, he was expensive to maintain because he still lived at home, and without skills, experience, or education to improve his chances for a better job, even his future contributions were not worth speculation. Although not quite analogous to those who constitute the surplus labor populations of the world, Brandon was still disposable, redundant, and interchangeable; it did not matter that, as a biracial, American-born citizen, he embodied the privileged categories of neoliberal multiculturalism. As both "privileged" and "stigmatized,"[49] Brandon was offered opportunity, but it came with obstacles. He was given the chance to become socially valuable; all he had to do was take "personal responsibility" for increasing his social worth and augmenting his human capital by making better (i.e., normative) choices. His value was illegible because he opted out.

Dead Ends and Detours

It would be untrue to Brandon to script him as a victim who was unable to access a better life. In fact, privileging the American Dream and the financial stability one needs to acquire it devalues the life he led and trivializes the choices he made. So I tried to reimagine how his choices were empowering. I imagined that it was a form of empowerment for him to perform Mexican American masculinity through hip-hop music, lowered cars, and baggy clothes. Although his attitudes and his attire could sometimes be read as stereotypical, they could also be read as evidence of an "oppositional social identity" because youth of color often take their (stereotypical) models of racial authenticity from popular culture.[50]

Performing racial masculinity could be read as a form of resistance if we read culture as political: "'Politics' must be grasped," as Lisa Lowe and David

Lloyd assert, "as always braided within 'culture' and cultural practices."[51] Robin D. G. Kelley insists that reserving the category of "resistance" for activists, organizations, and leaders underestimates and depreciates everyday forms of resistance, such as strategies to subtly subvert exploitation or artistic approaches to reclaim and "redecorate" public space. In fact, we may not only misread resistance as deviance, but in doing so we run the risk of patronizing youth, workers, and communities as childishly disobedient rather than consciously and deliberately defiant. As Kelley writes,

> If we are to make meaning of these kinds of actions rather than dismiss them as manifestations of immaturity, false consciousness, or primitive rebellion, we must begin to dig beneath the surface of trade union pronouncements, political institutions, and organized social movements, deep into the daily lives, cultures, and communities which make the working classes so much more than people who work.[52]

Kelley admits that many minority cultural practices might be considered "'alternative,' rather than oppositional," but even though leisure activities are created for pleasure, they often become (or can be read as) "political" in relation to where and when they take place.[53] Intention doesn't always matter. Brandon didn't need to be devoted to radically progressive politics to be valued by the kinds of epistemologies that motivate anti-racist, anti-capitalist projects and scholarship.

Yet like the story of racial exclusion, the narrative of resistance wasn't quite the right analytical framework for making sense of Brandon's life. I wasn't convinced that his clothes, music, and recreational activities could be considered resistant or oppositional or evidence of a latent political consciousness. I needed to imagine that he would have become, or at least could have become, a vital and valuable actor in the struggle for social justice. Although this perspective decriminalizes and depathologizes nonnormative racial masculinities, it ascribes value to his potential rather than his present. An effect of rereading Brandon's actions and attitudes as evidence of his potential to become an anti-capitalist, anti-racist "revolutionary-to-be" is that value can be attributed to him only by arbitrarily divorcing the person he was from the imagined, idealized person he could have been. He might have become an activist, although it seemed just as likely that he wouldn't. As Viet Nguyen asserts, "the subject who refuses to be hailed by dominant ideology can also refuse to be hailed by resistant ideology."[54] What did it mean that I had to recast who he was into someone he might never have become in order to narrate him as someone who should be valued?

Narratives of resistance sometimes betray an underlying assumption that acts of defiance will lead to (or at least support) progressive politics. For Saba Mahmood, reading "resistance" in this way can easily lead to a misreading of "agency." From this perspective, "agency" means resisting "dominating and subjectivating modes of power" because it is assumed that disrupting and frustrating norms is an innate need that motivates everyone all the time.[55] Mahmood asks us to think about whether "the category of resistance impose[s] a teleology of progressive politics . . . that makes it hard for us to see and understand forms of being and action that are not necessarily encapsulated by the narrative of subversion and reinscription of norms?"[56] Her questions and insights help me understand why calling Brandon "resistant" doesn't feel right either. If both dominant and oppositional discourses of value center norms—as either rules to live by or prescriptions for proper behavior to work against—then Brandon, who was nonnormative in many ways but intentionally oppositional to norms in hardly any, could only be evidence for someone else's value. Because he was the "negative resource" of normativity and respectability, he gave purpose to the work of activists and academics who protect and defend all the disillusioned members of disempowered communities. Our work is valuable, in part, because he was not.

As an academic, I was not just an innocent bystander in these relational processes of valuation and valorization. I shared my time and resources with my "disillusioned" and "disempowered" cousin to steer him toward a future that I imagined was more socially valuable than his present. Before we found out that Brandon would not graduate from high school, he asked me to tutor him. We met once a week for a couple of months, but even though he was receiving A's and B's on the assignments we worked on together, his overall grades weren't improving. I learned that this was because those were the only assignments he completed. I explained that the tutoring would work only if he did his homework every day, not just once a week with me. He apologized for wasting my time, and our tutoring sessions stopped. It never crossed my mind to ask him why he wanted tutoring. I assumed then that he wanted to graduate, but now I think he just wanted to talk.

He talked about pressures to graduate, get a good job, move out of the house, and become responsible. He talked about how he thought the students at his high school racially segregated themselves voluntarily and how he and his few close friends of different colors didn't have a group to join, a place to fit. He talked about how police were always following him, and he told me about how he felt left out and left behind when his parents became part of the middle class. We talked about wishing we knew our fathers' languages because we felt there were things our grandparents wanted to tell us that English could not communicate. We talked about growing up with white mothers and growing out of internalized racism. We talked about West Coast rap music, the different car cultures of Mexicans and Filipinas/os in Southern California, and the best place to buy Dickies. I talked about the future I wanted him to have: community college, universities, student organizations such as Movimiento Estudiantil Chicana/o de Aztlán (MEChA), and ethnic studies classes. He listened.

He told me he wanted to be a lifeguard in the first (and last) essay we worked on together in our study sessions. The assignment was to pick a career and research a path to achieve his goals. He had a list of questions he was supposed to answer: Why did you choose this occupation? What are the qualifications that you would need? And what do you see yourself doing in fifteen years? He decided he would like to be a lifeguard even though it was not an occupation that easily lends itself to becoming a career since it is temporary, seasonal, and pays only up to $10,000 a year.[57] It was an interesting choice because, at least the way I saw it, being a lifeguard would not change his life all that much. He wouldn't have much more disposable income than if he continued to work odd jobs in construction with his uncle (he'd probably have even less); he'd have to continue living at home; and the only upward mobility the job could offer was becoming a lifeguard II. I didn't dissuade him directly, but I did try to encourage him to think about other options, particularly ones that needed higher education.

He reluctantly obliged because he thought the teacher would like to read about that, too, but he also resisted, probably because, for Brandon, going to college didn't sound appealing. He wrote, "After lifeguarding there are several occupations that you could take up such as a paramedic, swimming coach, or a ski patroller, according to *Vocational Biographies*. That's not much to look forward to, but they are not the only options to take. You may have some other skills, so that's where a good education comes in for landing a better job."[58] He did not specify what that better job might be, possibly because better paying jobs didn't sound "better" to him. He chose a career that was not a career. To climb up the socioeconomic ladder, he had to drop out of his dreams and go back to school.

This is why contextualizing Brandon's life choices through his exclusion from decent-paying blue-collar work is inadequate; it implies that access to good-paying jobs or higher education would have enabled him to make different choices. But as his essay on the future he would never have suggests, he didn't really want a nuclear family with a house in the suburbs. He might not have taken one of those decent-paying blue-collar jobs even if they were still available. At the same time, Brandon constructed himself not only as someone who was not productive but also as someone who was not useless: "I am not quite sure but when you save a person's life I bet it makes you feel very good inside that is something I could see myself doing. Plus just being around the water and people all the time seems like something good for me."[59] He didn't want to work to pull himself up a corporate ladder; he wasn't interested in raises or promotions. He wanted to spend his time on the beach, feeling good on the inside if someone needed help, feeling good on the outside when everyone was safe. He wanted to be accountable to everyone and responsible for everyone.

There's nothing necessarily revolutionary in wanting to live this life, but choosing a seasonal career that would ensure downward mobility is not quite normative either. Brandon had a talent for choosing life's nonoptions, and because he often didn't make decisions according to American neoliberal logic, his decisions were usually illogical or unintelligible (but not necessarily "wrong") when evaluated through a cost/benefit or supply/demand analysis. He seemed to think of himself as someone who didn't fit into the life he had inherited, and while his efforts to redesign, evade, and defer the "American Dream" might not provide us with blueprints for redistributing resources, perhaps they can help us to think about the importance of redistributing dignity.

"A Politics of Deviance"

He was only nineteen. Sometimes, his age makes it difficult to ask the questions I have been asking. My analysis can seem imposing because, at nineteen, he was an unreliable predictor for the adult he might have been at age thirty-eight or sixty-two. But the expectations for the adult he was supposed to become not only disciplined him for most of his life, they also provided ways to measure his (real and speculative) value after he died—as if " 'living' is something to be *achieved* and not *experienced*."[60] So much of life and its supposed "seminal" moments are organized according to the universalized expectations of the family and its gendered roles in naturalizing private property (buying your first home), wealth accumulation (passing down inheritance), and the pleasures of domestic consumption (planning weddings and baby showers)—all of which conflate the reproductive labor upon which consumer capitalism depends with the unpaid but rewarding labor of love. The milestones of heteronormative life that Brandon would never be able to experience rendered his life tragic. He would not have children to carry on his family's name, and his death deprived his parents and sister of significant life moments with him. Our sadness sometimes even precluded our capacities to mourn his passing according to the life experiences he might have wanted for himself, which may not have included ones we imagined for him. We needed to disconnect the life he experienced from the life he had been failing to achieve.

It is difficult to value Brandon by the quality of his life experiences when time and space are organized through heteronormativity and dictated by capital accumulation.[61] However, by situating him in a "queer time and place," we can find ways of being and frameworks for valuing that "challenge conventional logics of development, maturity, adulthood, and responsibility."[62] As Judith Halberstam argues, "Queer subcultures produce alternative temporalities by allowing their participants to believe that their futures can be imagined according to logics that lie outside of those paradigmatic markers of life experience—namely birth, marriage, reproduction, and death."[63] Denaturalizing (hetero)normative time, space, and the life achievements they universalize enables us to extend value to—or at least suspend judgment of—all kinds of people who live outside the logics of capital accumulation and bourgeois reproduction. In Halberstam's words,

> All kinds of people, especially in postmodernity, will and do opt to live outside of reproductive and familial time as well as on the edges of logics of labor and production. By doing so, they also live outside the logic of capital accumulation: here we could consider ravers, club kids, HIV-positive barebackers, rent boys, sex workers, homeless people, drug dealers, and the unemployed. Perhaps such people could productively be called "queer subjects" in terms of the ways they live (deliberately, accidentally, or of necessity) during the hours when others sleep and in the spaces (physical, metaphysical, and economic) that others have abandoned, and in terms of the ways they might work in the domains that other people assign to privacy and family.[64]

In some ways Brandon lived in a "queer time and place," and in others he might even be considered a "queer subject."[65] Even though his experiences weren't necessarily comparable or similar to queers of color, a queer of color analysis "makes some sense" of his life without condemning or celebrating who he was or who he could have been.[66] Queer of color analysis, as defined by Ferguson, extends the "theorized intersections" of women of color feminism "by investigating how intersecting racial, gender, and sexual practices antagonize and/or conspire with the normative investments of nation-states and capital."[67] Put another way, both women of color feminism and queer of color critiques stress that sometimes "it may be necessary to overcome resistance in order to achieve resistance."[68] For Brandon, the failure to meet heteronormative and neoliberal expectations (and his reluctance to even try to attain them) was compounded by his racial background as Chicano/Mexican American. He was not just a lazy kid without a high school diploma who drank too much and lived off his parents. When Brandon defied normative investments in heteropatriarchy and American enterprise, he gave credence to racial stereotypes, which is partly why he also could not be fully valued through a politics of racial normativity.[69]

Brandon was always confusing me in ways I couldn't name. Trying to figure out the motives for his choices often eluded me because his actions and his attitudes were neither complicit nor resistant, as well as both at the same time. Imposing a normative framework onto his aspirations made his goals and desires difficult to decipher because he wanted to be unremarkable and live his life a little on the lazy side. He was only lackadaisically defiant, but we all read him as rebellious because he kept diligently deferring or sabotaging what was supposed to be his "American Dream." It was as if he followed a logic all his own—and maybe that was the tutoring lesson I was supposed to learn. Maybe I failed because I looked in all the wrong places to find methods, narratives, and strategies for ascribing social worth to his personhood, trying to make him fit into my over-researched reasons and rationales rather than making an effort to remember what he might have been trying to teach me.

I think he wanted to teach me how to make sense of what Cathy Cohen terms "a politics of deviance."[70] A politics of deviance makes sense of deviations from the norm differently rather than defensively. Such a politics would neither pathologize deviance nor focus most of its energies on trying to rationalize why people choose deviant practice over proper behavior. Rather than repudiating nonnormative behavior and ways of being, we would read nonnormative activities and attitudes as forms of "definitional power" that have the potential to help us rethink how value is defined, parceled out, and withheld.[71] Both Cohen and Kelley resist spinning a normative narrative that ascribing value to the devalued often demands. In different ways, they give us a language of value that translates "the cultural world beneath the bottom"[72] into lived practices and living alternatives to U.S. norms. Cohen argues that "ironically, through these attempts to find autonomy, these individuals, with relatively little access to dominant power, not only counter or challenge the presiding normative order with regard to family, sex, and desire, but also create new or counter normative frameworks by which to judge behavior."[73] Claims to empowerment through deviant and defiant behavior urgently unsettle the stubborn relationship between value and normativity, but they cannot always offer something more. Sometimes defiant or deviant practices critique the rules of normality (purposely or inadvertently) but don't necessarily break them; they might direct us toward necessarily nonnormative criteria for recognizing social worth even if they don't model or theorize alternative ways of living.

The something more insists that we hold ourselves accountable, too. A politics of deviance does not just set aside the impulse to discipline difference; it also centers the responsibility to reckon with those deemed dangerous, underserving, and unintelligible. Recuperating those deemed deviant means trying to make others' lives more acceptable and sympathetic, but *reckoning* with those who live in the spaces of social death means individually changing ourselves and collectively changing the world that made us all. As Avery Gordon writes, "Reckoning is about knowing what kind of effort is required to change ourselves and the conditions that make us who we are, that set limits on what is acceptable and unacceptable, on what is possible and impossible."[74] To make the unthinkable not just plausible but necessary, we have to reckon with restless ghosts and living people who share the status of "dead-to-others" and demand from us nothing less than transformation.

Brandon's unintelligible ethics of deviance might be neither unapologetically normative nor radically transformative, but it is definitely a way of living that interrogates and elucidates how normative understandings of morality and ethicality may sometimes mitigate oppositional politics and scholarship. When we take Brandon and others like him seriously, we are expected to suspend judgment of those who choose to drive down fatal roads because there is value as well as apprehension in taking risks and living differently—even if it means actively, accidentally, and unthinkably leaving the rest of us behind, empty and haunted. As Rubén Martínez reminds us, "The road may kill us in the end, but it's also the only way to get to where we're going."[75]

NOTES

NOTES TO THE INTRODUCTION

1. These photos were shot and captioned by Associated Press, Dave Martin, and Agence France-Presse/Getty Images, Chris Graythen, respectively. Van Jones, "Black People 'Loot' Food . . . White People 'Find' Food," *Huffingtonpost.com*, September 1, 2005, http://www.huffingtonpost.com/van-jones/black-people -loot-food-wh_b_6614.html.

2. Santiago Lyon, the director of photography for the Associated Press, cited by Aaron Kinney, "'Looting' or 'Finding'?," *Salon*, September 1, 2005, http://dir .salon.com/story/news/feature/2005/09/01/photo_controversy/index.html.

3. Tania Ralli, "Who's a Looter? In Storm's Aftermath, Pictures Kick up a Different Kind of Tempest," *The New York Times*, September 5, 2005.

4. For instance, Graythen emphasizes that he has an absolute definition of "looting":

> I wrote the caption about the two people who "found" the items. I believed in my opinion, that they did simply find them, and not "looted" them in the definition of the word. The people were swimming in chest deep water, and there were other people in the water, both white and black. I looked for the best picture. There were a million items floating in the water—we were right near a grocery store that had 5+ feet of water in it. It had no doors. The water was moving, and the stuff was floating away. These people were not ducking into a store and busting down windows to get electronics. They picked up bread and cokes that were floating in the water. They would have floated away anyhow. I wouldn't have taken it, because I wouldn't eat anything that's been in that water. But I'm not homeless (well, technically I am right now).
>
> I'm not trying to be politically correct. I don't care if you are white or black. I spent 4 hours on a boat in my parent's neighborhood shooting, and rescuing people, both black and white, dog and cat. I am a journalist, and a human being—and I see all as such. If you don't belive [sic] me, you can look on Getty today and see the images I shot of real looting today, and you will see white and black people, and they were DEFINITELY looting. And I put that in the caption.

Chris Graythen, "SportsShooter.com—Finding vs. Looting (word choice in AP caption)," *sportsshooter.com*, August 31, 2005, http://www.sportsshooter .com/message_display.html?tid=17204.)

5. The photographs together tell a certain story about the ways in which crime is recognized and racialized, but the story these photographs tell is not dependent on either photographer's intention. For instance, Chris Graythen's family lived in New Orleans; he took photos while he was helping his family and others get to safer ground. Race would not be the sole reason for his empathetic response. My analysis, however, focuses on the ways in which people understood the juxtaposition, how they interpreted the side-by-side comparison. The photographer's intentions are less relevant than his audience's perceptions.

6. Yen Le Espiritu, *Home Bound: Filipino American Lives across Cultures, Communities, and Countries* (Berkeley: University of California Press, 2003), 47.

7. Ibid.

8. See Erika Lee, *At America's Gates: Chinese Immigration during the Exclusion Era, 1882–1943* (Chapel Hill: University of North Carolina Press, 2003); Mae M. Ngai, *Impossible Subjects: Illegal Aliens and the Making of Modern America* (Princeton: Princeton University Press, 2004).

9. Jürgen Habermas, *Between Facts and Norms: Contributions to a Discourse Theory of Law and Democracy*, trans. William Rehg (Cambridge: MIT Press, 1998).

10. See also Jürgen Habermas, "On the Internal Relation between the Rule of Law and Democracy," in *Philosophical Perspectives on Law and Politics: Readings from Plato to Derrida*, ed. Patrick Hayden (New York: Peter Lang, 1999), 327–335. As Habermas reminds us, "However well-grounded human rights are, they may not be paternalistically foisted, as it were, on a sovereign. Indeed the idea of citizens' legal autonomy demands that the addressees of law be able to understand themselves at the same time as its authors. It would contradict this idea if the democratic legislator were to discover human rights as though they were (preexisting) moral facts that one merely needs to enact as positive law" (332).

11. Hannah Arendt, *The Origins of Totalitarianism* (New York: Harcourt Brace Jovanovich, 1973), 296.

12. Judith Butler, *Frames of War: When Is Life Grievable?* (London: Verso, 2009), 15.

13. For more on social death, see Orlando Patterson, *Slavery and Social Death: A Comparative Study* (Cambridge: Harvard University Press, 1982); Sharon Patricia Holland, *Raising the Dead: Readings of Death and (Black) Subjectivity* (Durham: Duke University Press, 2000); Ruth Wilson Gilmore, "Fatal Couplings of Power and Difference: Notes on Racism and Geography," *The Professional Geographer* 54, no. 1 (February 2002): 15–24; James Kyung-Jin Lee, *Urban Triage: Race and the Fictions of Multiculturalism* (Minneapolis: University of Minnesota Press, 2004); Raúl Homero Villa, *Barrio-Logos: Space and Place in Urban Chicano Literature and Culture* (Austin: University of Texas Press, 2000).

14. Holland, *Raising the Dead*, 15.

15. Ibid., 17–18.
16. Gilmore, "Fatal Couplings of Power and Difference," 16.
17. Holland, *Raising the Dead*, 18.
18. Ibid., 16.
19. Winona LaDuke, *Recovering the Sacred: The Power of Naming and Claiming* (Cambridge, MA: South End Press, 2005).
20. For more on the ways in which "gifting" freedom ensures unequal power relations through obligation and indebtedness, see Mimi Nguyen, *Refugee Passages* (Durham: Duke University Press, 2012).
21. Patterson, *Slavery and Social Death*, 209.
22. Ibid.
23. Ibid.
24. This quoted phrase comes from Patterson's discussion of manumission, which emphasizes that freedom is always framed as an unrequited gift. Patterson, *Slavery and Social Death*, 211.
25. Sara Ahmed, *Strange Encounters: Embodied Others in Post-Coloniality* (London and New York: Routledge, 2000), 2–3,
26. Ibid., 6.
27. Ibid., 5.
28. Ibid.
29. W. E. B. Du Bois, *The Souls of Black Folk* (New York: Penguin Books, 1995), 45.
30. Ruby C. Tapia, *American Pietàs: Visions of Race, Death, and the Maternal* (Minneapolis: University of Minnesota Press, 2011), 131.
31. Adam Nossiter, "Day Laborers Are Easy Prey in New Orleans," *The New York Times*, February 16, 2009.
32. Ibid.
33. Wendy Cheng and Michelle Commander, "Language Matters: Hurricane Katrina and Media Responsibility," in *Hurricane Katrina: Response and Responsibilities*, ed. John Brown Childs (Santa Cruz: New Pacific Press, 2005), 92–94; Jared Sexton, "The Obscurity of Black Suffering," in *What Lies Beneath: Katrina, Race, and the State of Nation*, ed. South End Press Collective (Cambridge, MA: South End Press, 2007), 120–132.
34. Nossiter, "Day Laborers Are Easy Prey in New Orleans."
35. Ibid.
36. Ibid.
37. Lindon Barrett, *Blackness and Value: Seeing Double* (Cambridge: Cambridge University Press, 1999), 19, 21.
38. Naomi Klein, *The Shock Doctrine: The Rise of Disaster Capitalism* (New York: Picador, 2008), 4.
39. Barrett, *Blackness and Value*, 28.
40. This is also an example of what journalist Naomi Klein calls "disaster capitalism." Klein, *The Shock Doctrine*, 6.

41. Jocelyn Noveck, "The Use of the Word 'Refugee' Touches a Nerve," *The Seattle Times*, September 7, 2005.

42. In the same interview, Jackson compared the federal government's response to Hurricane Katrina to its response to other national and international disasters, such as the 2004 tsunami. In this way, Jackson uses comparative methods to indict the government's devaluation of racialized spaces. Jesse Jackson, "A Racial Component?" *msnbc.com*, September 3, 2005, http://www .msnbc.msn.com/id/21134540/vp/9186615#9186615; Associated Press, "Calling Survivors 'Refugees' Stirs Debate," *msnbc.com*, September 7, 2005, http://www .msnbc.msn.com/id/9232071/ns/us_news-katrina_the_long_road_back/t/ calling-katrina-survivors-refugees-stirs-debate/#.Tq84lXExoXw.

43. Jackson, "A Racial Component?"; Associated Press, "Calling Survivors 'Refugees' Stirs Debate."

44. Mike Pesca, "Are Katrina Victims 'Refugees' or 'Evacuees'?" NPR, September 5, 2005, http://www.npr.org/templates/story/story.php?storyId=4833613.

45. Lydia Lum, "Swept into the Background," *Diverse*, December 15, 2005, 22.

46. Ibid., 23.

47. There are several texts that engage comparative racializations in innovative and critical ways. See Grace Kyungwon Hong and Roderick A. Ferguson, eds. *Strange Affinities: The Gender and Sexual Politics of Comparative Racialization* (Durham: Duke University Press, 2011); Helen Heran Jun, *Race for Citizenship: Black Orientalism and Asian Uplift from Pre-Emancipation to Neoliberal America* (New York: New York University Press, 2011); Moon-Ho Jung, *Coolies and Cane: Race, Labor, and Sugar in the Age of Emancipation* (Baltimore: Johns Hopkins University Press, 2006); Moon-Kie Jung, *Reworking Race: The Making of Hawaii's Interracial Labor Movement* (New York: Columbia University Press, 2006); Rachel Buff, *Immigration and the Political Economy of Home: West Indian Brooklyn and American Indian Minneapolis, 1945–1992* (Berkeley: University of California Press, 2001); Grace Kyungwon Hong, *The Ruptures of American Capital: Women of Color Feminism and the Culture of Immigrant Labor* (Minneapolis: University of Minnesota Press, 2006); Laura Pulido, *Black, Brown, Yellow, and Left: Radical Activism in Los Angeles* (Berkeley: University of California Press, 2006); Lee, *Urban Triage*; Natalia Molina, *Fit to Be Citizens? Public Health and Race in Los Angeles, 1879–1939* (Berkeley: University of California Press, 2006); George Lipsitz, *Dangerous Crossroads: Popular Music, Postmodernism, and the Poetics of Place* (New York: Verso, 1994); Gary Y. Okihiro, *Common Ground: Reimagining American History* (Princeton: Princeton University Press, 2001); Anani Dzidzienyo and Suzanne Oboler, eds., *Neither Enemies nor Friends: Latinos, Blacks, Afro-Latinos* (New York: Palgrave Macmillan, 2005); Claire Jean Kim, *Bitter Fruit: The Politics of Black-Korean Conflict in New York City* (New Haven: Yale University Press, 2000); Vijay Prashad, *Everybody Was Kung Fu Fighting: Afro-Asian Connections and the Myth of Cultural Purity* (Boston: Beacon Press, 2001); George J. Sanchez,

"'What's Good for Boyle Heights Is Good for the Jews': Creating Multiculturalism on the Eastside during the 1950s," *American Quarterly* 56, no. 3 (2004): 633–661.

48. Lisa Duggan, *The Twilight of Equality?* (Boston: Beacon Press, 2003), 14. For excellent analyses of neoliberal policies in both the global North and South, see Walden F. Bello, *Dark Victory: The United States, Structural Adjustment, and Global Poverty* (London: Pluto Press, 1994); Walden Bello, *Dilemmas of Domination: The Unmaking of the American Empire* (New York: Holt Paperbacks, 2006).

49. Jun, *Race for Citizenship*, 128–132.

50. Michel Foucault, *The Birth of Biopolitics: Lectures at the College de France, 1978–1979*, ed. Michel Senellart, trans. Graham Burchell (Houndmills, Basingstoke, Hampshire, England: Palgrave Macmillan, 2008), 243.

51. African Americans make up 20 percent of the unemployed but only 12 percent of the labor force. Latinas/os also make up 20 percent of the unemployed and are only 15 percent of the labor force. Algernon Austin, *EEOC to Examine Treatment of Unemployed Job Seekers*, February 16, 2011, http://www.eeoc.gov/eeoc/meetings/2-16-11/austin.cfm.

52. African American workers are entitled, as U.S. citizens, to take legal action against illegal hiring practices by proving their employer engaged in "criminal conspiracy" by hiring undocumented immigrants. In a recent case, *Williams v. Mohawk Industries, Inc.*, 465 F.3d 1277, 1289 (11th Cir. 2007), employees sued the flooring corporation under the Racketeer Influenced and Corrupt Organizations (RICO) Act, claiming that hiring undocumented immigrants depressed the wages of all workers. Although the case was settled, the workers could not prove that the wages of undocumented immigrants were connected to the wages of other workers.

53. U.S. Equal Employment Opportunity Commission, "Transcript of Meeting —EEOC to Examine Treatment of Unemployed Job Seekers," *eeoc.gov*, February 16, 2011, http://www.eeoc.gov/eeoc/meetings/2-16-11/transcript.cfm. At the time of this writing (October 2011), President Barak Obama was attempting to pass an American Jobs Act that would make it illegal to discriminate against the unemployed. The act has so far failed to pass the Senate.

54. Ibid.

55. Wendy Brown, "Neo-liberalism and the End of Liberal Democracy," *Theory and Event* 7, no. 1 (2003): par. 7, 15.

56. retire05, "Yippee! Katrina Victims Get More Money!," Weblog, *Sweetness and Light*, November 17, 2010, http://sweetness-light.com/archive/yippee-katrina-victims-get-more-money.

57. I'm thinking about entrapment in ways that are similar to Beth Richie's use of the concept of "gender entrapment." Richie argues that when poor black women are strongly invested in maintaining heteronormative households and relationships, they are actually much more vulnerable to domestic violence

and much more likely to be convicted of criminal activities. See Beth Richie, *Compelled to Crime: The Gender Entrapment of Battered Black Women* (New York: Routledge, 1996).

58. Undocumented workers' rights vary by state. For instance, in California, undocumented workers are entitled to minimum wage, overtime pay, workers compensation, and disability insurance. They are also protected by anti-discrimination law; however, they have no legal recourse to recover lost income if they are fired.

59. Klein, *The Shock Doctrine*, 521.

60. Cheryl L. Harris, "Whiteness as Property," *Harvard Law Review* 106, no. 8 (June 1993): 1777.

61. Ibid., 1713–1714.

62. Grace Kyungwon Hong, "Property," in *Keywords for American Cultural Studies*, ed. Bruce Burgett and Glenn Hendler (New York: New York University Press, 2007), 181.

63. Hong, *The Ruptures of American Capital*, 11.

64. Lisa Lowe, *Immigrant Acts: On Asian American Cultural Politics* (Durham: Duke University Press, 1996), 24–25.

65. Harris, "Whiteness as Property," 1716.

66. Ibid., 1725. Italics in original.

67. See the following: Tomás Almaguer, *Racial Fault Lines: The Historical Origins of White Supremacy in California* (University of California Press, 2008); Richard Griswold del Castillo, *The Treaty of Guadalupe Hidalgo: A Legacy of Conflict* (Norman: University of Oklahoma Press, 1990); Carl Scott Gutiérrez-Jones, *Rethinking the Borderlands: Between Chicano Culture and Legal Discourse* (Berkeley: University of California Press, 1995); Ian Haney López, *White by Law: The Legal Construction of Race* (New York: New York University Press, 1996).

68. López, *White by Law*, 79–109.

69. Ibid., 90.

70. Ibid., 240, n.2.

71. The complicated history of white ethnic groups is often cited as evidence that racial discrimination can be overcome (i.e., why can't people of color overcome discrimination as the Irish did?), but as the historian Matthew Frye Jacobson elucidates, reading this history as one of white races (rather than as one of white ethnics) illustrates that white privilege has been historically constituted and consolidated through its contentious history, not in spite of it. Matthew Frye Jacobson, *Whiteness of a Different Color: European Immigrants and the Alchemy of Race* (Cambridge: Harvard University Press, 1999), 8.

72. W. E. B. Du Bois, *Black Reconstruction in America, 1860–1880* (New York: Touchstone, 1995), 700–704.

73. David R. Roediger, *The Wages of Whiteness: Race and the Making of the American Working Class* (London: Verso, 1991), 57.

74. Ibid., 58–59.
75. Harris, "Whiteness as Property," 1744.
76. Ibid., 1753.
77. Ibid., 1777. Harris cites the following court cases as examples of the ways in which legal challenges to affirmative action treated whiteness as a vested property interest: *Bakke v. UC Regents* (1978); *City of Richmond v. J. A. Croson Co.* (1989); and *Wygant v. Jackson Bd. of Educ.* (1986).
78. George Lipsitz, *The Possessive Investment in Whiteness: How White People Profit from Identity Politics* (Philadelphia: Temple University Press, 1998), vii–viii.
79. This example is similar to the legally protected expectations that dismantled affirmative action, such as Alan Bakke's case against the University of California when he argued that he did not get into medical school because sixteen slots (of one hundred) were reserved for minorities. In *Bakke v. the UC Regents*, Bakke believed he was not admitted to medical school because of his race (according to his own criteria for judging which applicants were better qualified). He won his case because the sixteen seats reserved for people of color violated the property interest of his and future white applicants. Harris, "Whiteness as Property," 1769–1777.
80. Isabel Molina-Guzmán, *Dangerous Curves: Latina Bodies in the Media* (New York: New York University Press, 2010), 9.
81. See Robin Dale Jacobson, *The New Nativism: Proposition 187 and the Debate over Immigration* (Minneapolis: University of Minnesota Press, 2008).
82. Barrett, *Blackness and Value*, 17.
83. Ibid., 128.
84. Grace Kyungwon Hong, "Blues Imaginaries" (invited talk, University of Illinois at Urbana-Champaign, September 17, 2009). We also can think about "reckoning" with ghosts that haunt rather than breathing life into social death. See Avery F. Gordon, *Ghostly Matters: Haunting and the Sociological Imagination* (Minneapolis: University of Minnesota Press, 1997).
85. Holland, *Raising the Dead*, 18.
86. Derrick A. Bell, "Racial Realism," in *Critical Race Theory: The Key Writings That Formed the Movement*, ed. Kimberlé Crenshaw et al. (New York: New Press, 1995), 308.
87. Sara Ahmed, *The Promise of Happiness* (Durham: Duke University Press, 2010), 20.
88. Fiona I. B. Ngô, "Sense and Subjectivity," *Camera Obscura: Feminism, Culture, and Media Studies* 76, vol. 26, no. 1 (January 2011): 101.
89. For more on "survivability," see Achille Mbembe, "Necropolitics," trans. Libby Meintjes, *Public Culture* 15, no. 1 (Winter 2003): 11–40; Giorgio Agamben, *Homo Sacer: Sovereign Power and Bare Life* (Stanford: Stanford University Press, 1998); Giorgio Agamben, *Means Without End: Notes on Politics* (Minneapolis: University of Minnesota Press, 2000).

NOTES TO CHAPTER 1

1. Thomas Larson, "The Adult Boys of Rancho Peñasquitos," *San Diego Reader*, December 7, 2000. Larson's account is culled from the police report. He puts the ages of the migrant workers at 64–69.
2. Ibid.
3. Ibid.
4. Proposition 21 was passed with about 62 percent of the vote. "State Ballot Measures," *Vote 2000—California Secretary of State*, June 2, 2000, http://primary2000.sos.ca.gov/returns/prop/oo.htm.
5. Proposition 21 also required that juveniles be held in state correctional facilities and that convicted gang members register with law enforcement. Confidentiality protections and probation programs also were significantly altered. The measure was preceded by Proposition 184, the "three-strikes-and-you're-out" initiative, which mandated a life sentence upon conviction of a third felony. Proposition 184 passed in 1994.
6. On white injury, see Lisa Marie Cacho, "'The People of California Are Suffering': The Ideology of White Injury in Discourses of Immigration," *Cultural Values* 4, no. 4 (October 2000): 389–418.
7. In California, the initiative process allows citizens to change laws directly, without going through the Legislature. To change California statutes, initiative drafters need to collect signatures equal to 5 percent of the total votes cast for governor during the last election. To change the California Constitution, the signature requirement rises to 8 percent. Although touted as "direct democracy," such campaigns require large amounts of funding as well as legal counsel; as such, most propositions on the ballots that meet all the requirements are primarily drafted by wealthy citizens and politicians.
8. This is not only neoliberal but also historically specific. Welfare was originally set up for white women. See Dorothy E. Roberts, *Killing the Black Body: Race, Reproduction, and the Meaning of Liberty* (New York: Vintage, 1999).
9. Leti Volpp, "Divesting Citizenship: On Asian American History and the Loss of Citizenship through Marriage," *UCLA Law Review* 53, no. 2 (December 2005): 411.
10. Ibid., 409–412.
11. The race exclusions were lifted in 1952 with the McCarran-Walter Act, and the national origins system was abolished in 1965. However, the 1952 act also established exclusions based on sexual "deviance"—homosexuality and adultery. See Siobhan B. Somerville, "Sexual Aliens and the Racialized State: A Queer Reading of the 1952 U.S. Immigration and Nationality Act," in *Queer Migrations: Sexuality, U.S. Citizenship, and Border Crossings*, ed. Eithne Luibhéid and Lionel Cantú Jr. (Minneapolis: University of Minnesota Press, 2005), 75–91.
12. Ibid.; Siobhan B. Somerville, "Queer Loving," *GLQ: A Journal of Lesbian and Gay Studies* 11, no. 3 (2005): 335–370; David L. Eng, *The Feeling of Kinship: Queer Liberalism and the Racialization of Intimacy* (Durham: Duke University

Press, 2010), 23–57; Jasbir K. Puar, *Terrorist Assemblages: Homonationalism in Queer Times* (Durham: Duke University Press, 2007), 1–36; Chandan Reddy, "Time for Rights? Loving, Gay Marriage, and the Limits of Legal Justice," *Fordham Law Review* 76, no. 6 (2008): 2849–2872.

13. Asian women were excluded with the Page Law of 1875, and Chinese laborers were excluded with the Chinese Exclusion Act of 1882, which was not repealed until 1943. The Gentlemen's Agreement (1907–8) barred laborers from Japan. The 1917 Immigration Act established the Asiatic Barred Zone, and the 1924 Immigration Act established the Asia-Pacific Triangle. In both those acts, Asian nations were excluded through geographic restrictions. In 1934, the Tydings-McDuffie Act changed the colonial status of the Philippines, making all Filipinos no longer eligible to immigrate as nationals. For more about Asians' "nonnormative" relationships and residences, or what Nayan Shah calls "queer domesticity," see Nayan Shah, *Contagious Divides: Epidemics and Race in San Francisco's Chinatown* (Berkeley: University of California Press, 2001); Yen Le Espiritu, *Asian American Women and Men: Labor, Laws and Love* (Thousand Oaks, CA.: Sage Publications, 1997); Lowe, *Immigrant Acts*.

14. Ngai, *Impossible Subjects*, 258.

15. Ibid., 246.

16. Ibid., 260.

17. Ibid., 261.

18. Ibid.

19. Ibid. Ngai also notes that the act closed off the path to naturalization for parents of undocumented children, thereby further contributing to producing the "illegality" of Mexican immigration.

20. Ibid.

21. Ibid., 227; Kitty Calavita, *Inside the State: The Bracero Program, Immigration, and the I.N.S.* (New York: Routledge, 1992); Deborah Cohen, *Braceros: Migrant Citizens and Transnational Subjects in the Postwar United States and Mexico* (Chapel Hill: University of North Carolina Press, 2011); Kelly Lytle Hernández, *Migra! A History of the U.S. Border Patrol* (Berkeley and Los Angeles: University of California Press, 2010).

22. Rather than focusing on the status as the crime, illicit institutions and behaviors have been outlawed. For instance, it is no longer illegal to be a prostitute, but in many states brothels are illegal, and the act of sexually prostituting oneself is a crime.

23. Volpp, "Divesting Citizenship," 470. As Volpp explains, "the conduct- or behavior-based restrictions on citizenship that exist today, while usually conceptualized as neutrally based restrictions, are both constitutive of and the product of very specific identities that we understand as a matter of status."

24. John T. Philipsborn, appearing as attorney for amicus curiae of California Attorneys for Criminal Justice, Court of Appeal of the State of California Fourth Appellate District Division One, Case No. D 036456 (Superior Court No. SCD

154096). *Michael Rose v. Superior Court, San Diego County, Juvenile Division* and *Morgan Victor Manduley v. Superior Court, San Diego, The People of the State of California*, Amicus Curiae. December 14, 2000, 17.

25. Malika T. Djafar, "Dehumanizing Youth: When California Gave Up on Its Children," *Whittier Journal of Child and Family Advocacy* 3 (2003–2004): 151–170. In the end, Proposition 21 was not found in violation of the single subject rule. *Manduley v. Superior Court of San Diego County* 27 Cal. 4th 537. Cal. App *Manduley v. Superior Court* (2001) 86 Cal. App. 4th 1198 [104 Cal. Rptr. 2d 140] *Manduley v. Superior Court* (2002) 27 Cal. 4th 537, 571.

26. John T. Philipsborn, Amicus Curiae. December 14, 2000, 17.

27. The brief also argues that the draft of the proposition was different from the actual ballot and that the title of the initiative was misleading because it did not specify that the three strikes law would be altered in ways that would affect nongang adults (Philipsborn, 7–8, 17–18).

28. See Lizabeth N. de Vries, "Guilt by Association: Proposition 21's Gang Conspiracy Law Will Increase Youth Violence in California," *University of San Francisco Law Review* 37 (2003, 2002): 191–226. De Vries is a lawyer who specializes in elder abuse law, juvenile law, and civil rights law.

29. Ibid., 192–194.

30. Harry M. Caldwell and Daryl Fisher-Ogden, "Stalking the Jets and the Sharks: Exploring the Constitutionality of the Gang Death Penalty Enhancer," *George Mason Law Review* 12, no. 3 (2003–2004): 637.

31. Ibid.

32. Arnold P. Goldstein and Donald William Kodluboy, *Gangs in Schools: Signs, Symbols, and Solutions* (Champaign, IL: Research Press, 1998), 69.

33. Ibid.

34. Larson, "The Adult Boys of Rancho Peñasquitos."

35. Greg Moran, "Three Teens Sentenced for Assault on Migrants," *San Diego Union-Tribune*, July 24, 2002.

36. Valerie Alvord, "Law Challenged by 'Good Boys' Facing 16 Years," *USA Today*, September 15, 2000.

37. "Text of Proposition 21," *Vote 2000 — California Secretary of State*, n.d., §2(b), http://primary2000.sos.ca.gov/VoterGuide/Propositions/21text.htm.

38. Habermas, *Between Facts and Norms*, 450.

39. Ibid., 38. Habermas emphasizes that although citizens must imagine they would be the authors of law, the rule of law also relies upon the recognition that they are not: "However, the binding quality of legal norms does not stem solely from processes of opinion- and will-formation, but arises also from the collectively binding decisions of authorities who make and apply law. This circumstance makes it conceptually necessary to distinguish the role of authors who make and adjudicate law from that of addressees who are subject to established law. The autonomy that in the moral domain is all of a piece, so to speak, appears in the legal domain only in the dual form of private and

public autonomy." Habermas, "On the Internal Relation between the Rule of Law and Democracy," 330.

40. Denise Ferreira da Silva, "Towards a Critique of the Socio-logos of Justice: The Analytics of Raciality and the Production of Universality," *Social Identities: Journal for the Study of Race, Nation and Culture* 7, no. 3 (September 2001): 421–454; Arendt, *The Origins of Totalitarianism*.

41. Proposition 21 was passed statewide with 62.1 percent of the vote. Only five counties had a majority vote against the proposition. All five—Marin, San Francisco, San Mateo, Santa Cruz, and Alameda—are in the San Francisco Bay Area ("State Ballot Measures"). For the vote estimate for Rancho Peñasquitos, see Larson, "The Adult Boys of Rancho Peñasquitos."

42. "Profile of General Demographic Characteristics: 2000; 92129 5-Digit ZCTA," *U.S. Census Bureau*, n.d., http://factfinder.census.gov/servlet/QTTable?_bm=y&-geo_id=86000US92129&-qr_name=DEC_2000_SF1_U_DP1&-ds_name=DEC_2000_SF1_U&-_lang=en&-_sse=on. The median income in 2000 was $77,851 for the Rancho Peñasquitos zip code. Nationally, the median income was $41,994. "92129 - Fact Sheet - American FactFinder," *U.S. Census Bureau*, n.d., http://factfinder.census.gov/servlet/SAFFFacts?_zip=92129&_lang=en.

43. Alvord, "Law Challenged by 'Good Boys' Facing 16 Years."

44. For more examples of alternative viewpoints that explicitly condemn the attackers' actions, see Kimberly Epler, "Two Settlements Approved in Beating Case," *North County Times* (Escondido, CA, July 7, 2001); Ernesto Cienfuegos, "Vigilante Thugs Sentenced in Beating of Elderly Mexican Workers," *La Voz de Aztlán*, November 21, 2002, http://www.aztlan.net/vigilantethugs.htm; Larson, "The Adult Boys of Rancho Peñasquitos"; Norma de la Vega, "Laborer in Beating Case Living in Tijuana," *San Diego Union-Tribune*, January 2, 2002.

45. Jacquelyn Giles, "Will Prison Teach Teens Tolerance?" *San Diego Union-Tribune*, July 21, 2000.

46. Ibid.

47. Ibid.

48. Ibid.

49. Ahmed, *Strange Encounters*, 4.

50. When writing about ethnography, Ahmed speaks about the different techniques used to learn from and about "strangers." Giles' suggestions are similar to one such technique: "learning to be them." The knowledge produced about the Other by a scholar who learns "*how to be them*" potentially hides the power dynamics that produce the knowledge in the first place because learning from "them" makes it seem as though "they have authorised 'our' knowledge" (Ahmed, *Strange Encounters*, 71).

51. Ibid., 74.

52. Ibid., 55.

53. Giles, "Will Prison Teach Teens Tolerance?"

54. Ibid.
55. Alex Roth, "Teen-ager Charged in Rampage Speaks Out: Youth Calls Role in Attack on Latino Workers Minor," *San Diego Union-Tribune*, February 1, 2001.
56. Ibid.
57. Alex Roth, "Court Rejects Adult Charges in Migrant Beatings," *San Diego Union-Tribune*, February 8, 2001.
58. For more examples of media coverage of the case, see Michael Burge and Greg Moran, "Youngest Suspect in Migrant Attack Gets Bail," *San Diego Union-Tribune*, July 21, 2000; Greg Moran, "8th Youth in Beatings Faces Adult Charges," *San Diego Union-Tribune*, August 2, 2000; Greg Moran, "Migrants' Attackers to Be Sentenced: Youths Could Get as Much as 12 Years in Prison for Three-Hour Terror Spree," *San Diego Union-Tribune*, June 27, 2002; Alex Roth, "7 Teens Face Trial as Adults in Migrant-Camp Beatings," *San Diego Union-Tribune*, July 19, 2000; Alex Roth, "Teen Admitted Role in Attack, Affidavit Says," *San Diego Union-Tribune*, July 26, 2000.

    For more examples of news coverage of Proposition 21 in general, see "Prop. 21: No Youth Crime Remedy," *Los Angeles Times*, February 22, 2000; Ben Fox, "Teens Sentenced for Attack on Mexican Workers," *The Associated Press*, June 28, 2002; Maura Dolan, "Prop. 21 Argued Before Justices," *Los Angeles Times*, December 6, 2001; Maura Dolan and Greg Krikorian, "State Justices Uphold Juvenile Crime Law," *Los Angeles Times*, March 1, 2002; Robert Greene, "Cooley Issues Strict Guidelines for 'Direct Filing' Under Proposition 21," *Metropolitan News-Enterprise*, Los Angeles, March 14, 2002; "Juvenile Justice," *Online NewsHour*, February 29, 2000, http://www.pbs.org/newshour/bb/youth/jan-june00/justice_2-29.html; Greg Lucas, "Huge Changes Proposed for Juvenile Justice: Teenagers Would Face Adult Courts," *San Francisco Chronicle*, February 14, 2000; Rene Sanchez and William Booth, "California Toughens Juvenile Crime Laws: Rules to Treat Young Offenders More Like Adults," *The Washington Post*, March 13, 2000.
59. Karen S. Johnson-Cartee, *News Narratives and News Framing: Constructing Political Reality* (Lanham, MD: Rowman and Littlefield, 2005), 255.
60. The quotation comes from Frank Almaguer, Manduley's great uncle and U.S. ambassador to Honduras. See Alex Roth, "Leniency Asked for Teen in Camp-Raid Case: Relatives Say He 'Shamed . . . His Latino Heritage,'" *San Diego Union-Tribune*, August 10, 2000.
61. Greg Moran, "Four Migrant Attackers Sentenced," *San Diego Tribune*, June 29, 2002.
62. Carrie A. Rentschler, "Victims' Rights and the Struggle over Crime in the Media," *Canadian Journal of Communication* 32, no. 2 (June 2007): 219.
63. Ibid.
64. Ibid., 221.
65. Unlike the earlier Cuban refugees, Cubans arriving after 1980 were not always welcomed. The Marielitos, for instance, were darker and poorer and

portrayed as criminals. See María Cristina García, *Havana USA: Cuban Exiles and Cuban Americans in South Florida, 1959–1994* (Berkeley and Los Angeles: University of California Press, 1996); Yvette M. Mastin, "Sentenced to Purgatory: The Indefinite Detention of Mariel Cubans," *Scholar: St. Mary's Law Review on Minority Issues* 2, no. 1 (2000): 137–186.

66. María de los Angeles Torres, *In the Land of Mirrors: Cuban Exile Politics in the United States* (Ann Arbor: University of Michigan Press, 1999), 74–75. Since 1950, 90 percent of the refugees admitted into the United States emigrated from communist nations. Lynn Fujiwara, *Mothers Without Citizenship: Asian Immigrant Families and the Consequences of Welfare Reform* (Minneapolis: University of Minnesota Press, 2008), 59.

67. Torres, *In the Land of Mirrors*, 80, 174.

68. Roth, "Teen-ager Charged in Rampage Speaks Out."

69. Fred Dickey, "The Perversion of Hate: Laws Against Hate Crimes Are an Idea Gone Sour. Prosecutors Apply Them Unfairly and the List of 'Special Victims' Keeps Growing," *Los Angeles Times Magazine*, October 22, 2000.

70. Roth, "Teen-ager Charged in Rampage Speaks Out."

71. Ibid.

72. Ibid.

73. Laurence Steinberg, "Turning Poor Judgment into a Felony," *San Diego Union-Tribune*, February 11, 2001.

74. Kyle W. Kusz, "'I Want to Be the Minority': The Politics of Youthful White Masculinities in Sport and Popular Culture in 1990s America," *Journal of Sport and Social Issues* 25, no. 4 (November 2001): 401.

75. Jeff McDonald, "Some Suspects in Camp Attack Had Troubled Pasts: Neighbors, Friends Are Left Puzzled, Distressed," *San Diego Union-Tribune*, July 22, 2000.

76. Moran, "Three Teens Sentenced for Assault on Migrants."

77. Alex Roth, Jill Spielvogel, and Kim Peterson, "Teens Left Migrant for Dead, Court Told: Returned to Crime Scene to Hide Body, Prosecutor Says," *San Diego Union-Tribune*, July 20, 2000.

78. Ibid.

79. Alex Roth, "Judge Upholds Adult Trial for 8 Teens," *San Diego Union-Tribune*, September 13, 2000.

80. *Manduley v. Superior Court* 27 Cal.4th at 548.

81. Nicholas Espíritu, "(E)racing Youth: The Racialized Construction of California's Proposition 21 and the Development of Alternate Contestations," *Cleveland State Law Review* 52, nos. 1–2 (2005): 201. Espíritu is an attorney for the Mexican American Legal Defense and Educational Fund (MALDEF).

82. Ibid.

83. Philipsborn, Amicus Curiae. December 14, 2000, 22.

84. Mike Males and Dan Macallair, *The Color of Justice: An Analysis of Juvenile Adult Court Transfers in California* (Washington, DC: Building Blocks for

Youth, January 2000), 5, http://www.jjpl.org/Publications_JJ_InTheNews/ JuvenileJusticeSpecialReports/BBY/colorofjustice/coj.html.

85. Ibid., 7–8.

86. Christopher Hartney and Fabiana Silva, *And Justice for Some: Differential Treatment of Youth of Color in the Justice System* (Oakland, CA: National Council on Crime and Delinquency, January 2007), 34.

87. Barbara Herrnstein Smith, *Contingencies of Value: Alternative Perspectives for Critical Theory* (Cambridge, MA: Harvard University Press, 1988), 43.

88. "Sixth Teen Pleads No Contest to Migrant Beating," *10News.com*, May 29, 2002, http://www.10news.com/news/1486666/detail.html.

89. "Last of Group Plead No Contest to Migrant Beatings," *10News.com*, June 3, 2002, http://www.10news.com/news/1494218/detail.html.

90. Michelle Morgante, "Three More Teens Sentenced in Migrant Beating," *SignOnSanDiego.com*, July 23, 2002, http://legacy.signonsandiego.com/news/ northcounty/20020723-1223-ca-migrantattack.html.

91. "More Teens Sentenced for Migrant Attack," *10News.com*, November 20, 2002, http://www.10news.com/news/1796704/detail.html.

92. Moran, "Four Migrant Attackers Sentenced."

93. "Another Teen Sentenced for Migrant Attack," *10News.com*, July 30, 2002, http://www.10news.com/news/1584879/detail.html.

94. "Sentencing Held for Teens Involved in Migrant Attack," *10News.com*, June 28, 2002, http://www.10news.com/news/1536117/detail.html.

95. Larson, "The Adult Boys of Rancho Peñasquitos."

96. "Sentencing Held for Teens Involved in Migrant Attack."

97. Greg Moran, "Three Teens in Migrant Attack Are Sentenced: Activists Say Jail, Probation Too Lenient," *San Diego Union-Tribune*, November 21, 2002.

98. Ibid.

99. Cal. Penal Code, Title 7, Chapter 11, Section 186.22 (b)(1)(B): "The California Street Terrorism Enforcement and Prevention Act."

100. Thomas D. Elias, "California Sees Its First Juveniles Charged as Adults under New Law," *The Washington Times*, April 17, 2000.

101. Paradoxically, there is no lack of news coverage that portrays young men of color as criminal; there is just so little that portrays them complexly. This also has to do with the value of the victims' lives—youth of color are often victims and perpetrators. African Americans and Latinos are more often portrayed as criminal suspects by news media than as victims whereas whites are overrepresented as victims of crime and underrepresented as perpetrators of violent crimes. See Lori Dorfman and Vincent Schiraldi, *Off Balance: Youth, Race and Crime in the News* (Washington, DC: Building Blocks for Youth, April 1, 2001), 15–17.

For instance, even though news of school violence, especially school shootings, consistently make national headlines, social ecologist Mike Males found that between 1997 and 1999, thirty school killings went virtually unreported. Twenty-two of them involved youth of color attending schools with a majority population of color. Mike A. Males, *"Kids and Guns": How Politicians, Experts, and the Press Fabricate Fear of Youth* (Monroe, ME: Common Courage Press, 2000).

102. Raymond Smith, "Prop. 21 in Debut; Juvenile Charged: Riverside County Prosecutors Take a Case Directly to Adult Court under the Measure Passed by Voters on March 7," *The Press-Enterprise*, Riverside, CA, March 21, 2000.

103. "Juvenile Guilty in County's 1st Prop. 21 Case: Prosecutors Had Filed Charges against the Riverside Teen Less than Two Weeks after the Law Took Effect," *The Press-Enterprise*, Riverside, CA, April 19, 2000. Whether he would serve his term in jail, prison, or a correction facility for juveniles was not reported.

104. Elias, "California Sees Its First Juveniles Charged as Adults under New Law."

105. In addition to lowering the age that youth could be tried as adults for certain crimes, the proposition also authorized the death penalty for gang-related murders. As a gang member, Jesus Miranda faced the death penalty for killing Edgar Cruz, reported to be a rival gang member. Miranda was sentenced to prison for 94 years, 20 of which were for gang enhancement charges alone. Tracy Wilson, "Slaying Results in Life Term," *Los Angeles Times*, September 20, 2002.

106. Kevin Dolan, "Blinded by 'Objectivity': How News Conventions Caused Journalists to Miss the Real Story in the 'Our Lady' Controversy in Santa Fe," *Journalism* 6, no. 3 (2005): 392.

107. Johnson-Cartee, *News Narratives and News Framing*.

108. Rentschler, "Victims' Rights and the Struggle over Crime in the Media," 234.

NOTES TO CHAPTER 2

1. Mark Dow, *American Gulag* (Berkeley: University of California Press, 2005), 267.

2. For more on the ways in which Cambodian refugees have been regulated in the United States, see Aihwa Ong, *Buddha Is Hiding: Refugees, Citizenship, the New America* (Berkeley: University of California Press, 2003).

3. Melissa Cook, "Banished for Minor Crimes: The Aggravated Felony Provision of the Immigration and Nationality Act as Human Rights Violation," *Boston College Third World Law Journal* 23, no. 2 (Spring 2003): 293–329.

4. Bill Ong Hing, *Deporting Our Souls: Values, Morality, and Immigration Policy* (Cambridge: Cambridge University Press, 2006), 4–7.

5. Dow, *American Gulag*; D. L. Cheng, "Émigrés of the Killing Fields: The Deportation of Cambodian Refugees as a Violation of International Human Rights," *Boston College Third World Law Journal* 25, no. 1 (Winter 2005): 221–260; Yen H. Trinh, "The Impact of New Policies Adopted after September 11 on Lawful Permanent Residents Facing Deportation under the AEDPA and IIRIRA and the Hope of Relief under the Family Reunification Act," *Georgia Journal of International and Comparative Law* 33, no. 2 (Winter 2005): 543–572.

6. The 1980 Refugee Act enabled people who entered the United States without authorization to adjust their status if they were eligible for asylum. Even before the act, however, Cubans had this privilege until the Mariel Boatlift of 1980. Darker and poorer, the Mariel Cubans were also rumored to be insane or criminal; they were granted "parole" rather than asylum and legal residency; thus, their status was "excludable" or "inadmissible." Because the Mariel Cubans were not "admitted," they do not qualify for INS bond hearings to get out of INS detention and they are not entitled to "due process."

7. *Zadvydas v. Davis et al.* and *Ashcroft v. Ma,* 533 U.S. 678 (2001). Because Mariel Cubans were considered inadmissible or excludable, this court decision did not include most Mariel Cubans until 2003. Even so, it applies only within the Sixth U.S. Circuit Court of Appeals, and INS/BICE can move detainees to places where it does not apply. Dow, *American Gulag,* 289–290.

8. For more on criminalization and refugees, see Damien Lawson, "Refugee! Criminal! Terrorist!" *New Internationalist Magazine,* October 1, 2002, http://www.newint.org/features/2002/10/01/criminalization/; Teresa A. Miller, "Blurring the Boundaries Between Immigration and Crime Control after September 11th," *Boston College Third World Law Journal* 25, no. 1 (Winter 2005): 1–43; Jennifer M. Chacón, "Managing Migration Through Crime," *Columbia Law Review Sidebar* 109 (2009): 135–145; Bill Ong Hing, "The Immigrant as Criminal: Punishing Dreamers," *Hastings Women's Law Journal* 9, no. 1 (Winter 1998): 79–96.

9. For more on Cambodian refugees in general, see Sucheng Chan, *Survivors: Cambodian Refugees in the United States* (Champaign: University of Illinois Press, 2004); Ong, *Buddha Is Hiding.*

10. Lewis Yablonsky, *The Violent Gang* (Bloomington, IN: iUniverse, 2009), xxii–xxiii.

11. Barrett, *Blackness and Value,* 128.

12. The President's Commission on Organized Crimes was established under President Reagan by Executive Order 12435.

13. President's Commission on Organized Crime, *Organized Crime of Asian Origin: Record of Hearing III October 23–25, 1984, New York, New York* (New York & Hong Kong: Books for Business, 2001), v.

14. Sergeant Douglas Zwemke of the San Jose, California, Police Department, speaking to U.S. Senate Permanent Subcommittee on Investigations of the Committee on Governmental Affairs, *Asian Organized Crime, Hearing before the Permanent Subcommittee on Investigations of the Committee on Governmental Affairs,* 102nd Cong., 1st sess., October 3, November 5–6, 1991, 54.

15. William S. Sessions, Federal Bureau of Investigation director, speaking to U.S. Senate Permanent Subcommittee on Investigations of the Committee on Governmental Affairs, ibid., 15–16.

16. Captain Donald Saviers of the Westminster, California, Police Department, speaking to the President's Commission on Organized Crime, *Organized*

Crime of Asian Origin: Record of Hearing III October 23–25, 1984, New York, New York, 381–382.

17. Delaware Senator William V. Roth Jr., speaking to the U.S. Senate Permanent Subcommittee on Investigations of the Committee on Governmental Affairs, *Emerging Criminal Groups, Hearings before the Permanent Subcommittee on Investigations of the Committee on Governmental Affairs,* United States Senate, 99th Cong., 2nd sess., September 24, 1986, 50.

18. Question 12 in the Naturalization Civics Test Booklet is: "What is the 'rule of law'?" The possible answers are the following: 1) "Everyone must follow the law." 2) "Leaders must obey the law." 3) "Government must obey the law." 4) "No one is above the law." (U.S. Citizenship and Immigration Services, Learn About the United States: Quick Civics Lessons for the New Naturalization Test, July 2009, 4.) All the answers are correct.

19. Kim Ho Ma's appeal to the Board of Immigration Appeals regarding his application for asylum and withholding of deportation was denied December 31, 1997. Paul W. Schmidt, Decision of the Board of Immigration Appeals, October 26, 1998 (C.A. Ex. Rec. 162–168). Ma's applications were included in the U.S. Supreme Court Briefs for his Writ of Certiorari to the United States Court of Appeals for the Ninth Circuit, Joint Appendix, 54. *Janet v. Reno, et al. v. Kim Ho Ma* (2000). No. 00–38.

20. Allegedly, Chhay was a member of the Oriental Lazy Boys, a rival gang. Representations of his background are inconsistent, however; some reported he was a member of the Local Asian Boyz who wanted to leave the gang, while others wrote that he was not a gang member.

21. Dori Cahn and Jay Stansell, "From Refugee to Deportee: How U.S. Immigration Law Failed the Cambodian Community," in *Race, Culture, Psychology, and Law*, ed. Kimberly Holt Barrett and William H. George (Thousand Oaks, CA: Sage Publications, 2005), 243.

22. Ibid.

23. Ibid.

24. Most anti-gang legislation is enacted at the state and local levels, and most states' anti-gang laws define a gang by two criteria: 1) whether a group is *visibly* identifiable and 2) what kind of criminal activity was committed. Not all crimes legally define a group as a gang. California, for instance, names 25 specific crimes that would potentially define three or more adolescents and/or young adults as a criminal street gang. Committing any of the 25 crimes may only "potentially" define a group of teenagers as a gang because the group also needs to be identifiable. As in most states, California's relatively ambiguous identifying markers consist of a common name, sign, or symbol. A few states explicitly cite examples of the visual signs and symbols that would be evidence of gang membership. Georgia includes "tattoos, graffiti, or attire or other distinguishing characteristics"; New Jersey's definition incorporates a common "tattoo or other physical marking, style of dress or use of hand signs

or other indicia of association or common leadership"; and Arizona specifies tattoos as well as "clothing or colors." What these indicate is that gang membership, and criminal activity in general, is unrecognizable without a body of color. "Compilation of Gang-Related Legislation," *National Gang Center*, n.d., http://www.nationalgangcenter.gov/Legislation.

25. Kim Ho Ma's application for eligibility to apply for asylum or withholding of deportation, decision by Immigration Judge Anna Ho, September 12, 1997. Kim Ho Ma's application for Bond Redetermination, decision by Immigration Judge Anna Ho, December 31, 1997. Ma's applications were included in the U.S. Supreme Court briefs for his Writ of Certiorari to the United States Court of Appeals for the Ninth Circuit, Joint Appendix, 30. *Janet v. Reno, et al. v. Kim Ho Ma* (2000). No. 00-38.

26. Kim Ho Ma's application for Bond Redetermination, decision by Immigration Judge Anna Ho, December 31, 1997. Ma's applications were included in the U.S. Supreme Court briefs for his Writ of Certiorari to the United States Court of Appeals for the Ninth Circuit, Joint Appendix, 43. *Janet v. Reno, et al. v. Kim Ho Ma* (2000). No. 00-38.

27. This is similar to the confession that Foucault analyzes as a strategy of psychiatric power: "not so much the truth that he could say about himself, at the level of his actual experience, but a truth imposed on him in a canonical form: cross-examination of identity, the recall of certain episodes already known to the doctor." Michel Foucault, *Psychiatric Power: Lectures at the Collège De France, 1973–74*, ed. Jacques Lagrange, trans. Graham Burchell (Basingstoke, Hampshire, UK: Palgrave Macmillan, 2006), 159.

28. Kim Ho Ma's application for Bond Redetermination, decision by Immigration Judge Anna Ho, December 31, 1997. Ma's applications were included in the U.S. Supreme Court Briefs for his Writ of Certiorari to the United States Court of Appeals for the Ninth Circuit, Joint Appendix, 42–43. *Janet v. Reno, et al. v. Kim Ho Ma* (2000). No. 00-38.

29. Ibid.

30. Michel Foucault, *Abnormal: Lectures at the Collège De France, 1974–1975*, ed. Valerio Marchetti and Antonella Salomoni, trans. Graham Burchell (New York: Picador, 2003), 316. "[Psychiatry] becomes the discipline of the scientific protection of society; it becomes the discipline of the biological protection of the species."

31. Foucault, *Psychiatric Power*, 85.

32. Ibid., 85–86.

33. As Foucault writes, "The Psy-function was the discourse and the establishment of all the schemas for the individualization, normalization, and subjection of individuals within disciplinary systems." Ibid., 86.

34. Ibid., 52–53.

35. Lewis Yablonsky, *Gangs in Court* (Tucson, AZ: Lawyers and Judges Publishing, 2008), 51.

36. Ibid., 50.

37. Yablonsky, *The Violent Gang*, 239. Emphasis in the original.

38. Yablonsky, *Gangs in Court*, 58, 51.

39. Salt Lake County, Utah, Sheriff Aaron D. Kennard, speaking to Senate Committee on the Judiciary, *Gangs: A National Crisis: Hearing before the Senate Committee on the Judiciary on S. 54 A Bill to Reduce Interstate Street Gang and Organized Crime Activity, and for Other Purposes,* 105th Cong., 1st sess., April 23, 1997, 40.

40. Chairman Senator Orrin G. Hatch of Utah, speaking to Senate Committee on the Judiciary, *Gangs: A National Crisis*, ibid., 62.

41. Colleen Minson, a Salt Lake City resident, speaking to Senate Committee on the Judiciary, *Gangs: A National Crisis*, ibid., 46.

42. Also see Paul K. Longmore and Lauri Umansky, eds. *The New Disability History: American Perspectives* (New York: New York University Press, 2001).

43. Douglas C. Baynton, "Disability and the Justification of Inequality in American History," in *The New Disability History: American Perspectives*, 36.

44. Ibid.

45. Ibid., 37–51.

46. Ibid.

47. Ibid., 42.

48. Homosexuality was considered a mental illness by the American Psychiatry Association in the *Diagnostic and Statistical Manual* until 1973. The United States banned people with HIV/AIDS from entering for 22 years; the ban was enacted in 1987 and was not lifted until January 2010.

49. Dean Spade, "Resisting Medicine, Re/modeling Gender," *Berkeley Women's Law Journal* 18 (2003): 15–37.

50. Baynton, "Disability and the Justification of Inequality in American History," 33–52.

51. Ibid., 33–34.

52. Ibid., 44.

53. Ibid., 34.

54. Foucault, *Abnormal*, 312. Emphasis added. A condition is different than a predisposition because one could be "normal *and* predisposed to an illness," but the person "who has a condition, is not a normal individual" (312).

55. According to Foucault, around the 1860s–1870s, the "condition" was introduced by French psychiatrist Jean-Pierre Falret and was subsequently "reformulated a thousand times." Ibid., 311.

56. Ibid., 304, 308.

57. Ibid., 306–309.

58. Ibid., 310.

59. Ibid., 311.

60. Ibid., 312–313.

61. Yablonsky, *Gangs in Court*, 52.

62. Foucault, *Abnormal*, 313.

63. Ibid.

64. David T. Lykken, *The Antisocial Personalities* (Hillsdale, NJ: Lawrence Erlbaum, 1995), ix.

65. Kim Ho Ma's application for eligibility to apply for asylum or withholding of deportation, decision by Immigration Judge Anna Ho, September 12, 1997. Ma's applications were included in the U.S. Supreme Court Briefs for his Writ of Certiorari to the United States Court of Appeals for the Ninth Circuit, Joint Appendix, 30. *Janet v. Reno, et al. v. Kim Ho Ma* (2000). No. 00-38. Ma argued that he was eligible for asylum and withholding of deportation because he should not have been tried as an adult in his criminal trial (29–30). If he had been tried as a juvenile, his crime would not have been considered an aggravated felony; an aggravated felony is grounds for deportation.

66. Cahn and Stansell, "From Refugee to Deportee," 243.

67. Silva, *Toward a Global Idea of Race*, xv.

68. Mbembe, "Necropolitics," 25–26. Emphasis in the original. In this quotation, Mbembe is drawing upon Franz Fanon's analysis of the spatialization of colonial occupation.

69. Bello, *Dark Victory*, 27.

70. Ibid., 25.

71. Phrases such as the "third world," "newly industrialized country," and "developing nation" connote that poorer countries are following inevitable paths toward becoming like the United States, Europe, or Japan (i.e., toward becoming "modern nations"). Representing nations as following a predestined path toward modernization denies poor nations contemporaneity and hides the fact that "modern" nations and multinational corporations actively and violently keep poor regions impoverished by exploiting the people and the natural resources of vulnerable nations. For these reasons, I have chosen to use "global South" and "global North" instead of "third world" and "first world." These phrases are not without problems (as North and South also imply hierarchies), but I prefer them because they better capture how violent spatial practices maintain exploitation.

72. Bello, *Dark Victory*, 52.

73. Massimiliano Tomba, "Differentials of Surplus-Value in the Contemporary Forms of Exploitation," *The Commoner* 12 (Spring/Summer 2007): 33.

74. Ibid.

75. Ibid.

76. Bello, *Dilemmas of Domination*, 87.

77. George Caffentzis, "A Tale of Two Conferences: Globalization, the Crisis of Neoliberalism and Question of the Commons," presented at the Alter-Globalization Conference (San Miguel de Allende, Mexico: The Commoner, 2004), 4, http://www.commoner.org.uk/wp-content/uploads/2010/12/caffentzis_a-tale-of-two-conferences.pdf. It's important

to note that Caffentzis recognizes that communal property rights are not necessarily anti-capitalist even though they counter neoliberalism. Some forms of communal ownership can be appropriated and incorporated. For Caffentzis, the difference lies in whether the questions that guide the commons concerns the "efficiency, sustainability, and equity" of a property regime or "whether a particular commons increases the power of workers to resist capital and to define a non-capitalist future" (27). As he says, "radical developments inevitably create opportunities for alliances with powerful reformist forces within capitalism that are at least superficially supporting the same demand. These alliances pose many political problems and require an even deeper understanding of the differences between a capitalist and an anti-capitalist theory and practice of the commons" (27).

78. Midnight Notes Collective, "The New Enclosures: Planetary Class Struggle," in *Globalize Liberation: How to Uproot the System and Build a Better World*, ed. David Solnit (San Francisco: City Lights Books, 2004), 67.

79. Ibid., 66.

80. Ibid.

81. Ibid., 64–70.

82. George Caffentzis and Monty Neill, "Preface: The New Enclosures: Planetary Class Struggle," in *Globalize Liberation: How to Uproot the System and Build a Better World*, ed. David Solnit (San Francisco: City Lights Books, 2004), 62–63.

83. Locking up political prisoners is an example of using incarceration to neutralize social and political unrest. For more about political prisoners in the United States, see Dylan Rodríguez, *Forced Passages: Imprisoned Radical Intellectuals and the U.S. Prison Regime* (Minneapolis: University of Minnesota Press, 2006); Assata Shakur, *Assata: An Autobiography* (Chicago: Lawrence Hill Books, 1987); Dhoruba Bin Wahad, Mumia Abu-Jamal, and Assata Shakur, *Still Black, Still Strong: Survivors of the U.S. War against Black Revolutionaries* (New York: Semiotext(e), 1993). On the role of prisons in the U.S. economy, see Ruth Wilson Gilmore, *Golden Gulag: Prisons, Surplus, Crisis, and Opposition in Globalizing California* (Berkeley: University of California Press, 2007); Christian Parenti, *Lockdown America: Police and Prisons in the Age of Crisis* (London: Verso, 2000).

84. Randall Richard, "For Kim, There Is No Second Chance," Associated Press, November 6, 2003.

85. Lykken, *The Antisocial Personalities*, 199.

86. Donald W. Kodluboy, "Asian Youth Gangs," *School Safety* (1996): 8–12.

87. Bill Ong Hing, for instance, provides an account of Cambodian refugees that humanizes the deportees, but the process of humanization requires decriminalizing or rationalizing their actions (rather than, for instance, challenging values or laws). I am defining humanization here as the (re)presentation of

people in ways that minimize their unsympathetic status and emphasize their socially valuable qualities. Humanization represents someone as deserving to be recognized as a person. For Hing, explanations for Cambodian criminality all "seem to flow from refugee status itself" (88). Hing, *Deporting Our Souls*, 78–117.

88. Eric Tang, "Collateral Damage: Southeast Asian Poverty in the United States," *Social Text* 18, no. 1 (Spring 2000): 55–79.

89. Nathan S. Caplan, John K. Whitmore, and Marcella H. Choy, *The Boat People and Achievement in America: A Study of Family Life, Hard Work, and Cultural Values* (Ann Arbor: University of Michigan Press, 1989), 162–163.

90. Ong, *Buddha Is Hiding*, 86. Ong claims that Cambodians were ideologically blackened whereas the Vietnamese were ideologically whitened.

91. Miranda Joseph, "Family Affairs: The Discourse of Global/Localization," in *Queer Globalizations: Citizenship and the Afterlife of Colonialism*, ed. Martin Manalansan and Arnaldo Cruz-Malavé (New York: New York University Press, 2002), 80–81.

92. Letha A. (Lee) See, *Tensions and Tangles Between Afro Americans and Southeast Asian Refugees: A Study of the Conflict* (Atlanta: Wright Publishing, 1986), 147.

93. Jun, *Race for Citizenship*, 250.

94. Ibid., 145.

95. Ibid.

96. Ibid.

97. Arendt, *The Origins of Totalitarianism*, 295–296.

98. Detective William Oldham of the New York City Police Department, speaking to U.S. Senate Permanent Subcommittee on Investigations of the Committee on Governmental Affairs, *Asian Organized Crime, Hearing before the Permanent Subcommittee on Investigations of the Committee on Governmental Affairs*, 102nd Cong., 1st sess., October 3, November 5–6, 1991, 37.

99. Ibid., 39.

100. Douglas D. Daye, *A Law Enforcement Sourcebook of Asian Crime and Cultures: Tactics and Mindsets* (Boca Raton, FL: CRC Press, 1996), 263.

101. Ibid.

102. Ibid., 264.

103. Ibid.

104. Sergeant Douglas Zwemke of the San Jose, California, Police Department, speaking to U.S. Senate Permanent Subcommittee on Investigations of the Committee on Governmental Affairs, *Asian Organized Crime, Hearing before the Permanent Subcommittee on Investigations of the Committee on Governmental Affairs*, 102nd Congress, 1st session, October 3, November 5–6, 1991, 55.

105. David Coyoca, "Our New Neighbors," *Ninth Letter* 2, no.1 (Spring–Summer 2005): 165.

106. Senator William V. Roth Jr. of Delaware, opening statement to U.S. Senate Permanent Subcommittee on Investigations of the Committee on

Governmental Affairs, *Asian Organized Crime: The New International Crimi-nal, Hearings before the Permanent Subcommittee on Investigations of the Committee on Governmental Affairs*, 102nd Cong., 2nd sess., June 18, August 4, 1992, 5.

107. Oldham, 41.

108. The legislation did not extend to other places, such as the Philippines or Korea, which also had a high number of children fathered and abandoned by American servicemen. Elizabeth Kolby, "Moral Responsibility to Filipino Amerasians: Potential Immigration and Child Support Alternatives," *Asian Law Journal* 2, no. 1 (May 1995): 61–62.

109. See, for example, Robert S. McKelvey, *The Dust of Life: America's Children Abandoned in Vietnam* (Seattle: University of Washington Press, 1999).

110. Lowe, *Immigrant Acts*, 77.

111. Ibid., 63.

112. National Crime Prevention Council, *Powerful Partnerships: Twenty Crime Pre-vention Strategies That Work for Refugees, Law Enforcement, and Communities* (Washington, DC: National Crime Prevention Council, 1998), 11.

113. Jim Steinberg, "Lost in America Southeast Asian Youths Coming of Age; Gen-erations Struggle with Cultural Conflicts," *The Fresno Bee*, July 16, 1995.

114. Lieutenant Kenneth Adair, Garden Grove Police Department, California, Special Investigations, speaking to the President's Commission on Organized Crime, *Organized Crime of Asian Origin, Record of Hearing III, October 23–25, 1984, New York, New York* (New York: Books for Business, 2001), 325–326.

115. National Crime Prevention Council, *Powerful Partnerships*, 12.

116. Andrea J. Ritchie and Joey L. Mogul, "In the Shadows of the War on Terror: Persistent Police Brutality and Abuse of People of Color in the United States," *DePaul Journal for Social Justice* 1, no. 2 (Spring 2008): 181–182.

117. Ibid.

118. Richard Straka, "The Violence of Hmong Gangs and the Crime of Rape," *FBI Law Enforcement Bulletin*, February 2003, 15.

119. Ibid. The quotation is from Na Ly Yang, executive director of the Women's Association for Hmong and Laos in St. Paul, Minnesota.

120. Ibid., 16.

121. Ibid., 14.

122. Ibid., 14–15.

123. Ibid., 15.

124. For more on how culture and feminism are constructed as mutually exclu-sive, see Uma Narayan, *Dislocating Cultures: Identities, Traditions, and Third World Feminism* (New York: Routledge, 1997); Leti Volpp, "Feminism versus Multiculturalism," *Columbia Law Review* 101 (2001): 1181–1218; Julietta Hua and Kasturi Ray, "The 'Practice of Humanity': Neoliberal Constructions of Domestic Workers and 'Sex Slaves,'" *Feminist Media Studies* 10, no. 3 (Septem-ber 2010): 253–267; Saba Mahmood, *Politics of Piety: The Islamic Revival and*

the Feminist Subject (Princeton: Princeton University Press, 2005); Andrea Smith, *Conquest: Sexual Violence and American Indian Genocide* (Cambridge, MA: South End Press, 2005); Natalie J. Sokoloff and Christina Pratt, eds., *Domestic Violence at the Margins: Readings on Race, Class, Gender, and Culture* (New Brunswick: Rutgers University Press, 2005).

125. Straka, "The Violence of Hmong Gangs and the Crime of Rape," 16.

126. Carole Pateman, *The Sexual Contract* (Stanford: Stanford University Press, 1988).

127. Dow, *American Gulag*, 269.

128. Ibid., 269–270. Dow is quoting Morones here.

129. Senator Warren B. Rudman of New Hampshire, prepared statement for the U.S. Senate Permanent Subcommittee on Investigations of the Committee on Governmental Affairs, *Asian Organized Crime, Hearing before the Permanent Subcommittee on Investigations of the Committee on Governmental Affairs*, 102nd Cong., 1st sess., October 3, November 5–6, 1991, 202.

130. Mimi Nguyen, *Refugee Passages: War, Debt, and Other Gifts of Freedom* (Durham: Duke University Press, 2012).

131. Ibid.

132. Justice Antonin Scalia, Supreme Court transcripts, *Zadvydas v. Underdown* (No. 99–7791), *Ashcroft v. Ma* (No. 00–38) February 21, 2001, Washington, DC, 13.

133. Dow, *American Gulag*, 264.

134. The IIRIRA amended the definition of aggravated felony through lowering the threshold of imprisonment from five years to one year with the exception of "alien smuggling," which was lowered from five years to zero years (and which also carried an exception if the first time offense was for "smuggling" an immediate family member into the United States). Ma was affected by the amendment that lowered the term of imprisonment from five years to one year for a crime of violence, INA §101(a)(43)(F). Section 321 of IIRIRA amends INA §101(a)(43) so definitions of "aggravated felony" apply to convictions before, on, or after the date of enactment of September 30, 1996.

135. Before the enactment of the IIRIRA and the AEDPA, legal immigrants could be deported if they had been convicted for committing certain kinds of crimes: 1) a violent crime that carried a sentence of five or more years of imprisonment, 2) a crime defined as an "aggravated felony," or 3) a crime of "moral turpitude," which to this day still remains undefined in immigration law. After the enactment of the IIRIRA in 1996, mandatory deportation for a five-year or longer sentence for theft and/or violent crime changed to a one-year or longer sentence.

136. The IIRIRA clarified how "conviction" was defined, INA § 101(a)(48), so that "conviction" did not refer only to being found "guilty" and formally sentenced. An alien was also considered "convicted" if the judge had ordered some form of punishment even if adjudication was withheld. In addition, a "conviction" encompassed any admission of guilt (such as a guilty plea) or the

suggestion of an admission of guilt (such as a plea of no contest or if the suspect admitted facts that could lead to a finding of guilt). The term of imprisonment was clarified to refer to the years sentenced, not actual time served, regardless of whether the sentence was partly or wholly suspended.

137. Norton Tooby, criminal defense attorney in Oakland, California, has compiled several resources for other criminal defense lawyers with noncitizen clients "because the criminal conviction may guarantee an immigration disaster, at that point it is often already too late. If we don't solve the problem at its source—in criminal court—the damage may be irrevocable." In effect, the IIRIRA made immigration lawyers powerless because, as Tooby notes, "Although it may be possible to seek post-conviction relief from the conviction, the difficulties are often insurmountable." Hence, criminal defense lawyers with a noncitizen client *must* also perform the job of an immigration lawyer: "*Very often, the adverse immigration effects of a criminal case are far worse for the client than any jail or fine will be.* The normal criminal effects are frequently *secondary*, such as in the first example above, in which the criminal sentence was relatively harmless (probation with no jail), but the automatic and unavoidable immigration effects of the conviction were life-shattering and permanent. In these cases, the criminal defense strategy should be directed primarily to avoiding the immigration consequences, and only secondarily to minimizing the criminal judgment or sentence." Norton Tooby, *Law Offices of Norton Tooby,* http://criminalandimmigrationlaw.com (accessed April 11, 2010).

138. The IIRIRA reduced and then completely eliminated the 212(c) waiver of deportation established under the Immigration and Nationality Act. Under the 212(c) waiver, immigrants who had legally resided in the United States for at least seven years were granted a hearing before an immigration judge to request discretionary relief from deportation by demonstrating that their "positive" factors (such as family ties, U.S. military service, or evidence of rehabilitation) outweighed the "negative" factors (such as a criminal record or other violations to immigration law). The remaining options for deportation relief or postponement were not only severely restricted, they were absolutely unavailable to noncitizens convicted of committing an aggravated felony. If a crime is defined as a misdemeanor according to state law but an aggravated felony according to the Immigration and Nationality Act, then it is considered an aggravated felony. See Human Rights Watch, *Forced Apart: Families Separated and Immigrants Harmed by United States Deportation Policy,* vol. 19, no. 3(g), July 2007.

139. Foucault, *Abnormal,* 317. Italics mine.

140. Senator Warren B. Rudman of New Hampshire, prepared statement for the Permanent Subcommittee on Investigations of the Senate Committee on Governmental Affairs, *Hearing on Asian Organized Crime,* 102nd Cong., 1st sess., October 3, November 5–6, 1991, 202.

NOTES TO CHAPTER 3

1. George W. Bush, "Remarks to the Airline Employees in Chicago, Illinois, September 27, 2001," *Public Papers of the Presidents of the United States: George W. Bush, 2001*, vol. 2 (Washington, DC: Government Printing Office, 2001), 1170–1171.

2. I am using Jasbir Puar's notion of "reassembled." Puar, *Terrorist Assemblages*.

3. Ibid., 38.

4. Michel Foucault, *Society Must Be Defended: Lectures at the Collège De France, 1975–76*, ed. Mauro Bertani and Alessandro Fontana, trans. David Macey (New York: Picador, 2003), 247. Foucault distinguishes disciplinary power from biopower by explaining that biopower is not about the body but about life, not about the individual but about populations, not a disciplinary power but a "power of regularization" that is about "making live and letting die" (247). For a state that regulates its population through biopower, racism is its "basic mechanism of power" (254) and "the precondition that makes killing acceptable" (256). Biopower, or this power to make live and let die (not just justified but enabled by racism), exceeds the sovereign right to kill. Through technologies such as the atomic bomb and biological warfare, biopower surpasses human sovereignty; the right to kill certain bodies through technologies of biopower can also end *all* life (254). Furthermore, when the state insists upon exercising its sovereign power, upon its right to kill the other, as in the war on terror, it is also demanding that its subjects risk death (254). As Foucault posits, modern racism is a technology of biopower not only "modeled on war" but necessary to wage war in the modern era.

5. Ibid., 254, 265.

6. Moustafa Bayoumi, "Racing Religion," *CR: The New Centennial Review* 6, no. 2 (Fall 2006): 278.

7. Mbembe, "Necropolitics," 12.

8. Ibid., 40.

9. George W. Bush, "Address Before a Joint Session of the Congress on the United States Response to the Terrorist Attacks of September 11, September 20, 2001," *Public Papers of the Presidents of United States: George W. Bush, 2001*, vol. 2 (Washington, DC: Government Printing Office, 2001), 1141.

10. Ibid., 1142.

11. George W. Bush, "Remarks to Military Personnel and Families at Fort Stewart, Georgia, September 12, 2003," *Public Papers of the Presidents of United States: George W. Bush, 2003*, vol. 2 (Washington, DC: Government Printing Office, 2001), 1144.

12. Leo R. Chavez, *The Latino Threat: Constructing Immigrants, Citizens, and the Nation* (Stanford: Stanford University Press, 2008), 28. See also Leo R. Chavez, *Covering Immigration: Popular Images and the Politics of the Nation* (Berkeley: University of California Press, 2001).

13. Otto Santa Ana, *Brown Tide Rising: Metaphors of Latinos in Contemporary American Public Discourse* (Austin: University of Texas Press, 2002), 70.
14. Ibid.
15. Patrick J. McDonnell and Russell Carollo, "An Easy Entry for Attackers: Immigration Flaws Garner Attention as Authorities Track the Sept. 11 Hijackers' Movements through the United States," *Los Angeles Times*, September 30, 2001.
16. Peter Slevin and Mary Beth Sheridan, "Suspects Entered U.S. on Legal Visas: Men Blended In; Officials Say 49 Have Been Detained on Immigration Violations," *The Washington Post*, September 18, 2001.
17. James V. Grimaldi, Steve Fainaru, and Gilbert M. Gaul, "Losing Track of Illegal Immigrants: Once in U.S., Most Foreigners Easily Escape Notice of INS," *The Washington Post*, October 7, 2001.
18. Junaid Rana, *Terrifying Muslims: Race and Labor in the South Asian Diaspora* (Durham: Duke University Press, 2011), 61.
19. Undocumented Latinas/os "blended in" in different ways because the federal government never really needed to "see" or search for undocumented Latinas/os. It already knew where they would be: studying in school; cleaning, caretaking, and landscaping people's homes; working for contractors on government projects; or living in county jails and INS detention centers. Immigration law does not intend to keep undocumented workers out. Instead, it is designed to maximize corporate profitability by maximizing undocumented Latinas/os' legal vulnerability. This has been accomplished by intensifying the threat of deportability.
20. Janice Kephart, *Immigration and Terrorism: Moving Beyond the 9/11 Staff Report on Terrorist Travel* (Washington, DC: Center for Immigration Studies, September 2005), 7.
21. Puar, *Terrorist Assemblages*, 158.
22. Michael J. Whidden, "Unequal Justice: Arabs in America and United States Antiterrorism Legislation," *Fordham Law Review* 69, no. 6 (May 2001): 2827–2828.
23. Raquel Aldana, "September 11 Immigration Detentions and Unconstitutional Executive Legislation," *Southern Illinois University Law Journal* 29, no. 1 (Fall 2004): 8.
24. Ibid., 10. *Reno v. American-Arab Anti-Discrimination Committee* (1999) 525 U.S. 471 at 488.
25. Aldana, "September 11 Immigration Detentions and Unconstitutional Executive Legislation," 8–9.
26. Ibid., 8.
27. Jodi Melamed, "The Spirit of Neoliberalism: From Racial Liberalism to Neoliberal Multiculturalism," *Social Text* 24, no. 4 (Winter 2006): 1–24.
28. Ibid., 18.

29. Mahmood Mamdani, *Good Muslim, Bad Muslim: America, the Cold War, and the Roots of Terror* (New York: Three Leaves Press, 2004). Mamdani defines "culture talk" as the use of cultural difference to explain politics. Culture talk assumes that all cultures are defined by a "tangible essence": "It is no longer the market (capitalism), nor the state (democracy), but culture (modernity) that is said to be the dividing line between those who are modern and those who are premodern" (17–18). Mamdani argues that even if this suggests that "premodern peoples may not be held responsible for their actions," it still leads to the same conclusion: They must be "restrained, collectively if not individually—if necessary, held captive, even unconditionally—for the good of civilization" (18).

30. Sunaina Marr Maira, *Missing: Youth, Citizenship, and Empire after 9/11* (Durham: Duke University Press, 2009), 250.

31. Jasbir K. Puar and Amit Rai, "Monster, Terrorist, Fag: The War on Terrorism and the Production of Docile Patriots," *Social Text* 20, no. 3 (Fall 2002): 138.

32. Ahmed, *Strange Encounters*.

33. John Ashcroft, "Attorney General Prepared Remarks on the National Security Entry-Exit Registration System," *Department of Justice*, June 6, 2002, http://www.justice.gov/archive/ag/speeches/2002/060502agpreparedremarks.htm; "Fact Sheet: Changes to National Security Entry/Exit Registration System (NSEERS)," *Department of Homeland Security*, December 1, 2003, http://www.dhs.gov/xnews/releases/press_release_0305.shtm; "US VISIT and NSEERS," *GlobalSecurity.org*, n.d., http://www.globalsecurity.org/security/ops/usvisit-nseers.htm.

    The Department of Homeland Security suspended the reregistration requirement in December 2003 but kept the provision that certain foreign nationals must go through special registration upon entering the United States and report to immigration upon leaving. NSEERS is a predecessor for US-VISIT, a comprehensive entry-exit system, which was initiated by the DHS in 2004. All provisions of NSEERS in effect will be subsumed under US-VISIT when it is fully implemented.

34. Bayoumi, "Racing Religion," 278.

35. Ibid., 288.

36. Ibid., 272.

37. Leti Volpp, "The Citizen and the Terrorist," *UCLA Law Review* 49, no. 5 (June 2002): 1584. Along like lines, Puar argues the "binary-reinforcing 'you're either with us or against us' normativizing apparatus" enabled the "rehabilitation" of some gays and lesbians because a politics of homonormativity helped to emphasize the "sexual exceptionalism" of the United States (as "gay-safe") in relation to the Middle East (as purportedly not). Puar, *Terrorist Assemblages*, 39–41.

38. Elizabeth Llorente, "Illegal Immigration Down Since Terrorist Attacks," *The Record*, Bergen County, NJ, November 25, 2001.

39. Steven Greenhouse and Mireya Navarro, "The Hidden Victims: Those at Towers' Margin Elude List of Missing," *The New York Times*, September 17, 2001.
40. Puar, *Terrorist Assemblages*, 52.
41. Llorente, "Illegal Immigration Down Since Terrorist Attacks."
42. Anita U. Hattiangadi et al., *Noncitizens in Today's Military: Final Report* (Alexandria, VA: CNA Corporation, April 2005), 25.
43. Ibid.
44. Mark Stevenson, "U.S. Army Recruiter Crosses Mexico Border," Associated Press, May 9, 2003.
45. Jorge Mariscal, "The Militarization of Everyday Life: Latinos on the Frontlines, Again," *CounterPunch*, March 22, 2003, http://www.counterpunch.org/mariscal04012003.html.
46. *Population Representation in the Military Services: Fiscal Year 2002* (Washington, DC: Department of Defense, 2004), Appendixes B-25, B-30. The targeted recruitment of Latina/o youth and young adults of color is due in part to the military's claims that Latinas/os are underrepresented in the military. Latinas/os make up only about 10 percent of the military while constituting about 14 percent of the civilian population between the ages of 18 and 44. Such claims justify these selective recruitment practices even though Latinas/os in the military are overrepresented on the front lines.
47. 10 U.S.C. § 983
48. Many college and university departments, law schools, units, or centers have banned military recruiters' access to students in protest against, for instance, the military's former "don't ask, don't tell" policy or the selective recruitment of racial/ethnic students through such programs as the Hispanic Access Initiative.
49. *Population Representation in the Military Services*, Appendixes B-25, B-30.
50. Betsy Streisand and Samantha Levine, "Latin Heroes," *U.S. News and World Report*, April 14, 2003, 40.
51. Ibid.
52. "Fact Sheet: Naturalization through Military Service," *U.S. Citizenship and Immigration Services*, n.d., http://www.uscis.gov/military.
53. Executive Order 13269 enacted section 329 of the Immigration and Nationality Act. See INA Sec. 329. [8 U.S.C. 1440]; Executive Order no. 13269, "Expedited Naturalization of Aliens and Noncitizen Nationals Serving in an Active-Duty Status During the War on Terrorism," *Federal Register* 67, no. 130 (July 2002): 45287. Most of Executive Order 13269 was put into law through the Armed Forces Naturalization Act. The Naturalization and Other Immigration Benefits for Military Personnel and Families Act of 2003 also extended benefits to family members of soldiers granted posthumous citizenship. (This was not automatic under the executive order.) When introduced as a bill, this act was referred to as the "Naturalization and Family Protection for Military Members Act of 2003." See Hector Amaya, "Dying American

or the Violence of Citizenship: Latinos in Iraq," *Latino Studies* 5, no. 1 (April 2007): 3–24.

54. Margaret D. Stock, "When Your Client Fights for Uncle Sam: 'No Card' Soldiers and Expedited Citizenship," *Bender's Immigration Bulletin*, December 15, 2003. The executive order does not make undocumented immigrants legally eligible for service; however, it does enable lawyers to argue that Executive Order 13269 waives the process of attaining a green card.

55. Bruce Finley, "Military Eyeing 'Unknowns': Thousands in Ranks May Not Be Citizens," *The Denver Post*, February 24, 2004, 7. In a personal correspondence with Finley to confirm these numbers, I learned that Finley received this information through several correspondences with the Pentagon. All publications by the Department of Homeland Security, the Pentagon, and the various branches of the U.S. military regarding this issue cite Finley's story; no one denies or challenges his statistics. The Center for Naval Analyses published a report in 2005 on noncitizens in the military that, although not offering any evidence to counter Finley's findings, challenged his claims that "unknown" is synonymous with undocumented. The report based this on the services' findings that most of the "unknowns" in the Navy were officers, who are required to be U.S. citizens. However, Finley was primarily indicting the Army (not the Navy), which, he wrote, had enlisted the highest number of "unknown" soldiers at 9,055. A numerical estimate of undocumented immigrants in the U.S. military is not really possible. Because undocumented immigrants are ineligible to enlist, the information they provide will not be accurate. These conflicting representations and reports reveal an ambiguous attitude toward dealing with undocumented immigrants in the military.

A 2005 report by the Government Accountability Office states: "DOD records also showed that the personnel records of 12 percent of the noncitizens and nationals (almost 4,200 service members) indicated their country of birth was the United States. This finding was surprising because persons born in the United States are U.S. citizens, and it could not be explained by DOD officials." *Reporting Additional Servicemember Demographics Could Enhance Congressional Oversight* (Government Accountability Office, September 2005), 53.

Regardless of whether these statistics are accurate, there have been quite a few cases of undocumented immigrants serving the U.S. military, and if their undocumented status is disclosed, unlawful entry does not permanently disqualify them from serving. The military has a waiver for re-enlistment if soldiers are discharged or separated because of their undocumented status. The soldier must meet the legal status requirements when he or she applies for a waiver. "10 Steps to Joining the Military," *Military.com*, n.d., http://www.military.com/Recruiting/Content/0,13898,rec_step07_DQ_other,,00.html.

56. Florangela Davila, "Army Private Receives New Rank: U.S. Citizen," *The Seattle Times*, February 11, 2004; Finley, "Military Eyeing 'Unknowns.'" In

general, the U.S. public rarely hears about undocumented U.S. soldiers whose legal status has been exposed or about their cases for naturalization because the Department of Homeland Security usually defers decisions and disciplinary actions regarding undocumented soldiers to the military.

57. Amaya, "Dying American or the Violence of Citizenship."

58. Holland, *Raising the Dead*, 28.

59. Ibid., 30.

60. Martin Kasindorf, "Guatemala Native Put Off College to Join Marines," *USA Today*, March 24, 2003. This story states that Gutierrez received permanent residency in 1999. Heidi Specogna's documentary explains that Gutierrez immigrated as undocumented but was able to acquire permanent residency because he was mistaken for a minor. Heidi Specogna, *The Short Life of Jose Antonio Gutierrez* (Montréal: Atopia, 2007).

61. Kasindorf, "Guatemala Native Put Off College to Join Marines." The quotation was from Jackie Baker, Gutierrez's foster sister.

62. Specogna, *The Short Life of Jose Antonio Gutierrez*.

63. Amy Goldstein and Sylvia Moreno, "For Immigrants, a Special Sacrifice: War Takes Toll on Foreign-Born in Armed Forces," *The Washington Post*, April 7, 2003.

64. Valerie Alvord, "Non-Citizens Fight and Die for Adopted Country," *USA Today*, April 9, 2003.

65. Ibid.

66. Holland, *Raising the Dead*, 28.

67. "Fact Sheet: Naturalization Through Military Service."

68. "Families Conflicted about Posthumous Citizenship for US Troops Killed in Iraq," *New York Daily News*, March 20, 2008; "Immigrant U.S. Soldier Granted Posthumous Citizenship," *Good Morning America*, April 8, 2003, http://abcnews.go.com/GMA/story?id=125248&page=1; Mark Berman, "Immigrant Killed in Afghanistan Granted Posthumous Citizenship," *The Washington Post*, July 2, 2008; "Bill Seeks Citizenship for Binghamton Victims," *CNN.com*, April 9, 2009, http://articles.cnn.com/2009-04-09/us/ny.shooting.citizenship_1_citizenship-victims-binghamton?_s=PM:US.

69. The legislation passed the House but did not pass the Senate.

NOTES TO CHAPTER 4

1. Don Babwin, "Activists Back Mom Claiming Sanctuary: Facing Deportation, Elvira Arellano Takes Refuge in Church," *The Grand Rapids (Mich.) Press*, August 17, 2006.

2. Wendy Cole, "An Immigrant Who Found Sanctuary," *Time Magazine* 168, no. 26 (December 25, 2006): 80.

3. Sara E. McElmurry, "Elvira Arellano: No Rosa Parks: Creation of 'Us' versus 'Them' in an Opinion Column," *Hispanic Journal of Behavioral Sciences* 31, no. 2 (May 2009): 190–191.

4. "'I Fear God Much More Than I Fear Homeland Security': Chicago Pastor on Why He Is Allowing Mexican Mother to Stay in Church to Avoid Deportation," *Democracy Now*, New York, August 22, 2006, http://www.democracynow.org/2006/8/22/i_fear_god_much_more_than.

5. Mary Mitchell, "Blacks Know Rosa Parks and You, Arellano, Are No Rosa Parks," *Chicago Sun Times*, August 22, 2006; McElmurry, "Elvira Arellano: No Rosa Parks."

6. Mitchell, "Blacks Know Rosa Parks and You, Arellano, Are No Rosa Parks."

7. Ibid.

8. Arellano did in fact legally challenge the immigration laws. With the help of U.S. Senator Dick Durbin and U.S. Representative Luis Gutierrez, Arellano procured several one-year extensions to avoid deportation. Because this limited legal option helps an individual's predicament but does not help undocumented immigrants as a group, Mitchell also critiqued this legal avenue, contending that the extensions were evidence of Arellano's selfishness.

9. Mitchell, "Blacks Know Rosa Parks and You, Arellano, Are No Rosa Parks."

10. Ibid.

11. Silva, "Towards a Critique of the Socio-Logos of Justice," 440.

12. For more on the creation of "death-worlds," see Mbembe, "Necropolitics."

13. Bello, *Dark Victory*, 92.

14. Ibid., 88. Private U.S. investment abroad increased from $50 billion to $214 billion from 1965 to 1980.

15. Ibid., 4–5.

16. The Economic Recovery Tax Act of 1981, the Tax Equity and Fiscal Responsibility Act of 1982, and the Social Security Amendments of 1983 decreased personal taxes by $117 billion and increased Social Security by $11 billion. These tax reforms were mostly tax breaks for the wealthy in the form of federal tax cuts on incomes, estates, gifts, and businesses. Ibid., 92.

17. Michael A. Bernstein, "Understanding American Economic Decline: The Contours of the Late Twentieth-Century Experience," in *Understanding American Economic Decline*, ed. Michael A. Bernstein, David E. Adler, and Robert Heilbroner (New York: Cambridge University Press, 1994), 17, 20.

18. Thomas J. Sugrue, *The Origins of the Urban Crisis: Race and Inequality in Postwar Detroit* (Princeton: Princeton University Press, 1996), 3.

19. Robert L. Wagmiller, "Male Nonemployment in White, Black, Hispanic, and Multiethnic Urban Neighborhoods, 1970–2000," *Urban Affairs Review* 44, no. 1 (September 2008): 100.

20. Angela D. James, David M. Grant, and Cynthia Cranford, "Moving Up, but How Far? African American Women and Economic Restructuring in Los Angeles, 1970–1990," *Sociological Perspectives* 43, no. 3 (Autumn 2000): 404–405; Wendy Sigle-Rushton and Sara McLanahan, "For Richer or Poorer? Marriage as an Anti-Poverty Strategy in the United States," *Population* 57, no. 3 (2002): 509–526.

21. Bello, *Dark Victory*, 97.

22. Gilmore, *Golden Gulag*, 83–86.

23. Michael Tonry, "Racial Politics, Racial Disparities, and the War on Crime," *Crime and Delinquency* 40, no. 4 (October 1994): 482; Parenti, *Lockdown America*.

24. Gilmore, *Golden Gulag*, 18.

25. David Cole, *No Equal Justice: Race and Class in the American Criminal Justice System* (New York: New Press, 1999), 8; Parenti, *Lockdown America*. These different fines were a result of the Anti-Drug Abuse Act of 1986. The Fair Sentencing Act of 2010 reduced the disparity from a ratio of 100:1 to 18:1.

26. Cole, *No Equal Justice*, 8.

27. Drug offenders represented 49 percent of the growth, and public-order offenders represented 38 percent. Paige M. Harrison and Allen J. Beck, *Prisoners in 2004* (Washington, DC: Bureau of Justice Statistics, October 2005), 10.

28. Paige M. Harrison and Allen J. Beck, *Prisoners in 2005* (Washington, DC: Bureau of Justice Statistics, November 2006), 8.

29. Rodríguez, *Forced Passages*, 145.

30. Ibid., 40.

31. The Stop CAFTA Coalition, *Monitoring Report: DR-CAFTA in Year One* (Stop CAFTA Coalition, September 12, 2006), 30–32.

32. The Stop CAFTA Coalition, *DR-CAFTA Year Two: Trends and Impacts*, September 27, 2007, 9.

33. Ibid., 50.

34. Ibid., 9.

35. Ibid., 37–38.

36. U.S. Department of State, "Trade Regulations and Standards," in *Doing Business in Nicaragua: Country Commercial Guide for U.S. Companies*, 2011, http://nicaragua.usembassy.gov/chapter5.html.

37. Public Citizen, *Down on the Farm: NAFTA's Seven-Years' War on Farmers and Ranchers in the U.S., Canada and Mexico* (Washington, DC: Public Citizen's Global Trade Watch, June 2001), iv.

38. Ibid., vi. See also William Heffernan, *Consolidation in the Food and Agriculture Industry* (National Farmers Union, February 5, 1999), http://home.hiwaay.net/~becraft/NFUFarmCrisis.htm.

39. Diego Cevallos, "Crisis Drives Up Poverty Rate," *Inter Press Service*, May 23, 2009, http://ipsnews.net/news.asp?idnews=46957.

40. Public Citizen, *Down on the Farm*, iv.

41. According to a study by the Pew Hispanic Center, we can deduce that NAFTA dramatically increased the number of people entering the United States without authorization. The study notes that for each year between 1990 and 1994, an average of 450,000 people entered without authorization; from 1995 to 1999, the average increased to 750,000 a year, slowing down only slightly, to 700,000, from 2000 to 2004. Jeffrey S. Passel, *Estimates of the Size and*

Characteristics of the Undocumented Population (Washington, DC: Pew Hispanic Center, March 21, 2005), 1, 8.

42. Jeffrey S. Passel, *Trends in Unauthorized Immigration: Undocumented Inflow
Now Trails Legal Inflow* (Washington, DC: Pew Hispanic Center, October 2,
2008), 4–5.

43. Ibid. Undocumented immigration, generally, has remained stable or decreased since 2008, but this is more likely because of the financial crisis
in 2008 and the subsequent devaluation of the U.S. dollar as opposed to a
delayed effect of DR-CAFTA.

44. David Bacon, "Oaxaca's Dangerous Teachers," *Dollars and Sense*, no. 267 (October 2006): 24–28; David Bacon, "The Right to Stay Home," *David Bacon*,
July 14, 2008, http://dbacon.igc.org/Mexico/2008stayhome.html.

45. Bacon, "The Right to Stay Home." Dominguez is also a former migrant
worker and one of the founders of the Indigenous Front of Binational Organizations (FIOB). See also Mark R. Day, "Oaxacan Accepts Challenge: Who
Will Look After the Migrants?" *La Prensa San Diego*, December 30, 2010,
http://laprensa-sandiego.org/featured/oaxacan-accepts-challenge-who-will
-look-after-the-migrants/.

46. Ellen R. Shaffer and Joseph E. Brenner, "A Trade Agreement's Impact on Access to Generic Drugs," *Health Affairs* 28, no. 5 (August 2009): w957.

47. For instance, while Doctors Without Borders pays only $216 U.S. per person a
year to treat patients with HIV/AIDS with generic antiretrovirals, Guatemala's
social security system had to pay $4,818 U.S. per person to GlaxoSmithKline
for the same combination of drugs. "New Guatemalan Law and Intellectual
Property Provisions in DR-CAFTA Threaten Access to Affordable Medicines,"
Doctors Without Borders, March 11, 2005, http://www.doctorswithoutborders.
org/press/release.cfm?id=1490.

   In their study on DR-CAFTA's effects on access to generic drugs in Guatemala, co-directors of the Center for Policy Analysis on Trade and Health
Ellen Shaffer and Joseph Brenner found that every data-protected drug was
much more expensive than non-data-protected drugs within the same class.
For example, the antifungal Vfend costs 810 percent more than the non-data-
protected amphotericin B; Vfend cost 120,800 percent more than fluconazole,
which is also non-data-protected. Shaffer and Brenner, "A Trade Agreement's
Impact on Access to Generic Drugs," w962–w963.

48. Ellen R. Shaffer, Joseph E. Brenner, and Shayna Lewis, "CAFTA: Barriers to
Access to Medicines in Guatemala," *Health and Human Rights*, November
23, 2009, http://www.hhropenforum.org/2009/11/cafta-barriers-to-access-to
-medicines-in-guatemala/.

49. Shaffer and Brenner, "A Trade Agreement's Impact on Access to Generic
Drugs," w958.

50. Caffentzis, "A Tale of Two Conferences."

51. Burke Stansbury, "El Salvador: First in the Race to Implement DR-CAFTA, First to See Negative Effects of 'Free' Trade Agreement," in *Monitoring Report: DR-CAFTA in Year One*, 6–7.

52. The Stop CAFTA Coalition, *DR-CAFTA: Effects and Alternatives: The Stop CAFTA Coalition's Third Annual Monitoring Report*, 2008, 8.

53. Ibid.

54. The "Fighting back with the family" reference in the subhead refers to Cherríe Moraga's essay, "We Fight Back With Our Families" in Cherríe L. Moraga, *Loving in the War Years: Lo Que Nunca Paso por Sus Labios* (Boston: South End Press, 2000).

55. Cathy J. Cohen, *The Boundaries of Blackness: AIDS and the Breakdown of Black Politics* (Chicago: University of Chicago Press, 1999), 325.

56. Ibid., 334.

57. Ferguson, *Aberrations in Black*, 13.

58. In general, U.S. families no longer resemble the "ideal." See Thomas M. Shapiro, *The Hidden Cost of Being African American: How Wealth Perpetuates Inequality* (New York: Oxford University Press, 2005), 5; Melinda Chateauvert, "Framing Sexual Citizenship: Reconsidering the Discourse on African American Families," *The Journal of African American History* 93, no. 2 (Spring 2008): 198–222.

59. Ferguson, *Aberrations in Black*, 16.

60. Esther J. Cepeda, "4 Months in Church: 'I'll Stay': Son, 7, Off to Miami While Immigrant Mom Stays Put," *The Chicago Sun-Times*, December 15, 2006.

61. Ferguson, *Aberrations in Black*, 14; George J. Sánchez, *Becoming Mexican American: Ethnicity, Culture, and Identity in Chicano Los Angeles, 1900–1945* (New York: Oxford University Press, 1993); Eileen J. Suárez Findlay, *Imposing Decency: The Politics of Sexuality and Race in Puerto Rico, 1870–1920* (Durham: Duke University Press, 2000); Laura Briggs, *Reproducing Empire: Race, Sex, Science, and U.S. Imperialism in Puerto Rico* (Berkeley: University of California Press, 2002); Helen Safa, "Changing Forms of U.S. Hegemony in Puerto Rico: The Impact on the Family and Sexuality," *Urban Anthropology and Studies of Cultural Systems and World Economic Development* 32, no. 1 (Spring 2003): 7–41; Shah, *Contagious Divides*; Volpp, "Divesting Citizenship."

62. Oscar Lewis, *The Children of Sánchez: Autobiography of a Mexican Family* (New York: Vintage Books, 1963); Oscar Lewis, *La Vida: A Puerto Rican Family in the Culture of Poverty—San Juan and New York* (New York: Vintage Books, 1966).

63. Richard T. Rodríguez, *Next of Kin: The Family in Chicano/a Cultural Politics* (Durham: Duke University Press, 2009), 23.

64. Rodríguez, *Next of Kin*. Arguing along similar lines, Ferguson maintains that minority cultural nationalisms, or some forms of identity politics, can sometimes collude with state interests when heteronormativity and respectable domesticity are assumed to be universally valuable and, as such, universally

204   NOTES TO CHAPTER 4

desirable. As he writes, "State nationalism relegates particularities of race, gender, class, and sexuality to the private sphere and through this relegation is able to constitute itself as the terrain of universality. While cultural and revolutionary nationalisms have historically critiqued the state's relegation of race to the terrain of the private, calling attention to the state's illusory universality by exposing its surreptitious reliance upon racial difference, cultural and revolutionary nationalisms have colluded with the state by investing in gender and sexual normativity" (*Aberrations in Black*, 146).

    Ferguson's insights into minority nationalisms resonate with Yen Le Espiritu's contention that racialized immigrant communities "claim through gender the power denied them by racism" (*Home Bound*, 158). Espiritu notes that as a strategy of resistance against racism, Filipino immigrant communities construct white women as sexually immoral and promiscuous while characterizing Filipinas as virtuous and chaste, enabling Filipino immigrants to claim moral superiority over white women, white families, and (white) American culture. Yet in order to make this claim, Filipinas' sexuality must be strictly regulated, which has "the effect of reinforcing masculinist and patriarchal power in the name of a greater ideal of national and ethnic self-respect" (158).

65. Rodríguez, *Next of Kin*, 21.
66. See also Aída Hurtado, *The Color of Privilege: Three Blasphemies on Race and Feminism* (Ann Arbor: University of Michigan Press, 1996), 111.
67. Office of Policy and Research, *The Negro Family: The Case for National Action* (Washington, DC: U.S. Department of Labor, 1965). This report is commonly known as the Moynihan Report.
68. Ibid.
69. Chateauvert, "Framing Sexual Citizenship," 216.
70. Roderick A. Ferguson, "Of Our Normative Strivings: African American Studies and the Histories of Sexuality," *Social Text* 23, nos. 3–4 (Fall-Winter 2005): 89.
71. Richie, *Compelled to Crime*.
72. M. Jacqui Alexander, *Pedagogies of Crossing: Meditations on Feminism, Sexual Politics, Memory, and the Sacred* (Durham: Duke University Press, 2006), 23.
73. Ibid.
74. David Van Biema, "Sweet Sanctuary," *Time* vol. 170, no. 5 (July, 30, 2007): 45–47.
75. Sasha Abramsky, "Gimme Shelter," *The Nation*, February 25, 2008, 27. Johnson is affiliated with the United Church of Christ in Simi Valley, California.
76. Van Biema, "Sweet Sanctuary."
77. Diana Terry, *Hispanic Magazine* vol. 20, no. 8 (August 2007): 44.
78. Human Rights Watch, *Forced Apart: Families Separated and Immigrants Harmed by United States Deportation Policy*, vol. 19, no. 3(g), July 2007, 58.

The Human Rights Watch report cites the U.N. Human Rights Committee's comment on the Universal Declaration of Human Rights' proclamations on protecting the family. *Universal Declaration of Human Rights*, United Nations General Assembly, 217 A (III) (10 December 1948).

The U.N. Human Rights Committee states, "The right to found a family implies, in principle, the possibility to procreate and live together" and that "the possibility to live together implies the adoption of appropriate measures, both at the internal level and as the case may be, in cooperation with other States, to ensure the unity or reunification of families, particularly when their members are separated for political, economic or similar reasons." *CCPR General Comment No. 19: Article 23 (The Family) Protection of the Family, the Right to Marriage and Equality of the Spouses*, United Nations Human Rights Committee, July 27, 1990, available at: http://www.unhcr.org/refworld/docid/45139bd74.html (accessed 20 July 2011).

79. Dimitri Vassilaros, "Berthing Anchor Babies," *Pittsburgh Tribune Review*, May 7, 2007.

80. For works on images of immigrants in popular culture and the media, see Molina-Guzmán, *Dangerous Curves*; Angharad N. Valdivia, *A Latina in the Land of Hollywood and Other Essays on Media Culture* (Tucson: University of Arizona Press, 2000); Angharad N. Valdivia, ed., *Latina/o Communication Studies Today* (New York: Peter Lang, 2008); Angharad N. Valdivia, *Latina/os and the Media* (Malden, MA: Polity Press, 2009); Arlene Dávila, *Latinos, Inc.: The Marketing and Making of a People* (Berkeley: University of California Press, 2001); Clara E. Rodríguez, *Latin Looks: Images Of Latinas and Latinos in the U.S. Media* (Boulder, CO: Westview Press, 1997); Santa Ana, *Brown Tide Rising*; Kent A. Ono and John M. Sloop, *Shifting Borders: Rhetoric, Immigration, and California's Proposition 187* (Philadelphia: Temple University Press, 2002); Chavez, *Covering Immigration*; Leo R. Chavez, *Shadowed Lives: Undocumented Immigrants in American Society* (Fort Worth: Harcourt Brace College Publishers, 1998); Chavez, *The Latino Threat*.

81. Diana Terry, "The New Sanctuary Movement," *Hispanic Magazine*, August 2007, 43, 45.

82. Van Biema, "Sweet Sanctuary," 45.

83. Daniel B. Wood, "Rising Black-Latino Clash on Jobs," *The Christian Science Monitor*, May 25, 2006.

84. Rachel L. Swarns, "Growing Unease for Some Blacks on Immigration," *The New York Times*, May 4, 2006.

85. Monisha Das Gupta, *Unruly Immigrants: Rights, Activism, and Transnational South Asian Politics in the United States* (Durham: Duke University Press, 2006), 107.

86. Yvonne Abraham, "Immigration Hits Home in Lynn: Blacks Voice Fear of a Loss of Jobs," *The Boston Globe*, April 16, 2006.

87. Ibid.

88. For more on model minority discourse and social activism, see Gupta, *Unruly Immigrants*.

89. Robert G. Lee, *Orientals: Asian Americans in Popular Culture* (Philadelphia: Temple University Press, 1999), 145–161. Lee argues that we should examine the model minority myth not only in relation to the ways in which this stereotype disciplines non-Asian U.S. minorities, but also in relation to Asian Americans' legal vulnerability during and after World War II. Japanese internment illustrated all too clearly that U.S. citizenship did not make Asians immune to the abuses of state power. In addition, the Emergency Detention Act of 1950 formalized the government's capacity to intern noncitizen populations considered threatening. In this light, the passive, hard-working "model minority" Asian shares similar characteristics to today's overworked, underpaid, and largely uncomplaining undocumented Latina/o immigrants.

90. Victor Bascara, *Model-Minority Imperialism* (Minneapolis: University of Minnesota Press, 2006), 5.

91. Dresang and Johnson-Elie, "Immigration Rights Debate Unveils Rift."

92. Rachel L. Swarns, "Bridging a Racial Rift That Isn't Black and White," *The New York Times*, October 3, 2006.

93. Dresang and Johnson-Elie, "Immigration Rights Debate Unveils Rift."

94. Martin C. Evans, "The Immigration Debate: Blacks Weigh in on the Immigration Debate," *Newsday*, April 13, 2006.

95. Tomba, "Differentials of Surplus-Value in the Contemporary Forms of Exploitation," 35.

96. Ibid..

97. Ibid.

98. Clarence Lusane, *Race in the Global Era: African Americans at the Millennium* (Boston: South End Press, 1997), 6.

99. James Crawford, *Hold Your Tongue: Bilingualism and the Politics of "English Only"* (Reading, MA: Addison-Wesley Publishing, 1992).

100. Generally, living and working in nations other than the United States have been constructed as undesirable. See Jasbir Puar's discussion of the 2007 Human Rights Watch report, *Forced Apart: Families Separated and Immigrants Harmed by United States Deportation Policy*, in Puar, *Terrorist Assemblages*.

101. John R. Logan, *Urban Fortunes: The Political Economy of Place* (Berkeley: University of California Press, 1987); Robin D.G. Kelley, *Race Rebels: Culture, Politics, and the Black Working Class* (New York: Free Press, 1994); Robin D. G. Kelley, *Yo' Mama's Disfunktional! Fighting the Culture Wars in Urban America* (Boston: Beacon Press, 1997).

102. Miranda Joseph, *Against the Romance of Community* (Minneapolis: University of Minnesota Press, 2002), xxxv.

103. Ibid.

104. Mitchell, "Blacks Know Rosa Parks and You, Arellano, Are No Rosa Parks."
105. Ibid.
106. Evans, "The Immigration Debate."
107. Norman T. Feather, "Distinguishing between Deservingness and Entitlement: Earned Outcomes versus Lawful Outcomes," *European Journal of Social Psychology* 33, no. 3 (June 2003): 368.
108. Ibid., 367.
109. Harris, "Whiteness as Property."
110. Swarns, "Growing Unease for Some Blacks on Immigration."
111. Reddy, "Time for Rights?" 2853. As Reddy notes, "There is much to say about such symptomatic language, of the way in which rights are construed as goods, the nation as recipient of its citizens' labor and lives, and the state as little more than a disperser of those desired goods conceived as the purpose and end of social politics" (2854).
112. Ibid., 2853–2854. Italics in original.
113. Robin D. G. Kelley, *Freedom Dreams: The Black Radical Imagination* (Boston: Beacon Press, 2002), 81.
114. Ibid., 82.
115. Ibid., 109.
116. Ibid.
117. Randall Williams, *The Divided World: Human Rights and Its Violence* (Minneapolis: University of Minnesota Press, 2010), 18.
118. Esteban Magnani, *The Silent Change: Recovered Businesses in Argentina* (Buenos Aires: Editorial Teseo, 2009); Avi Lewis, *The Take* (New York: First Run Features, 2006).
119. Kelley, *Freedom Dreams*, 90.
120. Rafael Romo, "7 Arrested after Blocking Traffic to Raise Immigration Awareness," *CNN.com*, April 5, 2011.
121. Statement circulated during Georgia 7 arrests, The DREAM Is Coming Projects (April 2011).

NOTES TO THE CONCLUSION

1. The subtitle of this section, "Wreck in the Road," is the title of a song written by Rubén Martínez, which he performed with Los Illegals on April 22, 2000, at Espresso Mi Cultura in Los Angeles, California. Text provided by author. See also Rubén Martínez, *Crossing Over: A Mexican Family on the Migrant Trail* (New York: Metropolitan Books, 2001).

   This concluding chapter on "Racialized Hauntings of the Devalued Dead" was first published in *Strange Affinities: The Sexual Politics of Comparative Racialization*, ed. Grace Kyungwon Hong and Roderick A. Ferguson (Durham, NC: Duke University Press, 2011), 25–52. An earlier version appeared under the title " 'You Just Don't Know How Much He Meant': Deviancy, Death, and Devaluation," *Latino Studies* 5, no. 2 (Summer 2007): 182–208.

2. Trisha Martinez, "You Just Don't Know," Death and Funeral Notices: Martinez, Brandon Jesse, *San Diego Union Tribune*, March 29, 2000, B5.

3. Barrett, *Blackness and Value*, 19, 21.

4. Ibid., 28.

5. Gordon, *Ghostly Matters*, 202.

6. Isabel Molina-Guzmán, "Gendering Latinidad through the Elián News Discourse about Cuban Women," *Latino Studies* 3, no. 2 (July 2005): 182.

7. Ruby C. Tapia, "Un(di)ing Legacies: White Matters of Memory in Portraits of 'Our Princess,'" *Cultural Values* 5, no. 2 (April 2001): 263.

8. Ibid.

9. Shah, *Contagious Divides*, 254.

10. Joe Hughes, "Three Men Killed when Speeding Car Hits Trees; a Fourth Walks Away," *San Diego Union-Tribune*, March 25, 2000.

11. Ibid.

12. Although the site of the accident is not far from a possible racing strip (race locations changed weekly or daily), U.S. cars such as Brandon's 1984 Mustang —big, clunky, old, and slow—were not part of this particular racing culture, which raced late-model Hondas and Toyotas, most of which were altered to maximize speed and performance. However, as a young Asian man, Vanvilay fit the profile of a racer even though the car he was driving did not. To read more about the car culture of young Asian men, see Soo Ah Kwon, "Auto-exoticizing: Asian American Youth and the Import Car Scene," *Journal of Asian American Studies* 7, no. 1 (2004): 1–26.

13. Hughes, "Three Men Killed When Speeding Car Hits Trees."

14. Tom Krasovic, "Darr Legally Intoxicated, Says Examiner's Report," *San Diego Union-Tribune*, March 14, 2002.

15. Ibid.

16. Kusz, "I Want to Be the Minority," 412.

17. Ibid.

18. Robert Nowatzki, "Foul Lines and the Color Line: Baseball and Race at the Turn of the Twentieth Century," *NINE: A Journal of Baseball History and Culture* 11, no. 1 (Fall 2002): 83.

19. The media usually represent athletes of color in less sympathetic ways. See, for example, C. L. Cole and Alex Mobley, "American Steroids: Using Race and Gender," *Journal of Sport and Social Issues* 29, no. 1 (February 2005): 3–8. For a specific examination of the history of Latinos in baseball, including how Latino ballplayers have been racialized, see Adrian Burgos Jr., "Learning America's Other Game: Baseball, Race, and the Study of Latinos," in *Latino/a Popular Culture*, ed. Michelle Habell-Pallán and Mary Romero (New York: New York University Press, 2002), 225–239; Samuel O. Regalado, "Hey Chico! The Latin Identity in Major League Baseball," *NINE: A Journal of Baseball History and Culture* 11, no. 1 (Fall 2002): 16–24.

20. Tom Krasovic, "Padres Crushed by Loss of Darr: Teammates Speak of Personality, Potential," *San Diego Union-Tribune*, February 16, 2002.

21. Dana Nelson, *National Manhood: Capitalist Citizenship and the Imagined Fraternity of White Men* (Durham: Duke University Press, 1998), 204.

22. Tom Krasovic, "Bochy Hopes Team Can Learn from Tragedy," *San Diego Union-Tribune*, February 23, 2002.

23. Nelson, *National Manhood*. Because Nelson's analysis focuses on "the era of 'universal' white manhood suffrage" (1780s–1850s), the imagined white fraternity she examines literally refers to white men (xi). How "national manhood" could still be considered an imagined white fraternity in the contemporary period is probably best understood by defining "whiteness" as "a possessive investment in whiteness." George Lipsitz defines the "possessive investment in whiteness" as "a social structure that gives value to whiteness and offers rewards for racism"; thus, a possessive investment in whiteness reinforces and reifies racial inequalities, but it is not necessarily practiced and possessed by only white people. George Lipsitz, *The Possessive Investment in Whiteness: How White People Profit from Identity Politics* (Philadelphia: Temple University Press, 1998), viii.

24. Nick Canepa, "Padres Crushed by Loss of Darr: Words Just Can't Soften His Passing," *San Diego Union-Tribune*, February 16, 2002.

25. Tom Krasovic, "Darr Tragedy Leaves Team Trying to Go On," *San Diego Union-Tribune*, February 17, 2002; Krasovic, "Padres Crushed by Loss of Darr"; Krasovic, "Bochy Hopes Team Can Learn from Tragedy"; Bill Center, "On a Swing and a Miss, Padres End It at the Q; Rockies Stage Rally to Wrap Up an Era," *San Diego Union-Tribune*, September 29, 2003.

26. See Kusz, "'I Want to Be the Minority'"; Nelson, *National Manhood*; Robyn Wiegman, "Whiteness Studies and the Paradox of Particularity," *boundary 2* 26, no. 3 (Fall 1999): 115–150; Lipsitz, *The Possessive Investment in Whiteness*.

27. Bill Center, "Despite Tragedy, Positives Found; Darr's Death Put in the Past; Team Moves Forward," *San Diego Union-Tribune*, April 1, 2002.

28. Center, "On a Swing and a Miss, Padres End It at the Q."

29. Tapia, "Un(di)ing Legacies," 268.

30. Christine Martinez and Jesse Martinez Jr., "Death and Funeral Notices: Martinez, Brandon Jesse," *San Diego Union-Tribune*, March 29, 2000, B5.

31. Diana Taylor, *The Archive and the Repertoire: Performing Cultural Memory in the Americas* (Durham: Duke University Press, 2003), 147.

32. José Esteban Muñoz, "Ephemera as Evidence: Introductory Notes to Queer Acts," *Women and Performance: A Journal of Feminist Theory* 8, no. 2 (1996): 9.

33. Ann Cvetkovich, *An Archive of Feelings: Trauma, Sexuality, and Lesbian Public Cultures* (Durham: Duke University Press, 2003).

34. Karla F. C. Holloway, *Passed On: African American Mourning Stories: A Memorial* (Durham: Duke University Press, 2003), 181.

35. Taylor, *The Archive and the Repertoire*, 32.

36. Ibid., 33.

37. For our families, becoming middle class would not be automatically inherited. Because people of color have been subjected to redlining and restrictive covenants as well as excluded from the programs that enabled wealth accumulation during the New Deal and afterward, many middle-class families of color in the contemporary era are unstable. Douglas S. Massey and Nancy A. Denton, *American Apartheid: Segregation and the Making of the Underclass* (Cambridge: Harvard University Press, 1993), 36–37, 51–58; Melvin L. Oliver and Thomas M. Shapiro, *Black Wealth/White Wealth: A New Perspective on Racial Inequality* (New York: Routledge, 1995), 16–18, 39–41, 87–89; Lipsitz, *The Possessive Investment in Whiteness*, 5–18. Many are without significant assets to pass down intergenerationally, and racial discrimination in education and the workforce also makes it difficult to pass down occupational mobility (Oliver and Shapiro, 90, 157–158). For an excellent analysis of how housing policies and home ownership affect Latinas/os in the contemporary era, see Eileen Díaz McConnell, *No Place Like Home: The State of Hispanic Housing in Chicago, Los Angeles, and New York City, 2003* (University of Notre Dame: Institute for Latino Studies, June 2005), http://latinostudies.nd.edu/pubs/pubs/AHS_housing.pdf.

38. Mike Davis, *Prisoners of the American Dream: Politics and Economy in the History of the U.S. Working Class* (London: Verso, 1986), 208; Manuel Castells, *The Informational City: Information Technology, Economic Restructuring, and the Urban-Regional Process* (Oxford, UK: Blackwell, 1989), 308; Masao Miyoshi, "'Globalization,' Culture, and the University," in *The Cultures of Globalization*, ed. Fredric Jameson and Masao Miyoshi (Durham: Duke University Press, 1998), 255.

39. For an excellent analysis of the particular hardships of urban areas, see Lee, *Urban Triage*.

40. Richard T. Rodríguez, "On the Subject of Gang Photography," *Aztlán: A Journal of Chicano Studies* 25, no. 1 (2000): 109–143; Edward J. Escobar, *Race, Police, and the Making of a Political Identity: Mexican Americans and the Los Angeles Police Department, 1900–1945* (Berkeley: University of California Press, 1999); Jerome G. Miller, *Search and Destroy: African-American Males in the Criminal Justice System* (Cambridge: Cambridge University Press, 1997).

41. Philip L. Martin, "The United States: Benign Neglect toward Immigration," in *Controlling Immigration: A Global Perspective*, ed. Wayne A. Cornelius, Philip L. Martin, and James Hollifield (Stanford: Stanford University Press, 1994), 94.

42. Bello, *Dilemmas of Domination*.

43. Herman Gray, *Watching Race: Television and the Struggle for "Blackness"* (Minneapolis: University of Minnesota Press, 1995); Tang, "Collateral Damage"; Rodríguez, "On the Subject of Gang Photography."

44. According to Jorge Mariscal, "*The Army Times* reported that 'Hispanics' constituted 22 percent of the military recruiting 'market,' almost double their numbers in the population." Jorge Mariscal, "Military Targets Latinos: Tracked into Combat Jobs," *War Times / Tiempo de Guerras*, November 2003, 3, http://www.war-times.org/issues/13art5.html. In a separate article, Mariscal explains that "military service does not close the economic gaps separating the majority of Latinos from the rest of society but potentially widens them" because military job training, such as "small arms expertise and truck driving," do not translate into good paying jobs in the civilian economy. Jorge Mariscal, "The Future for Latinos in an Era of War and Occupation," *CounterPunch*, April 18, 2003, http://www.counterpunch.org/mariscal04182003.html. African American men and women constitute an overwhelming 22.4 percent of the military while constituting only 12.41 percent of the civilian population between the ages of 18 and 44. *Population Representation in the Military Services*, Appendix B-25. Latinas/os are especially overrepresented in potential combat positions; for instance, more than a quarter of Latinas/os in the Army and more than 20 percent of Latinas/os in the Marines serve the infantry. Ibid., Appendix B-30. In 2009, Latinas/os constituted 39 percent of the population in California prisons. *California Prisoners and Parolees 2009* (Sacramento: California Department of Corrections and Rehabilitation, 2010), 19.

45. Of course, these are not mutually exclusive; for instance, some men of color might support their partners or children through illegal economies. See Cathy J. Cohen, "Deviance as Resistance: A New Research Agenda for the Study of Black Politics," *Du Bois Review: Social Science Research on Race* 1, no. 1 (March 2004): 36.

46. Ferguson, *Aberrations in Black*, 11–18.

47. Bascara, *Model-Minority Imperialism*, xvi–xvii; Lee, *Urban Triage*, xix–xx.

48. Foucault, *The Birth of Biopolitics*, 243.

49. Jodi Melamed explains that privilege and stigma no longer neatly correspond with race: "Neoliberal multiculturalism breaks with an older racism's reliance on phenotype to innovate new ways of fixing human capacities to naturalize inequality. The new racism deploys economic, ideological, cultural, and religious distinctions to produce lesser personhoods, laying these new categories of privilege and stigma across conventional racial categories, fracturing them into differential status groups." Melamed, "The Spirit of Neoliberalism," 14.

50. Beverly Daniel Tatum, *"Why Are All the Black Kids Sitting Together in the Cafeteria?" A Psychologist Explains the Development of Racial Identity*, 5th ed. (New York: Basic Books, 2003), 61.

51. Lisa Lowe and David Lloyd, "Introduction," in *The Politics of Culture in the Shadow of Capital*, ed. Lisa Lowe and David Lloyd (Durham: Duke University Press, 1997), 26.

52. Kelley, *Race Rebels*, 3–4. Also see Victor Hugo Viesca, "The Battle of Los Angeles: The Cultural Politics of Chicana/o Music in the Greater Eastside," *American Quarterly* 56, no. 3 (September 2004): 719–739.

53. Kelley, *Race Rebels*, 47, 166.

54. Viet Thanh Nguyen, *Race and Resistance: Literature and Politics in Asian America* (New York: Oxford University Press, 2002), 157.

55. Mahmood, *Politics of Piety*, 14.

56. Ibid., 9.

57. Brandon Martinez, paper assignment for Mira Mesa High School, San Diego, California (1997), 2.

58. Ibid., 4.

59. Ibid., 2.

60. Holland, *Raising the Dead*, 16.

61. Judith Halberstam, *In a Queer Time and Place: Transgender Bodies, Subcultural Lives* (New York: New York University Press, 2005). As Halberstam explains, "queer temporality disrupts the normative narratives of time that form the base of nearly every definition of the human in almost all our modes of understanding" (152).

62. Ibid., 13.

63. Ibid., 2.

64. Ibid., 10.

65. Holland, *Raising the Dead*, 178–180.

66. I am referencing Hong's definition of "women of color feminist practice" as a "reading practice" and a "methodology for comparative analysis" (xi, xvi). Women of color feminist practice emerges to "make sense of that which is pathologized and/or rendered invisible by the epistemologies of nationalism" (xii). Hong, *The Ruptures of American Capital*.

67. Ferguson, *Aberrations in Black*, 4.

68. Steve Pile, "Introduction: Opposition, Political Identities, and Spaces of Resistance," in *Geographies of Resistance*, ed. Steve Pile and Michael Keith (London: Routledge, 1997), 24.

69. For an insightful analysis of family and nationalism, see Rodríguez, *Next of Kin*. For an excellent analysis of the impossibility of heteropatriarchal investments in poor communities of color, see Richie, *Compelled to Crime*.

70. Cohen, "Deviance as Resistance," 34.

71. Ibid., 38.

72. Kelley, *Race Rebels*, 12.

73. Cohen, "Deviance as Resistance," 30. Unlike Kelley, Cohen specifically does not define most acts of defiance and deviance as evidence of resistance because she reserves "resistance" for acts with political intent (39).

74. Gordon, *Ghostly Matters*, 202.

75. Rubén Martínez, performance of "Wreck in the Road" with Los Illegals on April 22, 2000, at Espresso Mi Cultura in Los Angeles, California.